The Emancipation of the
Polish Peasantry

The Emancipation
of the
Polish Peasantry

Stefan Kieniewicz

The University of Chicago Press
Chicago and London

Standard Book Number: 226-43524-5
Library of Congress Catalog Card Number: 79-92684
THE UNIVERSITY OF CHICAGO PRESS, CHICAGO 60637
THE UNIVERSITY OF CHICAGO PRESS, LTD., LONDON

CONTENTS

v

CONTENTS

CONTENTS

CONTENTS

FOREWORD

The history of the Polish peasantry during the past one and a half centuries has been an unceasing climb along a tortuous road leading from serfdom to citizenship and from compulsory labor on manorial estates to ownership of land. To recreate the story of this weary passage of eight generations of millions of toilers of the Polish soil requires nothing less than a writer of epics. Happily, the task has fallen to the extraordinary talent of one of the great modern Polish historians, Professor Stefan Kieniewicz.

His work is the epic neither of a single hero nor of a small elitist group, but of the most numerous social class, the majority of the nation. The reader may well ask the simple, elementary question: to what extent is the history of the Polish peasantry the history of the Polish nation? The answer, which could be inferred from the following pages, is that the relation between the two is not one of identity but of relative congruence. During most of the period under consideration Poland did not exist as an independent state. The discontinuity of political independence, however, did not destroy the continuity of national existence, a fact supported by cultural continuity as well as by the frequent attempts at political resurrection. Professor Kieniewicz traces, with consummate skill, the changes in Polish society that gradually brought the Polish peasants into the mainstream of national life. The acquisition of national consciousness on the part of the Polish peasantry went hand in hand with the solution of their fundamental social problems. In part this is the story of how they came to think and act as Poles. It is no wonder, then, that the history of the Polish peasantry is treated by Professor Kieniewicz as distinct from the history of the nation, although most of the crucial issues of national history are reflected in the discussion, albeit primarily through the prism of attitudes of or toward the peasants.

It is difficult to classify the history of the peasantry as presented by Professor Kieniewicz exclusively in terms of professional historical classification. We are told by the author that it ought not to be categorized as a work of economic history, and in fact it is much broader in scope than an economic historian's approach to the problem. It includes and combines in the best tradition of historical research and narration elements of economic history, intellectual history, and description and analysis of political and social institutions. One might say that the work represents social history par excellence, assuming that there were a significant measure of agreement among historians as to the subject and methods in that still amorphous field. In the absence of agreed criteria, it can only be suggested that many social historians might benefit greatly by following the example of Professor Kieniewicz and using his methods as a model for their work.

The reader might inquire with good reason why he ought to study the history of the Polish peasantry. Not every product of excellent scholarship can be read by the general public or studied even by the members of the profession. One would probably have to argue in favor of the Polish peasantry as a case study neither in terms of its uniqueness nor its typicality. The subject appeals to the general interest through a range of problems. In the period of serfdom the Polish pattern was very similar to the pattern prevailing in central and eastern Europe, particularly east of the Elbe River, and as such is helpful for our general understanding of a relatively late variety of serfdom. In the modern period the political awakening of the Polish peasantry and the growth of its educational, economic and organizational aspirations have a number of counterparts in eastern and southeastern Europe.

Professor Kieniewicz begins his narrative with an analysis of serfdom in independent Poland of the second half of the eighteenth century. He views as the central feature of the institution of serfdom the monopoly of land ownership in the hands of the gentry with most other characteristics of the institution deriving from this major social fact. Some economic historians tend to agree with him; others would offer alternative explanations, emphasizing perhaps more strongly the personal dependence of the serf or his outright ownership by his lord. A proponent of the latter view would consider the serf himself a form of capital, a much more valuable resource than the land during this period, and could therefore explain the choices available to the serf owner in terms of maximizing the returns from serf labor rather than from land use. But whatever may be the point of departure for the analysis of serfdom, Professor Kieniewicz has provided an extremely perceptive description and evaluation of the significance of the institution for the Polish peasantry. The author is also correct in pointing out that the various attempts of a voluntary or arbitrary nature to change some forms of the lord-peasant relationship during this period of enlightenment did not seriously undermine the institution of serfdom itself. Serfdom during this period was as compatible with money rent as with compulsory labor. The market was still too weak, new technology was lacking, and the peasantry were too politically ineffective to challenge seriously or to destroy the institution of serfdom. The emancipation of the serfs—a late-eighteenth-century brainchild of the most radical wing of the Polish patriots striving to save the political independence of the country—remained in the realm of ideas, "a heritage transmitted to the next generation," to use Professor Kieniewicz's apt phrase.

The process of emancipation of the serfs, which took place during the subsequent period, involved the solution of a number of issues. The main issues were the extent of the peasants' claims (or the strength of the peasants' right in the traditional rather than legal sense) to the land they tilled, personal freedom, and compulsory labor on the estates. Since the solution of the above issues depended upon the government rather than upon private transactions and contracts between lords and peasants, much depended upon the policies pursued by the partitioning powers—Russia, Prussia, and Austria. Their attitudes in turn were shaped at least in part by the general policies that they followed in dealing with their own peasantry and gentry. The development of the market and money economy had an additional impact upon the settlement of the issues. Factors such as these determined whether the granting of personal freedom to the Polish peasants was preceded by the disappearance of compulsory labor on the landowners' estates, or was enacted simultaneously, or was followed with a substantial time lag by the disappearance of compulsory labor.

The Polish peasantry as well as peasants in other parts of the world soon discovered that personal freedom alone was not a sufficient guarantee that they would be able to take advantage of their new status, especially when the bulk of the land remained in the hands of the landlords or when alternative opportunities to earn income were lacking. Personal freedom becomes meaningful only under conditions of free mobility and free competition—including competition for the services of the peasants. But in fact most of the land was apportioned to the landlords, and the attitude of the gentry remained fixed, and so the conditions imposed upon the freed peasants did not differ much from the conditions prevailing under serfdom.

Thus, almost invariably, the first phase of the Polish peasants' emancipation can be viewed as a trade-off of the use of land resources remaining largely with the landlords for the personal freedom granted legally to the peasantry. The differences in the conditions of emancipation that existed between the various regions of the former Polish state were primarily differences in degree and timing rather than differences in kind.

The second phase, that of the peasants' experience as legally free individuals, was marked by their efforts to secure ownership rights to the land or, in some cases, to regain the land they had tilled prior to the emancipation, which they had given up and ceded to the landlords in exchange for (or payment of) their personal freedom. Viewed in general terms, it was a period when the market forces exerted an increasing influence upon the development of the agricultural sector in general, including both the estates and the peasant economy. The market conditions forced the estates to become more competitive and profit oriented, to revise their cost structure and production specialization in order to accept more fully the criteria of economic efficiency. The same market forces provided opportunities for the peasants to acquire additional land and, in part, to counteract the imbalance of plentiful labor resources and scarce land resources within the peasant economy. The process of acquisition of more land by the peasants was accompanied by an intensified economic stratification within the peasantry. While some were able to prosper, many became impoverished. Nevertheless, domestic employment opportunities outside of agriculture and migration, both seasonal and permanent, provided some sort of safety valve for the distress of the Polish peasantry.

So summary a view of a historical period sounds dry and bloodless indeed; it obviously hides most of the drama of changing social relations. It is much to the credit of Professor Kieniewicz that within his narrative the dramatic experience of the peasants' struggle for land unfolds itself. It was a struggle waged in many forms, with various means, but with a single objective: land for the peasants. Whether these were pitchfork battles between the peasants and estate officials for the right to graze their flocks on the meadows, or skirmishes between peasants and soldiers summoned from the nearby garrison for the right to use the forests, or generation-long lawsuits of peasants against landowners for a miserable piece of land, or petitions reaching the capitals of the counties after unsuccessful attempts to redress the peasants' grievances in local government offices, or violent strikes of agricultural workers for higher wages and against the use of the overseer's stick or whip—they all provide the drama-filled background of the conflict between the peasant hut and the estate villa. Professor Kieniewicz brings both objectivity and compassion to the telling of that tale.

But while the story of a social class in its drive toward recognition by the society at large and integration with that society is a well-researched subject in historical literature, the Polish case has some special features. The complex, intertwining patterns of the struggle for national independence and social emancipation, brought into focus by the Polish peasant problem, contain many suggestive analogies to problems in other parts of the world. The linkage of the issues of peasant emancipation and Polish political independence can be traced back to the radical, Jacobin type of tradition subscribed to by some few participants in the famous Kosciuszko insurrection (1794). But for a good part of the following century, with rather minor exceptions, the cause of national independence was mainly the cause of the Polish gentry. Given the relative numerical strength of the Polish gentry, any realistic appraisal of the prospects of a fight for independent statehood had to include the gentry. Did the inclusion of the gentry, or the orientation on the gentry as the champion of national independence, exclude a consistent pro-emancipation attitude toward the peasants? At least until 1863 this was by and large the case. It means that for at least seventy years the class interests of the gentry prevented the majority of the nation from integrating their social and national interests. That such a state of affairs did not escape the notice of foreign governments is also clear. Needless to say, it was in their interest to maintain the dichotomy. Professor Kieniewicz dwells in great detail on the attempts of the Polish patriots to involve the peasantry in the political struggle for statehood. The attempts went in two directions, one to convince the gentry that a fair solution of the agrarian problems was in the national interest and therefore ought to override individual or group interests; the second, directed toward the peasants, promised them the support of any future Polish government in reaching a favorable solution of the agrarian problems. The history of most such attempts is one of futility, since an alliance of two classes opposing each other cannot be effected unless either an outside force is equally threatening to both or their contradictions can be resolved beforehand.

It was during the second half of the nineteenth century that the Polish peasantry gained allies among the members of the Polish intelligentsia. The populist movement in Poland was essentially a result of this alliance, with its emphasis on cooperation (consumer cooperatives included) and education of the younger generation. The value placed on education could be explained both by the realization that education provides new opportunities for social and economic advancement and by the reaction to policies of forced assimilation imposed by some of the occupying powers. Populism in Poland remained by and large a conservative movement, characterized by limited practical goals which combined economic self-defense of peasant interests with increased social self-awareness and national consciousness. These particular characteristics of the populist movement could be explained perhaps by the auxiliary rather than the primary role played by the participating members of the intelligentsia, the radical wing of which turned rather early toward a new alliance—with the urban working class.

The political weight and power of the Polish peasantry, although still stronger in its potential than in its reality, was growing in part as a result both of the relative economic and social decline of the gentry and of increasing political suffrage in various countries. It was becoming clear that ultimate assertion would come from sheer numbers combined with self-awareness. Thus, to ignore the peasants in the national struggle became impossible, and various political groups within the ideological spectrum attempted to win the Polish peasants to their standards. The peasantry responded with qualified and circumspect support, never putting its actual weight behind one particular group. In spite of the fact that the Polish peasantry was economically differentiated, there is very little evidence, except perhaps for the revolutionary period of 1905–6, for claims that different groups within the peasantry allied themselves with opposing groups of other social classes. The Polish peasantry, during the period discussed by Professor Kieniewicz, never lost sight of its major social goal—true emancipation with land—and only in the last part of the period did it begin to emerge as a political force potentially instrumental in the achievement of its own aims and also of the aims of the nation at large.

ARCADIUS KAHAN

PREFACE

On taking up the subject of the Polish agrarian problem, I feel
bound to explain that I do not consider myself a specialist in
economic history. All my life I have been interested chiefly in
the story of politics; I have made my profession the study of
Polish national insurrections in the partition period. The study
of economics came later, as a methodological necessity. Poland
in the nineteenth century was an agrarian country. Poland's
struggle for independence was most closely connected with social
problems; the nation's fate depended on the attitude of the rural
masses, and this, in turn, depended on prevailing social conditions. In writing on the Polish insurrections of 1846, 1848, and
1863, I was eventually obliged to occupy myself with agrarian
problems as well: the conditions of life of the Polish peasants, the
class struggle, and the agrarian programs of political parties.
These topics obliged me, in turn, to occupy myself with still
more basic problems: the social structure in the Polish country-

side and the development of agriculture as compared with analogous phenomena in neighboring countries. The study of these
questions was favored by the general interest in economic problems prevalent in socialist countries. If I have contributed slightly
to a deeper understanding of some of these subjects, I remain,
nonetheless, a dilettante in economics; that is, I am interested,
above all, in their political aspects.

Why should Polish agrarian problems be of interest to American students? These are problems which do not have their
counterpart in American history, although a relationship does
exist, inasmuch as poor rural conditions in central and eastern
Europe forced millions of peasants to cross the ocean to become
citizens of the United States. The emancipation of the Polish
peasant is indeed a closed chapter of history. But this closed
chapter has had its consequences, which are felt to this day. In
addition, agrarian problems similar to those of nineteenth-
century Poland are still topical in many regions of Asia and Latin
America, influencing world politics of today. Learning a little
about the mechanics of agrarian problems in Europe in the past
century may be of some use not only from the point of view of
comparative history but also as a step toward the understanding
of some problems of the present.

This book concerns territories that belonged to the Polish
state or were inhabited by Polish peasants. They embrace almost
all of the basins of four eastern European rivers: the Oder, the
Vistula, the Niemen, and the Dnieper. The period studied leads
from the feudal epoch to the emancipation of the peasants and
its first consequences—that is, from the end of the eighteenth
century to the early part of the twentieth century. The closing
date, 1918—the date of the rebirth of an independent Poland—
also marks a turning point in the economic and political conditions of the country.

In a synthesis covering 150 years of history, it seemed super-
fluous and impractical to present all the sources upon which
particular statements have been based. Instead, a selection of
the most important primary and secondary sources has been
included at the end of the book, preceded by a brief discussion of
bibliographical material and historiography.

An appendix has also been added, containing the texts of the
most important legislation concerning the peasant emancipation,

from 1791 to 1864. The Prussian, Austrian, and Russian emancipation acts were much too lengthy to be entirely reproduced, and so only their vital passages have been included.

Polish and other European measures, weights, and money have been converted to American units, although some allusions to Polish *morgi* and *włóki* remain here and there, for the sake of local color. A number of Polish terms have been retained, together with English translations or definitions. Some of these terms have no exact English counterparts, and literal translation would lead to misunderstanding. This chiefly concerns three terms: *folwark* ("big farm forming a part of a landlord's estate"); *pańszczyzna* ("compulsory labor"); and *uwłaszczenie* ("the granting to the peasants of title to their holdings"). I hope it will not be impossible to gain acceptance for these three terms in English texts, at least among specialists in economic history.

The present volume is a slightly rearranged version of a course of lectures delivered in 1968 at the University of Chicago. I wish to express my indebtedness to my American hosts, my colleagues in the Department of History, who did so much to make my contacts with the New World easier, and to the students, who seemed to take interest in these lectures and with whom I found it a pleasure to associate. I also wish to acknowledge with particular gratitude the judicious and perceptive remarks made on my manuscript by Professors William McNeill and Arcadius Kahan, who helped make my script more understandable for American readers.

The Emancipation of the
Polish Peasantry

POLISH TERRITORIES AFTER 1815

INTRODUCTION

It has often been stressed that the countries east of the Elbe, which are now part of the socialist bloc, had a common feature in the past which distinguished them from other European countries. In all this vast area between the Elbe and the Volga, the Baltic and the Black Sea, the distinctive feature, toward the end of the feudal era, was the persistence of compulsory labor (*Fron, Robot, pańszczyzna*, or *barshtchina*) in the countryside.

Compulsory labor was not a causal factor. It was the consequence of an economic system evolved in the sixteenth century which rested on two pillars: the serfdom of the peasants and the manorial farm (*folwark*).

To an outsider, the most striking feature of these territories at the end of the eighteenth century was the coexistence of large- and small-scale cultivation. We must distinguish between the scale of the cultivation and the size of the property. In western Europe in feudal times, there were regions with large (latifundian)

3

farms predominating, and others with mostly small, peasant farms. But even in those countries in which most of the land belonged to the gentry, it was subdivided and cultivated by small, independent farmers: tenants, leaseholders, or sharecroppers. There were, of course, manorial farms in England and northern Italy, but they were run mainly by hired labor.

Meanwhile, in central and eastern Europe, there were no small holdings—or rather, they were very scarce. All the land belonged to feudal masters—king, bishop or abbot, lord or gentleman, and occasionally a rich burgher. In this region of the exclusively large estates, all the arable land was divided into two parts: (1) the manorial farm, and (2) the village land, given in usufruct to individual peasants. The village land was meant to provide for the subsistence of the peasants; the manorial farm was tilled by the compulsory labor of the same peasants, working for the master. This was the so-called manorial farm–compulsory labor (*folwark-pańszczyzna*) system, a phenomenon peculiar only to the feudal epoch, for which serfdom was a necessary condition.

Historians of law have debated widely the essence of feudal serfdom. They have distinguished three elements of the institution: personal dependence, judiciary allegiance, and territorial subordination. These are legal subtleties that miss the heart of the matter, which is that the gentry was monopolist in its possession of land. Everything else springs from this fact. The peasant living on a gentleman's land was his subject; he was attached to the land, governed by the laws of the domain, obliged to work on the manorial farm. Some theoreticians have argued that the property rights to village lands under this system were divided: the lord had the *dominium directum*, the right of ownership of the land; the peasant enjoyed the *dominium utile*, or the right to its use. This again is a fallacy. Under feudal conditions, especially in eastern Europe, the peasant's *dominium utile* was an illusion. He could be driven away, or displaced, or charged with additional duties, according to his master's whim.

This feudal system was to disintegrate in the first half of the nineteenth century, giving way to capitalism. The consequences of such an evolution were twofold: the emancipation of the peasants (that is, the abolition of serfdom) and the decline of compulsory labor. These are two distinct, although connected, processes. The disappearance of serfdom and *pańszczyzna* did not

4

end the division of land into manorial and village areas. It only changed the relationship between the two areas. The former serf, who had previously owed compulsory labor, now became an independent farmer, the owner of his land. The *folwark* became a capitalist enterprise run by hired labor. A new social class appeared in the countryside, almost unknown to the feudal epoch: the farmhands, the rural proletariat.

The eventual issue was always the same, from Mecklenburg to the Ukraine, from Estonia to Yugoslavia. There were, however, tremendous differences in the rate of the evolution and in the details of the new arrangements. These differences were due to varying rates of economic evolution and to differing political conditions. Respecting Poland, two important facts must be stressed.

1. The process of emancipation came at a time when Poland was deprived of its independence. The reform was carried out not by the Poles themselves but by the three partitioning powers: Russia, Prussia, and Austria. Hence the numerous parallels between the agrarian situation in Poland and in neighboring Russian, Prussian, and Austrian provinces—practically the whole of central and eastern Europe.

2. Agrarian problems, as has been said before, were an important element in the Polish struggle for independence. One ought to speak of an interdependence of two processes: insurrection hastening reform, and class struggle leading to insurrection. One ought not to forget that the peasants were not mere pawns in a contest between landlords, patriots, and partitioning powers. The peasants had their own goals and acted accordingly.

1

THE ENLIGHTENMENT PERIOD

The Rent Reforms

The economic system based on compulsory labor spread throughout Poland during the sixteenth century. It began to show signs
of crisis in the seventeenth century, it began to disintegrate in
the eighteenth century, and it was eventually suppressed in the
nineteenth century. The first visible signs of a crisis consisted in
a steady decline of Polish agriculture. Between 1620 and 1720
the population of the Polish state dropped more than 30 percent,
and the tilled area at least 20 percent. The output of agriculture
sank from five "grains" to three (measured as the ratio of the
amount of crops to the sowings). The disastrous wars of 1648–60
contributed to the decline, but its first symptoms were visible
even before 1600 and must be attributed to the ruthless exploitation of the peasant masses by the ruling class.

A change for the better could be observed in the second quarter
of the eighteenth century. Population was growing again, and

new areas were brought under the plough. Improvements in agricultural techniques, as well as the necessity for social reforms, began to be discussed. Projects of this kind began to multiply in the second half of the eighteenth century, the so-called Enlightenment period, coinciding with the reign of the last Polish king, Stanislaus Augustus Poniatowski (1764–95). The numerous important changes occurring at that time in the spheres of politics and culture cannot be treated here. It is enough to say that there was a general trend toward modernization of the state apparatus, so that it could better defend itself against external danger. These efforts were of no avail, and Poland lost its independence in the course of the three partitions of 1772, 1793, and 1795. The changes occurring in agrarian conditions were an important part of the whole Enlightenment movement; and although they were not durable, they can be considered a first trial, a preface to the later period of Reform, in the nineteenth century, and should be treated in detail.   .

The first years of Poniatowski's reign, down to the first partition, were years of political and social commotion, ending in a civil war. But after 1772, a period of stabilization followed, lasting about twenty years, which rendered economic progress possible. The towns were growing; numerous manufactures were set up; the incomes of the middle class were rising; possibilities of investment were at hand—as well as opportunities, for the peasant, of leaving the village. Such circumstances could have resulted in an incitement toward abandoning the natural economy and passing from compulsory labor to more modern methods of farming.

But another element was at work. After 1772, as a result of the first partition, Poland was cut off from its main trade thoroughfare: the Vistula, the port of Gdansk, and the Baltic. The traditional sea route of Polish grain, leading to the markets of London and Amsterdam, was now barred by the Prussian customs. King Frederick II restricted Polish exports; hence a decline of prices of grain on the local markets, a drop in profits for the producer, and a tendency, among some of the gentlemen-farmers, to shift the risk of farming onto someone else—namely, the peasant.

The older historical literature laid particular stress on another stimulus to economic progress, the spirit of the Enlightenment. Patriotic and humanitarian sentiments induced many of the big landowners to advocate various kinds of reform—social, agrarian, economic—in the hope of inciting a rise in the economy and bettering the condition of the serfs. This may well have played a part in getting reforms started, but it was hardly the central element.

The two proposals which were the most important in effecting changes in the conditions of peasant life in the eighteenth century were (1) the rent reforms, and (2) the strengthening of the peasants' rights to the soil.

The rent reforms, generally speaking, consisted in commuting compulsory labor (*pańszczyzna*) into annual (more often quarterly) payments in cash (*czynsz*). Such reforms were frequent enough in various parts of eighteenth-century Poland, but they were dissimilar in nature as far as their motives, their scope, and their results were concerned. As to the motives, they were chiefly to be found in the self-interest of the landlord.

I stated earlier that the Polish rural economy of the time was based on the *folwark* system, working with compulsory labor. This is true only to some extent. There were some regions and some categories of estates without any compulsory labor, or with very little of it.

These were the very backward regions, lying so far from the market or growing such poor crops that it was not worthwhile to run manorial farms. Thus in the sub-Carpathian area, as well as in the woodlands of Byelorussia, there were no manorial farms to speak of. The peasants were pledged to only slight charges in cash or kind, and the charges were not easily collected, since the mountaineer or the woodcutter could easily escape his landlord's justice.

On the other hand, there were some other regions of a relatively high level of cultivation where compulsory labor ceased to pay. Among these was the Żuławy district, in the delta of the Vistula— a region of particularly rich slime land, protected from flooding by a system of dikes and drains. For centuries it was a property of the crown, divided into big peasant farms. The peasants' only obligation was the payment of rent. Not far from the lower Vistula was the Warmia district, a vast domain of the bishop, which was similarly leased. Then too, in so-called Royal Prussia— name given to the territory of eastern Pomerania (chief town, Gdansk) after its reincorporation into Poland in 1466—down the lower Vistula on the fertile riverside soil, numerous manorial farms had long been accustomed to employing hired labor. It was profitable because of the proximity of the seaport of Gdansk.

A third category of villages without compulsory labor consisted of those inhabited by the petty gentry: small farmers of gentry origin who were, as gentlemen, full owners of their land although they tilled it with their own hands. From the economic point of view, they were independent small farmers. These were the so-called *zaścianki*, immortalized in Mickiewicz's *Pan Tadeusz*—a phenomenon frequent in northeastern Masovia, Podlasie, southern Lithuania, and western Byelorussia but occurring in other parts of the country, too. There were no serfs in a *zaścianek* and consequently no compulsory labor.

On the contrary, compulsory labor was used not only in peasant environments but also in towns—I mean of course little towns ("rotten boroughs"), which were supported mainly by agriculture and belonged to private estates. These poor burghers, earning little from handicrafts and trade, often leased a piece of land from their landlords in exchange for manual labor on the local *folwark*. In such instances, there was an obligation to work, though without serfdom.

Summing up, the absence of compulsory labor was due either to very backward or to very advanced conditions; or, in some cases, to the juridical status of the population. Consequently, a generally progressive trend in agriculture could bring about entirely different effects, according to the niveau of individual regions. In an economically developed region, a boom in agriculture could induce the landlord to adopt a system of hired labor, and one of the possible ways of doing this was to commute compulsory labor into rent. But in more backward regions, the same boom in agriculture incited the landlords to set up manorial farms where there had been none previously—and this meant, on the contrary, the commuting of rent into compulsory labor. This happened in many regions of Lithuania, particularly in the crown estates. Toward the end of the preceding century, after a long period of economic depression, most of the farms in those domains were simply suppressed, and rent introduced in place of labor. But under King Poniatowski the tide changed: manorial farms reappeared, and compulsory labor with them. Needless to say, the peasantry protested violently; riots and even armed revolts occurred.

The more important process, however, in eighteenth-century Poland, was the conversion to rent. This operation ought to be considered from two sides: the landlord's and the peasant's. From the landlord's point of view, the decisive argument in favor of the rent reform was that it would be profitable, but this was seldom the case. Even such a progressive author—and friend and protector of peasants—as Stanisław Staszic (1755–1826) had to admit that Poland could not afford a compulsory rent reform: it had to depend on the enlightened good will and the patriotic intention, and only in particular instances on the interest of the landlord. What circumstances, then, could induce the landlord to eliminate compulsory labor? All or part of it? There were a number of different circumstances: Compulsory labor, at times, was inefficient; or one had too much gratuitous labor to be able to use it; or, on the other hand, it was difficult to get any gratuitous labor at all. Each of these situations could lead to a different kind of rent reform.

Compulsory labor was likely to become inefficient in latifundia which could not be run by their magnate owners; they were either leased by single manorial farms or by tenants belonging to the poorer gentry, or they were administered by estate agents and stewards. In both cases, the go-between function of tenants and administrators deprived the magnate of a good portion of the income wreaked from the peasant serf. At times when corn prices were low (because of Prussian customs) and when there seemed to be a rise in industrial growth, it sometimes appeared profitable to let the peasant sell the corn and to collect rent money directly from the serfs, bypassing the go-between, and being able, thus, to invest part of the income in manufacturing, in banking, and often in politics. This is the main reason why most of the rent reforms were introduced in big latifundia, by magnates, bishops, and also the crown. One should of course also take into account those of the enlightened aristocracy who were in touch with progressive ideas, prone to reforms of any kind, and able to afford the cost of experimentation. But, in fact, these reforms were more advantageous to a magnate than to a gentleman of middle-sized fortune. The owner of a single village could always extort from his peasants enough labor to make a good living for himself.

11

Some distinct cases should be examined here. In some situations, the landlord was, so to speak, compelled to introduce rent— e.g., for colonists, or new settlers. If a landlord wanted to ameliorate his estate—to bring barren soil under cultivation, to clear backwoods land or drain meadows—he was bound to guarantee the settler the fruit of his labor. The process of colonization was particularly brisk in western and northwestern Poland, on both banks of the Noteć River; numerous new settlements arose in the second half of the eighteenth century. The colonists were mostly newcomers from Germany, and they were called *Haulünder-clearings* (*olendrzy*). They were granted land exclusively for rent, without compulsory labor. Similarly, on the opposite outskirts of the Commonwealth, in southeast Ukraine, generous steppe lands were brought under cultivation in consequence of the pacification of the Crimean Tartars by Russia. Ukrainian peasants immigrating to the vast Korsuń estates of Prince Poniatowski, one of the king's nephews, were granted free use of the soil for the first years; afterward they paid rent. It would have been difficult to compel them to labor, so long as on the Russian side of the frontier similar settlers were under no such compulsion.

Now let us examine another category of commutations to rent not connected with either latifundia or with new settlements. In southern, or Little, Poland, a region of dense population and mostly middle-sized domains, sources tell us of rather frequent commutations of labor into rent; not for entire villages but for individual peasants, and for short, temporary periods. The procedure was called *lease instead of labor* (*najem za pańszczyznę*); though of course it was not a lease, by any means. The peasant paid his master in advance, for a year or a quarter, an appointed sum and was, in consequence, freed from labor until the end of his term. It was by no means a free compact; the master could always retract his agreement, or refuse to prolong it. As a matter of fact, he designated the individuals who would be thus freed from labor—for a time, and until further notice. For what reason did the landlords introduce such arrangements? They simply did not need as much labor as the estates could supply. As we read in a diary of the time, the landlord simply "bathed in compulsory labor." He commuted a portion of it: sometimes in distant villages, where the peasants lost much time in traveling to work and back; sometimes in parts of the villages, usually for the well-to-do, most productive farmers, who were apt to pay rent promptly. Or, in still another way, he sometimes commuted a certain number of compulsory labor days into payment in cash. Such manifestations of a rent system could hardly be called economic progress. They were partial and susceptible of recall; in some instances they only denoted an arbitrary raise of peasant charges: if the landlord noticed that his serfs were getting some cash from the local market, he accordingly made arrangements to divert this money to his own cash drawer.

This remark leads us to the further statement that the introduction of rent did not always coincide with the interest of the peasants. From the peasant's viewpoint, as a matter of fact, the crucial premise of a rent reform was the necessity of payment. And this depended, in turn, not only, and not so much, on the amount of rent as on the peasant's opportunity to accumulate the money. To pay rent, the peasant had to sell the products of his farming; consequently, a sufficiently capacious local market had to be at hand if the rent system was to work at all. The best results in commutation to rent were attained, therefore, in regions neighboring larger cities or commercial routes. Let us cite two examples. The first is the city of Poznan, which owned some suburban villages which were farmed out to a single tenant and brought little profit. As early as about 1740, a reform was introduced: the manorial farm was suppressed and all the peasants were converted into rent payers. The operation proved profitable for both sides. The welfare of the villagers rose, as well as the income of the city. This was due to the presence of a big city market in Poznan. Another, and later, instance is a big estate on the Niemen River in Lithuania. The Niemen was an important trade route for corn and timber. The owner of Merecz, Father Paweł Brzostowski, a wealthy canon of the Wilno chapter, was an enlightened writer and a friend of peasants. He not only suppressed compulsory labor in his estates but he gradually liquidated all manorial farms. He introduced a kind of village self-government and a local militia, he opened schools and hospitals, and he was unanimously praised as his serfs' father and benefactor. Nevertheless, Father Brzostowski boasted that the income of the Pawłów estate (Merecz was changed into Pawłów) had also considerably risen. There was a great deal of self-advertising in Brzostowski's declarations; but even so it seems that the Pawłów experiment was a successful one. And it would not have been successful at all, had Pawłów not been situated on the big Niemen trade route.

These observations help us to understand the attitude of the peasants toward all these reforms—introduced, one should not forget, of the landlord's own free will. It seems, in many instances that the peasants passively submitted to the new arrangements; but they also quite often petitioned for the introduction of rent, and, not infrequently, they demanded it. They also revolted, when compulsory labor was introduced again after a period of rent paying. Contrary examples, however, can also be cited of peasants protesting against a commutation to rent or begging, after a period of rent paying, to be allowed to return to compulsory labor. The best-known case is that of the Bieżuń estate of Great Chancellor Andrzej Zamoyski (1716–92)—a philanthropist, an enlightened magnate, and a politician. The peasants repudiated his attempts at reforms—which led some pamphleteers and historians to proclaim that the villagers were not yet mature enough for such benefactions and certainly did not deserve them. There could, of course, have been other reasons for the peasants' negative approach to manorial reforms as in the Bieżuń case. The rent could have been fixed too high. Or it could even have been moderate, but local conditions might have made it impossible for the peasants to sell their harvest advantageously. There could have been another reason still: The refusal of a rent reform, the demand for a return to compulsory labor, became, for the peasants, a weapon of class war. Let us imagine the situation of a landlord who has just abolished compulsory labor, allotted the manorial grounds to single farmers, and generalized the practice of rent. Now the peasants demand the reintroduction of compulsory labor! It is a horrible nuisance, and an expense, to turn back to the old system, to establish new manorial farms; better to come to terms with the peasants—that is, to lower the rents. The peasants understood this situation perfectly, and they bargained accordingly.

To put an end to our conjectures, we shall emphasize two main characteristics of rent reforms in Poland of the eighteenth century. First, they all had a local character, since they were, in principle, acts of free will on the part of the landlords. Numerous as they were, they should be considered exceptions. Compulsory labor remained the majority rule till the end of the eighteenth century. Second, the reforms were transitory, and they always could be recalled so long as the peasant (rent payer) remained a serf, a subordinate of the landlord. Pawłów, mentioned above, gives us a striking example. Father Brzostowski, the benefactor of Pawłów, became involved in the Kościuszko insurrection; he was obliged to emigrate and to sell his estates. Ten years later, he returned to the country and visited Pawłów again. His former serfs greeted him tenderly, even with tears. But nothing remained of his reforms. The new landlord did not feel himself bound to respect his predecessor's arrangements. There was no self-government left; there were no schools and no hospitals; and the peasants were again subject to compulsory labor. This was the case in many villages, though by no means in all. The reforms of the Enlightenment period did not disappear without leaving a trace; but they did not originate a decisive trend toward emancipation. They fitted entirely into the serfdom system.

The Peasants' Right to the Soil

Parallel to, and independently of, the rent reforms of the eighteenth century, a second tendency could be observed in Poland: the strengthening of the peasants' rights to the soil. What were these rights, and what could they be under the feudal system? The peasant, as a serf, had no rights. He could be deprived of his land, his charges could be raised, and he could be summoned to discharge various duties in his landlord's castle; he could also—but the cases were few (fewer than in Russia)—be sold "down the river" to another master. The great majority of peasants, not only in Poland but in all the countries east of the Elbe, had no guarantee against willful removal from their land, or equally willful alteration of their charges. They had no right to sell or cede their land to another peasant or to mortgage it in any fashion. And finally, they had no right to pass this modest inheritance to their children. It is true that it was the custom, after a peasant's death, for his land to be assigned to one of his sons. But this was only a custom and not a legal rule. The landlord was not obliged, either legally or morally, to respect the order of succession; he could choose between the sons, or sons-in-law, of the deceased; he also could, and often did, pick out another peasant, especially when there were no adult children ready and

15

able to perform the duties of the former possessor. The peasant's situation was often defined, especially by German officials, and later also by historians, as a "weak right to the soil." The expression is somehow artificial; the right concerned was so weak as to be equivalent to no right at all. It seems that the term was created in opposition to another term: a "strong right" of the same peasant.

Instances of strong right were also known in central Europe, even under the feudal system. The peasant endowed with such a right was considered the hereditary possessor (though not the owner, in the modern sense) of his soil. He was bound by contract (an oral or a written one) to perform certain duties in labor, or to pay rent, but as long as he acquitted himself thereof he could not be driven away. He also had the right to cede his piece of soil, for money, to somebody else, provided the landlord found the successor apt to work and gave his consent. Such a set of privileges could really be considered strong, in comparison with the lot of the majority of Polish peasants possessing only weak rights. Of course, one ought to add that even these strong rights were not very strong, since under this system the peasant remained a serf and was often subject to compulsory labor.

Nevertheless, this so-called strong right was considered a privilege, and many a peasant was ambitious to strengthen his right to the soil, in one manner or another. How could it be done? The feudal system knew an institution called *act of purchase* (*zakupieństwo*): the peasant gave his landlord a sum of money, and he was granted in return the right of inheritance, of irremovability, etc. The purchaser could be a new settler—and we have seen that most of the new colonists in the eighteenth century agreed to settle only on such terms. But an older inhabitant of the village could also "purchase" such a right—that is, he could claim such a favor. The fulfillment of such a claim depended entirely upon the landlord's good will.

Such acts of purchase occurred in preceding centuries, but they became more frequent in the Enlightenment period. The main novelty was that the procedure of purchase was now spreading, not as a result of peasant initiative, but of state politics. Particularly in Prussia, under the reign of Frederick II, and in the Polish provinces conquered by Prussia, such as Silesia and Pomerania, the state tried to compel the peasants to purchase the "stronger rights." The same tendency was also to be observed in the Polish Commonwealth, namely, in the possessions of the crown.

What could have been the motives of the state in promoting such a procedure? They were fiscal and economic in nature. Fiscal, because the act of purchase meant the payment of a substantial amount of money by the peasant to the crown or, in a latifundium, to the magnate. It seems, however, that the economic motive was really the more important. The new point of view consisted in making the peasant—the purchaser—more interested in his farming, so that he would improve his farming methods and, perhaps, make some investments. Therefore the act of purchase imposed on a village or on a larger estate was often combined with a rent reform, the abolition of compulsory labor.

Historians of law have often considered these acts of purchase equivalent to granting the right of property, or at least a kind of property, to the peasants. This was, of course, an illusion. The soil supposedly purchased did not become the property of the peasant. It was still burdened by numerous charges; the so-called owner remained a serf and could be deprived of the purchased land for many reasons: refusing to perform his duties; proving to be a poor farmer, or considered so; showing disobedience toward the landlord; and even—if the landlord proclaimed the peasant guilty of propagating revolt—giving a bad example to the village. The stronger rights, though purchased at a high price, remained, after all, a favor of the landlord, a privilege, and not a right in the legal sense. The best proof thereof was the relatively small amount of enthusiasm, among the peasants, for profiting from the opportunity offered by the state. The Silesian peasants in particular showed no eagerness at all to pay the required sums for the stronger rights. The state officials used pressure, but the procedure dragged on, and after twenty years it was far from being completed. It is, again, not easy to establish with any degree of certainty what the real motives of the peasants' opposition were. Was it that they considered the so-called stronger rights of little positive value? Or perhaps they thought—and not entirely without reason—that the future would bring them the full ownership of the soil on more advantageous terms; or that if the landlord proposed a reform he sought his own interest and not that of the peasant. Such motives of behavior reappeared more distinctly among peasants of the nineteenth century.

The Political Programs

We have spoken, up to this point, about changes occurring in the peasants' conditions under the influence of economic factors and in consequence of privately undertaken reforms. Let us now review the various proposals for bettering the peasant's condition espoused by pamphleteers and politicians of the Enlightenment period. Such projects usually appealed to the gentry's humanitarian feelings, patriotism, and common sense, since a reform of the peasant's status was thought necessary for the improvement of agriculture. The actual design of these reformers lay elsewhere. They were promoting a general transformation of Polish society: the overthrow of the oligarchical regime, the improvement of the state apparatus, and the admission of the middle classes to political rights. The agrarian reform was to constitute only a part of a vast program aiming at the salvation of the commonwealth, which was more and more threatened by its neighbors. These programs varied in their scope and degree of radicalism; they aimed, in general, much further than the timid and partial reforms actually introduced. So let us distinguish at once these two spheres of political and economic thought which influenced each other but did not coincide: the partial and feasible reforms, on the one hand; the bolder but somewhat utopian projects, on the other.

The first of these projects, was set forth in a book attributed to the king-in-exile Stanislas Leszczyński, written about 1733 and published anonymously in 1749 under the title *The Free Voice Securing Freedom* (the king's authorship has been questioned by some recent searchers). *The Free Voice* advocated the necessity of abolishing serfdom and commuting labor into rent. It was, at the time, one might say, a "voice calling in the wilderness."

In the first year of Poniatowski's reign (1767), a pamphlet, singular in more than one respect, was circulated in manuscript; it was called "The Petition of Torczyn," from the name of the little Volhynian town where it was supposedly circulated. This petition was set forth in the name of the peasants themselves; it enumerated their grievances against the gentry and categorically demanded a substantial bettering of their position. It urged not only abolition of serfdom and compulsory labor but peasant participation in political life. The peasants, so it said, would willingly participate in the defense of the country, but if their wrongs were not redressed they would claim their rights, arms in hand. The style and content of this curious text show clearly that it was not from a peasant's pen. Numerous conjectures have been advanced concerning the authorship of this petition without convincing success. Probably, as suggested by E. Rostworowski, the author was an unknown intellectual of plebeian descent, acting on his own initiative. Unfortunately, we are not aware of the existence of such intellectuals on the eve of the Enlightenment period.

An incident which could have added some weight to the Torczyn petition was the violent peasant uprising, one year later, on the Ukrainian outskirts of the Commonwealth. This was the Humań massacre, so called because in the town of Humań and its neighborhood some 30,000 people lost their lives: landlords and their families, employees, petty gentry, and Jews. A civil war had just begun between the Confederation of Bar (which united the conservative magnates, hostile to reforms) and King Poniatowski, who was supported by Russia. "Poland's defense against foreign intervention" was one of the slogans of the confederates. The civil war gave the Ukrainian peasants one more occasion to shake off the yoke of the Polish gentry. The upheaval was stifled by royal forces, with help from the Russians. It nevertheless had numerous reverberations in Lithuania, Silesia, and elsewhere and profoundly impressed the gentry's mind. A reform of the peasant's status was considered, after that, by many authors, not only an act of humanitarianism or political wisdom but also a measure of prudence—the means of preventing a new outburst of the peasants' wrath.

Just before the Humań upheaval, the peasant question was talked over in the Polish parliament, or *Sejm*. New cardinal laws had to be elaborated, this time under Russian guarantee, and some progressive politicians, including the king himself, sought to introduce among them some ameliorations for the peasants. These attempts were of no avail; on the contrary, the serfdom of the peasants was solemnly included in the cardinal laws. The only resolution in favor of the peasants voted in this session of 1768 was to the effect that the landlords were now forbidden to sentence their serfs to death. This was to be done, henceforth, only in courts of justice. Numerous historians have dwelt on the importance of this bill of 1768—but it seems that it actually effected very little change. The most common practice, when a serious criminal offense was committed by a peasant—murder, violence, arson, or the like—was to transfer the case to the court of the nearest town. The procedure of these municipal courts was sharp and efficient; the landlord could rely upon having the culprit tortured and hanged without delay, and without encumbering himself with his neighbor's blood. And it was not unusual for a landlord or his bailiff to beat a stubborn peasant so severely that death ensued, even *after* the 1768 bill was passed.

The next attempt to change the peasant's condition was due to Andrzej Zamoyski, the proprietor, mentioned above, of the Bieżuń estate. The *Sejm* entrusted Zamoyski, in 1776, with the task of putting in order some of the existing laws. Two years later, Zamoyski submitted his project. He solemnly insisted upon not introducing any novelties; he merely wanted to reestablish good ancient laws and usages. Such phraseology was necessary for the conservative ears of the *Sejm*. Zamoyski sincerely wanted to introduce reforms; he referred, therefore, to ancient prescriptions, dating from the fifteenth century, when the serfdom was much milder than in later times. He suggested, among other things, liberating from serfdom the peasants settled on contract (in England one would say *copyholders*); granting the second and fourth sons of every peasant the liberty to move into town, in order to learn crafts; and legalizing the current though forbidden contracting of marriages between persons of different conditions: gentry, burghers, and peasants. These were rather timid proposals; they provoked, nevertheless, violent opposition among the middle gentry. The Zamoyski Code had powerful adversaries, but the peasant reforms—it was charged that Zamoyski wanted to dishonor the gentry's blood by marriages with villeins—contributed to its fall. In 1780, the project was unanimously rejected by the *Sejm* and prohibited from being proposed again.

Some years elapsed, however, and the attitude of the enlightened public slowly began to change. The necessity of reforms, both political and social, was acknowledged more and more generally. During the four-year *Sejm* (1788–92) numerous pamphlets were circulated, debating, among other things, the agrarian question. Hugo Kołłątaj (1750–1812), one of the leaders of the Patriotic party, as early as 1788 stepped forth with the slogan "The soil to the landlord, and free work for the peasants." This meant, in fact, the abolition of serfdom but without granting the peasants any right to the soil—a program which was to be put into effect much later. Two pamphlets anonymously published by a very young radical of plebeian descent, Joseph Pawlikowski (1770–1829), expanded eloquently upon the suffering of the peasants but did not propose any definite scheme of reform. Stanisław Staszic, the chief representative of the Polish bourgeoisie, was more explicit. One should, however, distinguish in his writings the theoretical views and the practical program. By conviction, Staszic was an adversary of compulsory labor; he thought it would be only just to let the peasant become owner of his soil. But such a program must have appeared utopian even to Staszic's eyes. In practice, he confined himself to proposing that the landlords grant their serfs personal freedom and commute compulsory labor into rent. It was essential that such views be printed and widely discussed; but discussion was not sufficient to alter the legal state of things.

The debates during the four-year *Sejm* were crowned by the Constitution of 3 May, 1791. Article 4 of this famous text* was dedicated to the peasants. It has been often stressed that the Constitution of 3 May did almost nothing for the peasants. It is clear that this point of view ought to be revised, particularly when one examines not only the bare text of the law but its genesis and the successive stages of discussion carried on in secret by a small group of parliamentary leaders. Only in recent years has the archival documentation pertaining to the elaboration of the Act of 3 May been opened to the public. It has enabled us to study, among other things, the course of discussion concerning the peasant question. Orginally, it seems, Article 4 was to contain more liberal stipulations: liberty of movement as well as a state guarantee for all contracts between the peasants and the landlords. This formulation was due to the initiative of the king himself. In later wordings, these promises acquired substantial limitations, owing largely to the influence of Ignacy Potocki (1750–1809), the most outstanding of the "enlightened"

* See Appendix, section *A*.

magnates of the time. As a first stage, the liberty of movement was restricted to fugitives, that is, to persons who had illegally left the village and established themselves elsewhere; they were not to be threatened with a forcible return to serfdom. There was much talk about the length of prescription in such cases: twenty-five, fifteen, or only ten years? Eventually, the matter was dropped entirely; there remained in Article 4 only a vague declaration, that runaways returning to their village should be considered, in future, personally free. Another proposal, due also to the king, that the retired soldiers, after ten years of service, should acquire personal freedom, was also canceled. Instead, at the suggestion of Kołłątaj, the leader of the radical wing, another phrase was adopted: The "farm laborers" are to be brought under the protection of the law and government. This protection, in the final text, was particularly to pertain to any new contracts concluded between the landlords and the villagers. It was emphasized, as well, that newly established settlers would be considered, henceforward, personally free.

How ought we to evaluate Article 4 of the Constitution? It is obvious that it consisted chiefly of generous phrases, vaguely commending the villagers for their honesty and industry. The granting of personal freedom was limited to a narrow category of peasants; the state guarantee to a still more narrow group of contracts—those which would be signed in the future. But, on the other hand, one should not disregard the fact that the same Article 4 did break, for the first time in centuries, and in the name of the state, the absolute domination of the landlord over the serf; it established, at least theoretically, the right of the government in the affairs of the private estate (right of control, if not of intervention).

More important still, the view recently expressed on the subject by most specialists is that the Constitution of 3 May should be regarded as the framework for future reform. It was actually rather brief and vague; numerous clauses expressly begged for a development. The leaders of the Patriotic party, who had sponsored the Act of 3 May, perfectly understood this aspect; they purposely aimed at a continuation, an expansion, of the legislative work. Kołłątaj himself, in a memorable speech in June 1791, declared openly that an economic constitution should follow the political Constitution of 3 May, elaborating, among other things, a reshaping of state finances, a policy of investments, and, as an indispensable condition of such a policy, a new settlement of the peasants' status. Such views, however, were far from being unanimously approved in a House composed entirely of gentlemen-landlords. Contradictory interests came into play. The Constitution was not enacted in a closed chamber, and its repercussions were extensive and often unexpected. Many villagers reacted in a singular way: they interpreted Article 4 as granting them personal freedom, whereas it actually permitted them only to change their residences or to sign formal contracts with their masters. Hence, numerous illegal migrations, petitions, and refusals to work. Occasionally there were even mutinies. These reactions were viewed with apprehension in the House, and even the king, who was considered, not without reason, a partisan of moderate social reform, insisted upon repressing such peasant offenses with military aid. This climate did not stimulate the *Sejm* to initiate further concessions in social matters, and so most social legislation was simply postponed.

There was, however, one urgent question which had to be decided immediately: What was to be done with the crown estates? These were vast domains of which a small part served as subsistence for the royal court. The larger part was distributed for life to favorites of the crown—mostly magnates—who paid a small percentage of their revenue to the treasury. For various political reasons, the arrangement was now to be canceled: most of the crown estates were to be taken from their possessors and sold into private hands. Hence a new problem: What should be the lot of the inhabitants of these domains? Peasants in crown estates were considered a privileged section of the villagers. They were serfs, it is true, and mostly pledged to compulsory labor; but they enjoyed stronger (if not very strong) rights to the soil, and remained, as subjects of the crown, under the crown's jurisdiction. If they felt injured by their immediate master, the *starosta*, they could appeal to the royal court (*Referendaria*). This juridical protection of the state was not very efficient, for two reasons. First, the state itself was feeble in Poland; and second, it represented the interests of the gentry. Nevertheless, the privilege of appeal, refused to the rest of the peasants, was not to be scorned. What was to be the lot of these serfs of the crown when the estates passed into private hands? Some patriot members of the *Sejm* demanded that they be given a state guarantee of their possessions. In other words, that the state should grant them the strong right. This proposition, however, was not adopted in the House, and therefore the crown peasants were to be left unprotected. The problem remained theoretical, since the sale of the crown estates was not carried out, after all. Nevertheless, this attitude was characteristic of the *Sejm*, as a representative of the gentry.

The new regime established on 3 May 1791 fell after fifteen months. It was abolished by Russia, supported by the conservative wing of the oligarchy, allied under the banner of the so-called Targowica Confederation. Shortly afterward, a new insurrection broke out, headed by Tadeusz Kościuszko (1746–1817). It was a last attempt at saving the state and the nation. In 1794, Kościuszko assumed dictatorial power and appealed to all citizens to defend their country: the gentry, the middle classes, and the peasants.

Kościuszko was a democrat; he had fought in the American Revolution; he remained a fervent admirer of American democracy and of the American conduct of the War of Independence. He was convinced that a free nation fighting for its liberty was unconquerable. Poland should therefore become a free nation; the peasants, particularly, should be freed from all bondage. This was theory—but there were also practical considerations, of a twofold nature. On the one hand, Kościuszko faced powerful armies: Russia and Prussia, in the first instance. He needed new recruits, especially peasants, who would enlist willingly and fight even against odds for a comprehensible aim. But, on the other hand, Kościuszko was no revolutionary, no partisan of social upheaval which would, for example, take the nobles' estates and give them to the lower classes. No; in Kościuszko's view, the gentry—if one excepted the small Targowica group—was a patriotic element. One was obliged to rely on the gentry's help and should therefore take care not to estrange or discourage them.

There were, besides, more practical reasons. A social revolution in the midst of a serious war would indeed be a risky enterprise. A normal functioning of the estates was essential for the waging of war. It had begun in March; what would one eat in autumn if the sowing were not done properly? Promises for the peasants

24

were all right, but it was essential that they not interrupt their work. These were the diverse considerations which were to influence and shape Kościuszko's social program.

After having proclaimed the war for liberty and independence in Krakow on 24 March, Kościuszko stepped forth against the Russians with a small corps of 4,000 regular army. He ordered a levy of recruits in the neighboring countryside and formed with the peasants, taken from the plough and armed only with scythes, an auxiliary detachment of 2,000 men. In the first battle at Racławice on 4 April, these peasant recruits fought gallantly, captured a number of guns, and significantly contributed to victory. But this victory was a tactical, not a strategic, success, since the road to Warsaw remained barred by superior Russian forces. Nevertheless, the battle at Racławice was widely reported throughout Poland, and the heroic role played by the scythemen was skillfully used by insurrectionary propagandists. Ostentatiously, Kościuizko put on the peasant russet coat, and he granted nobility to the hero of the day Wojciech Bartos, giving him the gentleman's name of Głowacki.

Such were the propaganda gestures; but legal enactments had to follow, and this was a delicate matter. Several proclamations by Kościuszko, issued in the next few days and addressed to the peasants as well as to the gentry, denoted irresolution, if not inconsequence. Only on 6 May did Kościuszko make his decision, and from the camp of Połaniec he published his famous manifesto, which was to put the peasant problem on an entirely new basis.

The most important clauses of the Połaniec Manifesto can be summarized as follows: (1) There would be a general granting of personal freedom to the peasant serfs. (2) There would be a partial reduction of compulsory labor, amounting to one day per week (if a peasant had been obliged to work three days a week, he would now work only two; if two days, henceforth only one). Such an abatement favored mostly the lower categories of compulsory laborers—that is, the poorer groups of villagers. (3) There would be total liberation from compulsory labor for the soldiers of the insurrectionary army and their families. This was an indispensable provision, since the villagers complained that their masters were obliging them to perform compulsory labor in the place of the enlisted men. (4) In order to control and enforce, if necessary, the regulations above, a new institution was to be created: the so-called surveyors (*dozorcy*), appointed for territories with 4,000–5,000 inhabitants, with the exclusive mission of setting in motion the new arrangements and of settling disputes between the landlords and peasants. These surveyors could belong to the gentry but they could also be chosen from the middle classes. (5) And finally, the manifesto closed with a proposition aimed at preserving the normal functioning of the domains. The peasants, though freed from serfdom and (partially) from compulsory labor, were asked to continue to work on the manor farms—this time, however for just wages. And the landlords were exhorted to treat their serfs, who were now to become hired farmhands, more kindly.

This set of regulations seemed realistic enough, in the sense that it took into account the necessity of supplying food, it considered the interests of both landowners and villagers, and it removed the most painful handicaps of the peasants without attempting to destroy the gentry. The essential problem now was how such a new arrangement could be swiftly and efficaciously put into effect.

Two different approaches can be distinguished in the historiography of the Połaniec Manifesto: on the one hand, a fervent apology of this enactment, describing it as the ultimate will of a free Polish state, opposed to the more conservative legislation of the partitioning powers, and extolling it as an act of perfect and final justice; on the other hand, the skeptical approach: the manifesto was partial, hence ineffective—and, above all, it was not actually put into effect, because of systematic sabotage on the part of the gentry. This last charge was a serious one; and minute research has been devoted in recent years to establishing in what measure, and with what consequences, the manifesto was applied. As could easily be foreseen, the results of such an inquiry have not been homogeneous.

The insurrection of 1794 lasted from March until October, less than seven months. It embraced a large part of the country, from Krakow to Courland, from Bydgoszcz to Volhynia. The course of the campaign, however, was variable; from month to month, the Poles conquered and then lost new territories. It would be difficult to name a region, with the exception, perhaps, of the country between Warsaw and the Bug River, which was held by the insurgents for more than a couple of months. This should be considered an important obstacle to the realization of the manifesto, the functioning of the surveyors, etc. And as for the application of the manifesto's provisions on territories under the insurrection's rule, no uniform picture emerges from the sources. Cases may be quoted of scrupulous control of these provisions and their realization, of convincing and efficacious activity by the surveyors, of noticeable effects of the patriotic propaganda among peasants, and of the peasants' willing participation in the national war. But other cases are known as well, where the institution of surveyor remained a mere formality; where the local authorities, civil and military, did not bother at all about the peasants' welfare; and where the families of peasant volunteers were still driven to work on the *folwark*—with obviously negative effects on the political attitude of the rural masses.

This attitude of the peasants in the war of 1794 is a subject much discussed, and it has been appraised in various ways, depending upon the attitudes of the authors toward democracy. It is a fact that the numerous sections of peasant recruits and volunteers, armed with scythes (or more often with pikes), did not play the decisive role attributed to them by the postwar legend. Decisive battles were fought and won—or lost—by the regular army, into which many peasants had been incorporated. The scythemen and pikemen were no hobby for Kościuszko; it was a necessity, in the presence of a painful scarcity of armaments, to employ units with no firearms. Some of these units, though, proved really useful, as in the defense of the Narew Line, where poorly armed volunteers managed to hold their sector of the front line and to secure the flanks of the main army during the siege of Warsaw by the Prussians. Kościuszko's appeal to the peasants did not ensure victory, although it certainly reinforced the insurgent army. More important, in the long run, was the tradition of this appeal to the peasants—a tradition which was to influence the program, the attitudes, and the behavior of many social groups in Poland, during the following century and even later. The banners of the scythemen units bore, by Kościuszko's order, this significant inscription: "They nourish and they defend" (*Żywią i bronią*). The same slogan was adopted by numerous partisan units of peasant stock, fighting in the war

27

against Hitlerism. This shows the persistence of some types of historical tradition.

We should not abandon the subject of Kościuszko's insurrection before considering still another aspect of the peasant problem: the maximal program of the left wing. The insurrection was a period of active political struggle, and, particularly in Warsaw (among the intelligentsia and the lower middle classes), radical tendencies were evolving, inspired chiefly by the suggestive example of the French Revolution. These were the so-called Polish Jacobins, to whom Professor B. Leśnodorski recently dedicated a valuable monograph. The Jacobins advocated a more energetic conduct of the war, as well as drastic measures against the traitors of the Targowica group, including the king himself. Some Jacobins initiated proposals for solving agrarian problems. These proposals are worthy of note, not because they were—or could have been—put into effect, but because they pointed to new courses of evolution; they presaged, so to speak, future programs which might have some possibility of being effected.

We have seen that, during the eighteenth century, political programs and their practical realizations oscillated between two main proposals: the abolition of or at least the diminution of serfdom; and the commuting, or restraining, of compulsory labor. It was agreed that the peasant should be freed, but no further thought was given to his material condition. Now the Jacobins were taking further steps: they advocated, albeit timidly, the necessity of granting the liberated peasants the full ownership of their soil. One of the radical Warsaw journalists, Alojzy Orchowski (1767–1832), proposed that every peasant who enlisted in the insurgent army or had two sons serving in the army should be declared the owner of his plot of land. The landlord should be indemnified by the state. The Targowica traitors, however, should be deprived of all indemnity. Toward the end of the insurrection, on 20 October 1794, a motion was brought by Kołłątaj himself, in the Supreme National Council, to the effect that war veterans, wounded soldiers, and orphan children of fallen insurgents should be granted plots of land "in eternal and hereditary possession." Time was lacking, unfortunately, for voting on or for carrying out such a program. Other projects were also advanced in the radical press, relating to the appointing of peasants to some functions in the parish self-government—

for example, as surveyors or as officers in the local courts of justice; some even discussed the possibility of peasant representation in a future *Sejm*. None of these proposals was taken seriously; even their existence was forgotten; only in recent times has a careful investigation of the radical press divulged such tendencies.

The Polish Commonwealth died out because of its predominantly feudal economic structure. The ruling class—the *szlachta* —was unwilling to abandon traditional methods of exploiting peasant labor; and neither the peasants themselves nor the middle classes were able to enforce an abolition, modeled after the French pattern, of feudal privileges. Changes occurring in the Polish countryside—limitation of compulsory labor and strengthening of the peasants' rights—were partial and temporary. The same can be said of reforms introduced by the Patriotic party. New approaches were outlined and new programs proposed with, as a central theme, the liberation of the serf. But all these can best be regarded as guide lines for the next generation; they had little effect during the Enlightenment era.

2

THE FIRST YEARS OF
FOREIGN RULE

The significant feature in the next—the partition—period in Polish agrarian history was that agrarian relations were henceforth framed, not exclusively by the Poles themselves, but more and more under the influence and pressure of a foreign state—or, rather, three foreign states and their bureaucracies. At that time there existed a tremendous difference between the old Polish state, which was practically deprived of all authority by the propertied gentry, and the three absolutist and bureaucratic monarchies of Russia, Prussia, and Austria. The Polish state in its last years showed a tendency to modernize its structure in an attempt to render it more efficient. In peasant affairs it advocated a series of liberal, although timid and partial, reforms. The partitioning powers, on the other hand, had long since established the regulation not only of political but of social relations, and especially of class relations, between landlords and serfs. This was done in the spirit of the so-called Enlightened absolutism, a tendency aiming not to overthrow the feudal structure but to remodel it. The state functions were to remain, in substance, in the hands of the feudal ruling class. Of course, such state interference was bound to cause opposition among the more conservative groups of the gentry, who were not prone to accept the new burdens imposed by the state and generally to subject themselves to state control. And in this respect it often happened that the partitioning state felt itself more akin to the Polish gentry—an alien and politically unreliable element—than to its own Junkers or *pomeshtchiki*. Thus the partitioning state frequently promoted, or put to the test, peasant reforms of a more radical character in the annexed Polish territories than in the central provinces of Russia, Prussia, and Austria.

One constant element of this policy was a tendency to win the sympathy of the Polish masses, by satisfying some of their needs and requirements, at the expense of the gentry. At the time of the third partition, in 1795, there was, however, an important obstacle to such a policy. Monarchal Europe waged a bitter war against revolutionary France. The coalition cabinets were anxious to combat the Jacobin contagion in their own countries; as a matter of fact, they had fought Kościuszko's insurrection under the pretense of trampling down Jacobinism in Poland. In these circumstances, they were not likely to inaugurate agrarian reforms in Poland similar to those introduced by the French National Assembly of 1789.

Next in importance is the fact is that the three partitioning powers were far from following uniform policies with their new Polish subjects, especially in agrarian problems. There were, of course, some common features, arising from the fact that Russia, Austria, and Prussia all represented feudal, absolutist, and bureaucratic monarchies. Hence a general tendency to limit the very broad, traditional self-government of the gentry; to introduce a foreign administration; to support the big landowners rather than the petty ones; and to bring the crown estates as well as the church domains under direct state administration. Nevertheless, the chief goal of the three powers was to assimilate the new provinces and to introduce in Poland arrangements already tested elsewhere. Moreover, whereas Russia, Prussia, and Austria were at that time on very different levels of economic and social development, it was inevitable that they should impose on their Polish acquisitions different, if not contrasting, patterns of evolution. And this applied above all to social, that is, peasant problems. So we are obliged to speak not of one social policy of the partitioning powers but of three, very different policies.

Changes in Russia

Catherine II (1763–96) annexed, in the three partitions of 1772, 1793, and 1795, the eastern provinces of the Commonwealth extending to the Niemen, the Bug, and the Zbrucz rivers. From the ethnographic viewpoint, these territories were not predominantly Polish. The Polish, or Polonized, element consisted of the gentry and a part of the middle classes. There were some regions settled by Polish peasants, but the majority of the peasant class consisted of Lithuanians, Byelorussians, and Ukrainians. It seems likely that the new Russian regime would have taken advantage of this fact and insisted on the Russian (Byelorussians and Ukrainians did not exist, as distinct nationalities, in the eyes of St. Petersburg) character of the country, despite its Polish gentry. No such tendency, however, was evident at first. Old Russia, after all, was a landlord (*pomeshtchik*) state, and so it had to leave the authority to the landlord. Also, in Lithuania and Ukraine the landlords were Poles, and the local governments kept a Polish character. Numerous participants in the Kościuszko insurrection were imprisoned and sent to Siberia, and many estates were confiscated or sequestrated; but such repressions did not affect the majority of the gentry. On the contrary, and especially under the reign of Catherine's successor, Czar Paul (1796–1801), local self-government was again left to the gentry. The landlords in each county were given the right to elect their judicial and administrative officials, who were subordinate, of course, to the Russian officials and to the Senate in Petersburg. Anyone who has read Mickiewicz's poem *Pan Tadeusz* (1834) will remember this milieu of officials: the chamberlain, the judge, the notary, the assessor—all of them Polish landlords on H.I.M. service. *Pan Tadeusz*'s plot is situated in Nowogródek County, the heart of Byelorussia. The peasants vaguely alluded to in the poem are Byelorussians—although they take no part in the story.

The truth is that the condition of the peasants in the provinces which were under Russian rule underwent a change for the worse, in comparison with their former condition under Polish rule. The

Russian peasant-serf was, properly speaking, a slave, on a level with cattle, entirely in his master's power. Acts such as flogging and torturing refractory peasants, violating peasant women, and selling away single members of a family also occurred in Poland, but as exceptions. In Russia they were current practice. Moreover, the landlord had the authority to send a recalcitrant peasant to the Siberian mines.

Such now became the lot of Byelorussian and Ukrainian peasants. In the definition of their charges, a similar change for the worse set in. In Poland compulsory labor was usually exacted from each plot of land, that is, from each peasant family: so many days per week from so many acres. In czarist Russia, as one knows from Gogol's works, the estates were valued not in acres but in "male souls," specified every ten years or so in the "revision." This was the base of the famous "soul tax": one ruble yearly for each male soul, paid by the landlord to the state. Since the landlord had to pay the tax for the male, he could also oblige him to work, and therefore compulsory labor, under Russian rule, was counted not per acre but per capita, and it grew proportionally with the increase in population. Particularly on the Ukrainian black soils, after the opening of the Odessa port on the Black Sea, the cultivation of wheat became very lucrative, and this had a fatal effect on the charges and conditions of the peasantry. The czarist government, moreover, was strong, and it held the masses in obedience much more efficaciously than the old Polish government. One Polish memoirist frankly admitted, in the first years of the nineteenth century, We Polish landlords in Ukrainian provinces can only praise the new régime; we are free to live by our old Polish customs and to lead a secure country life—we are no longer afraid of a new Humań massacre!

Besides augmented charges and aggravated penalties, one more burden was now forced upon the peasants: the military service. The draft lasted for twenty-five years and was particularly heavy. And since it was the landlord who appointed and delivered the drafted men from his village to military quarters, it is easy to see that every conscription could become a measure of oppression, if not of punishment, against a refractory or simply an inconvenient serf.

Thus, in order to depict the peasant's situation in the provinces annexed by Russia, we must use the bleakest terms.

The Prussian System

The Prussian system was similar to the Russian, inasmuch as it rested on the landlord class, or the Junkers. The chief of the county (*Landrat*), was elected by and from among the landlords. His was the task of maintaining order, collecting taxes, and drafting recruits. But the king of Prussia was in need of a large army and a full treasury, and so he attached much importance to a large and healthy population of prompt taxpayers and sound recruits. Hence the policy called "Protection of the Peasant" (*Bauernschutz*), which amounted to state control of the landlord's activities on his estate. The peasant was not to be overburdened; his charges were to be defined and not transgressed. This policy was equivalent to the granting of a stronger right to the soil, and it was advocated by the state in Polish provinces like Silesia and Pomerania. But it was only theory, because its application depended upon the local *Landrat*, who was a Junker, chosen by Junkers as their trustee and plenipotentiary.

An analogous policy was to be followed in the Poznan province annexed in the second partition. When the Prussian army entered Poland in 1793, some German colonists tried to refuse to pay rent to their Polish landlords. The new authorities, however, reminded the country folk that they were serfs, as before, and that they owed obedience to their masters. Shortly afterward, the Kościuszko insurrection broke out, and numerous landowners joined in. At that time, in Prussian bureaucratic circles, there was some talk of making an appeal to the loyalty of the peasants against the treacherous *szlachta*, but it was not put into effect. The conflict with revolutionary France restrained the Berlin government from espousing any kind of social demagogy. After the eventual fall of Poland, nothing much was changed in the new Prussian provinces, and there were no experiments with introducing the *Bauernschutz*. On the contrary, the General Country Law (*Allgemeines Landrecht*) introduced in 1798 maintained the feudal class structure and the institution of serfdom. It also stated that in particular cases the courts of justice should follow the local common law. This meant, as far as Polish provinces were concerned, following the old practices of the Polish gentry.

Some innovations were introduced, however. The judiciary in every estate was to be administered, henceforth, by a justice (*Jus-*

tiziarius) appointed and paid by the landlord but supervised by the *Landrat*. This amounted to state control of the dominial judicature. Second, an interdiction was enacted against evicting the peasants from their lands, except for stubbornness and disobedience, and then only after a conviction in court. This provision, however, remained a dead letter. Third, in the state domains some attempts at rent reforms were undertaken although with little success. Only in the Warmia district, a region of predominantly state-owned big peasant farms, was rent reform carried through.

In sum, the Prussian state attempted merely timid reforms in its Polish provinces. Their results were insignificant. The Prussian regime was, for the Polish gentry, a prosperous era; later it was referred to as the "golden Prussian time." Corn prices were booming and credit was easy, which encouraged the landlords to increase their production. To do this, they enforced compulsory labor and enlarged the *folwark* at the peasants' expense. The government did not impede this tendency, and if it tried, the effort was feeble. In theory, the Prussian *Bauernschutz* was superior to the Russian serfdom (*krepostnitchestvo*). In practice, however, the Prussian state did not provide the peasant an efficient protection.

The Josephinist Reforms

The Austrian reforms were on another scale. Here the government did promote substantial change, some of which was put into effect. But all this happened somewhat earlier, before 1790 and the French Revolution. Galicia, the part of Poland annexed by Austria during the first partition of 1772, was the biggest and most densely populated area. Therefore, in comparing reforms undertaken after the first partition, we see that it was the Austrian reforms which exercised the deepest influence on Polish life.

These reforms are generally linked with the personality of Joseph II, the classical representative of Enlightened absolutism, who—first as German emperor and co-ruler with his mother, Maria Theresa, and after her death as independent ruler in Austria (1780–90)—endeavored to reshape and modernize nearly every sphere of public life. Josephinist reforms have often been taxed by Polish conservative historians as aiming especially at the undermining of the Polish gentry, that is, of the Polish nationality. This is, of course, a one-sided view. The reforms in question extended to the whole empire, and their conception was elaborated in Bohemia and the Alpine lands, that is, in provinces economically more developed than Galicia. Hence the difficulty in applying some of the new provisions to backward territories. It will be seen that Joseph II was far from attempting to overthrow the nobility's wealth and privileges, although this intention was imputed to him in earlier times. To clarify the matter, two points should be made. (1) Joseph's initiative was obviously instrumental in enforcing these radical changes, but the general conception of the reforms, the elaboration and realization of the numerous edicts and decrees, was due to a large and well-trained bureaucracy. (2) It would be one-sided, not to say false, to regard Josephinism as reforms thought through somewhere in the imperial palace and mechanically imposed from above on a bewildered and recalcitrant community. This is an especially false view of agrarian reforms. The idea of an agrarian reform did indeed arise, like the Prussian *Bauernschutz*, in government centers, from fiscal and demographic considerations. It was also prompted by economic arguments: compulsory labor was becoming less and less economical, and community-owned grounds were an obsolete custom, incompatible with modern agriculture. But it seems that mass movements, and particularly the peasant upheavals in Bohemia in 1767 and 1775, also had some influence on the imperial decisions. Other, more passive provinces like Galicia were to profit from the Bohemian class struggle.

Galicia was annexed to the Hapsburg Empire at the time the fiscal and social reforms destined for other provinces were on the way to elaboration. Hence the haste to introduce at least some of these reforms in Galicia. One of them was a new land tax. It was based on income declarations (*fasje*) made by the landlords, which were, so to speak, uncontrolled. The result was that the gentry managed to shift as much of the new fiscal burden as possible onto the peasant's back. Later and more accurate calculations helped to correct these abuses, but only in part.

The general goal of the Josephinist regime was to regulate the peasant charges due to the landlords and to the state according to one basic principle so that all burdens should be shared equally. Such an arrangement was nicknamed *Urbarialreform* (a pseudo-Latin neologism, of doubtful etymology). The way to an *Urbarium* was a thorny one, especially in Galicia. Maria Theresa began by removing (or, rather, prohibiting) some of the most drastic abuses of the serfdom system. One of her edicts forbade the beating of peasants; another forbade forcing the peasants to purchase given quantities of liquor in the dominial inn. The peasants were also allowed, when allegedly harmed, to present their complaints to the *Kreishauptmann,* or chief of the "circle" (county). The crown lands in Galicia were annexed at once, that is, taken under state administration. It was seen that in Prussia the crown estates could well serve as a model for experimenting in reforms difficult to impose on private owners. The same was true in Austria. In some Austrian provinces, for example, in Bohemia, the manor farms on rich lands were subdivided among the peasants, in exchange for rent, and compulsory labor ceased to exist. This so-called Raab system (named after its inventor, a high Viennese official) was not introduced into Galicia. The treasury was in need of money, and for that reason most crown lands in Galicia were rapidly sold into private hands, with no concern for the lot of the peasants.

After Maria Theresa's death Joseph II proceeded more energetically with various reform projects. Numerous laws were enacted in the 1780s, in behalf of agrarian relations; not all of them were enforced, because of the resistance not only of the gentry but also of a part of the bureaucracy closely connected with aristocratic circles. These laws can be reduced to three main tendencies.

The first was equivalent to the Prussian *Bauernschutz* and granted the peasant a stronger right to the soil. All land belonging to the gentry, as well as to corporations (church, university, etc.), was divided into two categories: the dominical and rustical lands (the lord's and the villein's). The character of a given plot of land could not be willfully changed; such a change required the agreement of political authorities (the *Kreis*). A plot of rustical soil could not willfully be taken from the peasant, and if it was abandoned the landlord was bound to settle another peasant thereon. On the other hand, a plot of dominical soil did not lose its character, even if given into a peasant's possession. Such land could always be taken away from the peasant and incorporated again into the manor farm at the gentleman's whim. The peasant could be deprived of his rustical land, by decision of the *Kreishauptmann,* in cases of disobedience or maladministration, but the "waste plot" (*pustka*) would pass to another peasant. This arrangement did not guarantee possession to any given peasant; it only guaranteed the inviolability of the totality of peasant possessions.

The second trend of Josephinist reforms aimed at a definition as exact as possible of what was to be understood by *Robot*, or compulsory labor. The famous *Robot* Law of 1786 explained minutely how many hours the peasant should work on a *Robot* day— in summer and in winter; what kind of work should be counted not per hour but per quantity of work done (e.g., felling); how transport service should be calculated in *Robot* days; etc. An important paragraph established the maximum of *Robot* at three days a week. This provision favored the wealthier peasants; the poorer ones had seldom ever been obliged to work more than three days a week.

The third important point of the Josephinist reform was an indispensable corollary to the first two. It granted the peasants the right to sue their masters before the state administration. It is true that the right was restrained by a number of formalities: the injured peasant first had to lodge his complaint at the Dominial Office, and only if he did not get satisfaction in a given time could he appeal to the *Kreis*. Bound to this provision was a reorganization of the dominial authorities. Every landlord had to appoint two officials: a judge (*Justiziarius*) and a police officer (*Mandatarius*). Both were officials of a mixed character—paid by the landlord but also bound to execute the orders of the *Kreishauptmann*. And finally, a kind of self-government was introduced in the village, with a mayor (*wójt*), chosen from among the peasants by the landlord, and two aldermen (*ławnicy*), elected by the peasants themselves. The competence of these village officials was questionable.

The above regulations did not touch the two pillars of the feudal system, serfdom and compulsory labor, although they imposed some limitations on both. All this legislation, however, was considered in Vienna only as a first step, an introduction, to the projected *Urbarialreform*. Its turn came in the late eighties. First, a cadastre was rapidly carried through in Galicia (the Josephinist cadastre), determining how much land and of what quality every peasant possessed and what gross income he should consequently enjoy. This cadastre was to form the basis for a general rent reform, united with a sweeping abatement of peasant charges. By virtue of the *Urbarialpatent* of 10 February 1789, every peasant was to pay from his theoretical income 12.2 percent to the state and 17.8 percent to the landlord—altogether, 30 percent. The remaining 70 percent, and even more, if he knew how to raise his income, should be his own. The poorest categories of peasants as well as those who were settled on dominical soil were excluded from this reform; it also provided, in Bohemia and Galicia, a transition stage lasting until autumn 1791.

Most certainly, this *Urbarialreform* would have drastically and, what is more important, not uniformly, reduced the gentry's income. It seems evident that 17 percent of the peasant's cadastre revenue would not have sufficed to pay the hired labor henceforth needed on the manor farm—even with the half-compulsory help of the poorer element of the village. The Austrian bureaucracy was not ignorant of this fact. It simply assumed that the landlords would subdivide part of their domains for rent; this would establish a new balance between the village land, as a source of rent, and the *folwark*, as an enterprise consigning the same rent in the form of wages. Theoretically the aims were blameless: More peasants would attain wealth and independence; the gentry would not be deprived of their property titles, and, moreover, they would gain in better and more modern husbandry. Joseph's reform, it should be stressed, did not aim to destroy feudalism; nevertheless, it cleared the way for a capitalist evolution.

Theories are one thing and practice another. There is doubt that the new system could have functioned in backward Galicia, a province with natural economy still prevailing. But proof has not been furnished, since the new law never entered into life. Its promulgation provoked varied reactions, all equally dangerous. On the one hand, the peasants began to move, especially in Bohemia and Carinthia. They refused to give assent to the new cadastre, they ceased to perform the *Robot*, and here and there they rioted. On the other hand, the gentry and, more important, the aristocracy protested violently, and not only in Poland. There were also political difficulties, external and internal: the war with Turkey, a threat of war from Prussia, ferment in Hungary, and an open insurrection in Belgium. So the Viennese bureaucracy simply took fright and prevailed upon Emperor Joseph, already on his deathbed, to cancel the *Urbarialreform* (5 May 1790). (Joseph's successor, Leopold II, was to adopt the opposite policy of cajoling the big landowners of various nationalities.) Shortly after, the French Revolution broke out, and any radical change in social relations was deemed unthinkable. Austria entered a period of police regime which was to last fifty years.

The earlier laws of Maria Theresa and Joseph II were never recalled. Thus, the inamovability of the peasant, the three-day maximum of compulsory labor, and the right of appeal to the *Kreis* remained in force in Galicia. But the application of these laws, and the relations of the bureaucrats to the peasants changed markedly. Two examples from the later nineties may be quoted here. First, the landlords and their stewards were again granted the right to beat their peasants. And second, any transaction commuting compulsory labor into rent was bound henceforth to be authorized by the county, which meant, in effect, that it would not be authorized. Summing up, Galicia, as opposed to other parts of Poland, was subjected toward the end of the eighteenth century to an extensive reform which could have substantially bettered the peasants' situation. This reform, however, was stopped halfway, and in consequence the social relations in the countryside remained, so to speak, frozen for a period of more than fifty years—a state of things pregnant with consequences.

Gorzkowski and Kościuszko

The agrarian policies of the three partitioning powers were one side of the problem; the other was the attitude of Polish society itself. There was, as we have seen, little generosity on the part of the propertied classes toward the peasant, although there was a conspiring element, active in the first years after 1795. We shall not dwell on the various clandestine associations of that time. It is sufficient to state that most of them had no definite social program. The most important, the Society of Polish Republicans, urged the abolition of all estate privileges—that is, among other things, the abolition of serfdom. It also emphasized the necessity of winning the peasants to the national cause. It did not say precisely by what means this aim could be attained. The conspirators, composed of intelligentsia, ex-officers, burghers, and landowners, were neither numerous nor very influential, and they did not wage any propaganda among the villagers.

Against this background, there was a glaring exception: Franciszek Gorzkowski (1760–1830). He was a native of Warmia, of gentry extraction, and by profession a land surveyor; he had long mingled with the village people and was well aware of all their grievances. He had studied in France and become imbued with Voltairianism, and he was an enthusiast of the French Revolution. He distinguished himself as a radical pamphleteer during the four-year *Sejm;* he served under Kościuszko and belonged to the Jacobin wing. After Poland's fall he became affiliated with the conspiracy in Warsaw, but he acted on his own, with only occasional help from friends. He took a job, again as land surveyor, in the Podlasie region, at that time under Austrian occupation, and began a propaganda campaign among the peasants which was directed against both foreign enemies and Polish landlords.

The peasants were illiterate; they could be reached only by oral persuasion. Therefore Gorzkowski instructed friends in effective ways of talking with peasants, and he distributed leaflets containing illustrations whose aim was to enliven the agitation. One of these illustrations depicted the large number of peasants in comparison with the handful of privileged persons, to allay the peasants' fears. In another leaflet, images of the life of a serf and of a free citizen were put in contrast. Gorzkowski advocated an agrarian revolution. All the peasants in the country would revolt on a chosen day and hour. The village community would appear arms in hand before its master and ask him whether he would join the movement. If so, he would be spared and his estate left him for his livelihood; if he opposed, he would be suppressed. Village detachments would form a peasant army which would combat the Austrians, and the French would surely come to the rescue. Poland would be a free country: no lords and no manors—only free, independent peasant farms! Such talk seems to us, and actually was, in the circumstances, childish and utopian. The first landlord who learned of this agitation denounced Gorzkowski to the authorities. The Jacobin agitator was arrested along with two of his collaborators, a former noncommissioned officer and a peasant. All three were imprisoned in the ancient Wawel castle, in Krakow. After five years of inquiry, Gorzkowski was sentenced to the gallows, but at the same time he was pardoned, released, and expelled from the country. This happened in 1802. The war was over, for a time; the conspiracies seemed to have dissolved, and

Gorzkowski's foolish enterprise no longer presented any political or social danger. One should perhaps use the definition *premature*, rather than *foolish* or *utopian*, for Gorzkowski's activities. Fifty years later, his slogans would resound mightily in numerous Polish provinces, and they would rightly be considered appropriate at that time.

From those same years, at the end of the eighteenth century, one event, or one text, is still to be mentioned. It emanates from the emigration, or, more exactly, from the last Polish leader, Kościuszko.

Imprisoned after the disaster of Maciejowice, Kościuszko had been kept in the Peter and Paul fortress, in St. Petersburg. Emperor Paul granted him his freedom, but Kościuszko was required to give a pledge that he would not fight against Russia again. He traveled to America, where he had numerous friends and admirers, including Washington and Jefferson. The next year he appeared in Paris. He did not engage in politics, but he demonstrated a vivid interest in the Polish legion, then fighting in Italy under the French banner. He was listened to by politicians in exile and entered into connections with the Republican Society in Warsaw. Then came Bonaparte's coup d'etat of the 18th *Brumaire*. The French Revolution was coming to an end, and it appeared that Bonaparte would seek a compromise with monarchal Europe. Kościuszko evidently lost his faith in the possibility of establishing a free Poland with the help of France. He decided to step forth with a new program.

In 1800, an anonymous pamphlet appeared in Paris, with the mystifying address Perekop-on-the-Don. It bore the suggestive title "Can the Poles regain their independence?" The brochure was widely circulated, although it was destroyed by the police of Fouché (no copy of this first edition is known to exist at present). People ascribed the text to various authors; today it is known that it was written by Joseph Pawlikowski, the fervent Jacobin already mentioned, who served at that time as a private secretary to Kościuszko. The text was evidently inspired by Kościuszko.

" 'Can the Poles regain their independence?' asked the former 'Chief of the Nation.' Of course, yes—as did the Swiss, the Dutch, and the Americans. In order to vanquish, there is only one condition: The whole nation should rise to fight. And in order to mobilize the whole country, one must make the whole people free. One should not await a time when peasants are civilized enough to be free. On the contrary, it is freedom which will civilize them. A folk of free citizens is invincible; it has no need of foreign help." These were simple and enticing words. They simplified the problem, inasmuch as they did not concretely specify how a liberation of the masses could be accomplished. There was only one weighty argument in that declaration: The two problems, Poland's independence and social freedom, were linked together and would ever be interdependent. At the time, the brochure had little influence; rather, it was understood simply as an affirmation of self-dependence—*Polonia fara da se*—an affirmation soon to be denied by facts. And thus Kościuszko's program became a kind of last will, a message to the next generations who would be mature enough to comprehend such a program and undertake its realization.

3

THE DUCHY OF WARSAW

In 1806, Napoleon's Grand Army crushed the Prussians at Jena and Auerstädt and entered Poland. A second campaign ensued, this time with Russia, ending with the compromise of Tilsit, in 1807. A new Polish state was formed, from only a part of Prussian Poland, named the Duchy of Warsaw, an area of 40,000 square miles with a population of 2.6 million, extending in a narrowing belt from the upper Warta to the lower Niemen. This territory was augmented in 1809, in consequence of a new war, with some parts of Austrian Poland, amounting to about 65,000 square miles with 4 million inhabitants. It was only a small part of prepartition Poland, and, moreover, it was not a fully independent state but a vassal of the French Empire. As a result of Napoleon's disastrous Moscow campaign, the Duchy of Warsaw was occupied by Russians early in 1813, and two years later it was divided again at the Congress of Vienna.

The Napoleonic episode lasted only six years, but it exerted on Poland's fate a multifarious, powerful, and long-lasting influence. At present, we are concerned only with its effect on agrarian problems, and this can be defined in terms of the contact between two different state structures: bourgeois France and feudal Poland.

The December Decree

France under Napoleon was a country freshly transformed, ploughed up by the Great Revolution—a country of formally equalized citizens and with estate privileges eliminated. Some of these revolutionary institutions were to be imposed on Poland by the French conqueror, and reforms of this kind, once carried out, were not likely to be withdrawn even with a change of regime. Thus the French influence was to shatter the Polish feudal system from above, so to speak, by government regulation, not by changing the economic structure.

The Constitution of the Duchy of Warsaw established by Napoleon on 22 July 1807 read, in Article 4, "Slavery will be abolished. All citizens are equal in the eyes of the law. Personal freedom will be protected by the courts." Napoleon boasted more than once of having suppressed slavery in Poland. But Polish historians argued at length that Napoleon was ignorant in Polish matters; that there had been no slavery in Poland at that time, only serfdom; and that Article 4 gave an erroneous impression of Polish social relations. This juridical controversy was unbecoming; to a foreign observer some aspects of Polish serfdom could well have looked like slavery. The actual sense of the article was clear enough: it canceled every form of the peasant's personal dependence on the landlord. This regulation remained in force after the fall of the Duchy of Warsaw. The Constitution of 1815 granted to the Kingdom of Poland read, in Article 17, "The law extends equal protection to all citizens, regardless of estate or condition." And in Article 24: "Every Pole is free to move with his person and property, according to rules designated by law."

Another paragraph of the 1807 Constitution introduced the Napoleonic Code, the main chart of the French bourgeoisie. The Napoleonic Code was also to survive the fall of its legislator. But the results of the introduction of constitution and code in feudal Poland proved unforeseen by their protagonists and adversaries alike.

The formal equality of citizens before the law was actually put into effect for the burghers (with some exceptions, concerning Jews). This equalization, however, proved impracticable in respect to peasants. There were serious economic, social, and political problems. (1) Economic: To guarantee the peasants effective freedom, it was necessary for the whole system of compulsory labor to give way to a more-or-less capitalistic wage system, and this required credits and investments. The Duchy was meanwhile in a state of war and of acute economic depression. Prices were falling, all credit was suspended, most of the real estate was on the verge of bankruptcy, and all the resources of the country were absorbed by the army. This was hardly a time for profound economic reforms. (2) Social: In France, the revolutionary reforms, including agrarian reforms, were carried through by the bourgeoisie, which replaced the nobility at the top of the social structure. The Polish bourgeoisie was far from being able to play such a role. It was small and economically feeble. Under the Napoleonic regime, the gentry was to remain the leading social force. And the gentry, of course, was traditionally unsympathetic to plans for strengthening peasants' rights. (3) Political: For reasons concerning world politics, which need not be developed here, Napoleon based his system in the Duchy of Warsaw on the support of the aristocracy. The Warsaw government was almost exclusively composed of latifundists, who were not likely to advocate reforms damaging to the interests of the landlords.

An animated discussion began in 1807, when the peasant question was put on the agenda. The Polish Jacobins (or former Jacobins) exposed their point of view in confidential memoranda, in pamphlets, and in the press. They were aware, of course, that the Napoleonic regime excluded a social revolution; but they tried to influence Polish public opinion and, similarly, French official circles with their appeals to better the peasant's condition. Most of them advocated a program of gradual change. The first step had already been taken with the abolition of serfdom; rent reform was recommended as the next step, to include the granting to the peasants of full property rights to the land tilled for their own use. This point of view was aptly developed in a book published in 1807 written by Wawrzyniec Surowiecki (1769–1827), the distinguished economist: *Consideration on the Serfs, and a Project of Freeing Them.*

46

The Polish left was deliberately excluded from power by Napoleon and could not influence the new legislation. But in the new ministry there were individuals who, aristocrats though they were, understood the need of a policy favorable to the peasants, in the spirit of Enlightened absolutism—that is, in the interests of the state and its treasury and army. We should list among them Stanisław Małachowski (1736–1809), president of the State Council and former speaker of the four-year *Sejm*, and Prince Joseph Poniatowski (1763–1813), the dead king's nephew, now minister of war. This party proposed to guarantee the peasants a strong right to the soil, and the unalterability of their prestations (charges).

Propositions of this kind were actually advanced in the State Council, but they were not supported by the majority. Another viewpoint prevailed, represented by the minister of justice, Felix Łubienski (1758–1848). He was one of the new aristocrats, who were quite ready to cooperate with the new French system, provided, of course, that it would be to the exclusive advantage of the big property owners. Łubienski's chief work was the famous Royal Decree of 21 December 1807 (we shall henceforth refer to it as the December Decree).* It can be summarized in five points:

1. The peasants were free to move if they wished. This was a confirmation of Article 4 of the constitution.
2. The peasants were required to notify only the landlord and the village mayor (the mayor was, in most cases, an agent of the landlord) of their plans to move.
3. The landlord could not evict the peasant from his land before the lapse of one year after the decree's issuance. This provision was later interpreted to mean that after this one year had elapsed the landlord acquired the right to evict any peasant.
4. Officials were to be appointed who would be authorized to register all new contracts negotiated between landlords and peasants concerning possessions and charges. Such registered contracts would be considered legally binding.
5. A peasant abandoning his land could take nothing with him; the land, the buildings, and the livestock and farming equipment would become the landlord's property.

* See Appendix, section *B*.

This was, obviously, an ambiguous text, containing positive as well as negative provisions, from the peasants' viewpoint. Point 5, which denied the peasant rights to his land and appurtenances, was the most portentous one. Unfortunately, all the negative paragraphs were put into effect; the positive ones were not.

Some historians have represented the December Decree as an artful intrigue of Łubienski, cunningly veiling under benevolent phrases a blow aimed at the peasants' rights to the soil. It seems probable, however, that even Łubienski did not realize, at the time, the full meaning of his decree. But the meaning soon appeared clear to the gentry. It perceived that the decree gave it a powerful means of control over the peasant. This was the main reason why the December Decree was to remain in force for forty years; it accorded too well with the landlords' interests to be overridden by any political power.

The decree represented one of the possible modes of adaptation of the Napoleonic Code (the bourgeois code) to Polish feudal relations. In a feudal society the soil belonged to the lord. The peasant could possess a stronger or weaker right to the same soil, but his right was subordinated to the lord's right. The bourgeois, or capitalist, code did not acknowledge any such multiplication of conflicting rights. It recognized only one kind of indivisible property, the capitalist kind, which could, indeed, be voluntarily and temporarily transferred to another person, for example, by act of lease. The State Council had to resolve, once and for all, the question who was to be considered the owner (the bourgeois owner) of the village lands. Should it be the landlord or the peasant? It is not surprising that it decided in favor of the former. It only later developed that the adjudication of this right gave the landlord the additional right to drive the peasant from his home—that is, the right of eviction.

The right of eviction put the peasant in a most unfavorable position in relation to his former master. He could not very well demand a bettering of his condition or even protest against an aggravation of charges, because he was always in danger of being driven away. As long as the landlord retained a monopoly in land ownership, he retained the upper hand and could dictate his conditions. This concerned, inter alia, the problem of compulsory labor. If the landlord was not interested in substituting some other charge for it, the peasant was defenceless. And the majority of the Polish landlords showed no interest in labor reform for a long time. Therefore the provision of the December Decree concerning officially registered contracts between landlords and peasants remained a dead letter. The landlord had no need for such contracts, and the peasants had no means at all for imposing them.

This set of circumstances was responsible for a specific feature of Polish agrarian evolution. In most European countries the emancipation of the peasants was accomplished by one single legislative act (although its terms might specify a lapse of time), and so serfdom disappeared simultaneously with compulsory labor and other forms of feudal exploitation. But in central Poland, emancipation took another course. Serfdom was abolished in 1807, but compulsory labor continued until 1861. The succession of reforms was similar in Latvia and Estonia, and also in Hungary, but for different reasons. The Negro emancipation in the United States also gave freedom to the slaves without giving them rights to the soil. Indeed, in contrast with the European emancipation, the American emancipation converted the slaves into farmhands without giving them any property rights at all.

The Agrarian Structure in 1810

Always much more important than the texts of legal enactments are their consequences; so we must ask, What happened in the Polish countryside as a result of the December Decree, particularly in the first years after its proclamation? From the theoretical standpoint, three different tendencies were to be expected: (1) The now-freed peasant would profit from his freedom and would emigrate in search of better conditions. (2) The peasants, threatened with eviction, would be more and more exploited. (3) The landlord would profit from his now-legalized eviction right and would start to enlarge his domain.

Passing from conjecture to documentation, we find traces of all three tendencies, but none of them was actually widespread. Numerous memoirs of gentry origin do speak of peasant migrations, and the facts are confirmed in official correspondence. It was a very natural first reaction for serfs, suddenly freed, probably distrustful of the future, to break with their former masters, to find shelter in other regions, and to try to wipe out the past.

This tendency, however, did not appear uniformly; migrations were most numerous in the Płock district, and it seems that the main reason was the ruin of the countryside, which had been the theater of the last campaign. It had been ruthlessly deprived, by levies and by plundering, of its seed corn and cattle. Migrations, thus, were an established fact, but they were not a significant issue. The fact is that the peasant had nowhere to go to make a living. Industry in the Duchy did not play an important role, and there was little demand for labor in the cities. The state had begun, for military reasons, important fortification works and employed tens of thousands of men in earth-digging. But this kind of labor had no advantages at all; the journeymen were poorly paid, undernourished, and maltreated. Of course, there remained the army, with its high demand for cannon fodder; supported by patriotic slogans, it was attractive in a way, thanks to its democratic character. Enlistment, however, was possible only for the young bachelors; it did not assure subsistence for wives and children. The great majority of those peasants who left their villages as a consequence of the emancipation simply settled on other estates, under conditions imposed by new landlords. The December Decree had announced a legal registering of these new contracts, but the landlord cared little for such formalities, and the peasant had to yield. Now, as before, these contracts were mostly oral and without any fixed term of duration. The conditions were often defined as "conforming to local usage."

Did these conditions actually worsen, in the first years after 1807? It was often claimed, and not least by conservative politicians, who were most ready to criticize emancipation, that the reform did, indeed, only make the peasants' lot worse. A witticism by Martin Badeni, one of the ministers (to the effect that Napoleon took the chains from the peasants' legs—together with their boots), was incorporated in many textbooks. Statistical data, however, are lacking concerning the actual scope of the reform's aggravation of the peasants' problems, at least for the first few years. One ought not to forget that war—three campaigns in six years, fought on Polish soil—was also responsible for it.

As to the policy of the landlords in the face of the new arrangements, private archives of some of the bigger estates give us some knowledge about the general trend. It does not appear that the big property owners immediately embarked on a policy of eviction—of scattering the peasants and seizing the village fields. On the contrary, the chief preoccupation of the landowners in those years seems to have been the problem of wastelands, abandoned farms. To incorporate these lands into the *folwark* would have required investments and, in addition, turnover capital with which to finance hired labor. But, as mentioned earlier, agriculture was in a state of crisis. Corn prices had fallen after the trade route to England was cut off by the introduction of the Continental Blockade; credit was tight, since most estates were heavily mortgaged; and taxes and levies-in-kind were doubly heavy, as was usual in times of war. The only sensible way to farm at that time was to cut expenses and withdraw, as much as possible, into a natural economy. That is, compulsory labor seemed, until the end of the war, the most practical system, and it is small wonder that it prevailed.

In order to get a general view of the changes that occurred in the countryside as a first result of the emancipation, we shall consider two statistical censuses which were carried out in the Duchy of Warsaw in 1808 and 1810. These censuses have been acknowledged by statisticians as noteworthy achievements of the Polish administration. But the use of their data for historical purposes has proved delusive, for many reasons. The two operations were not performed very skillfully; they were not organized on a uniform basis—for example, they did not pertain to the same territory (the Duchy was enlarged in 1809); and finally, they did not take enough material into consideration. The first census of 1808 was not based at all on contemporary evidence but on a conscientious recast of earlier depositions (*indaganda*), dating from 1805–1806. The second census (1810) is the more accurate and authentic, but data concerning the social structure are lacking for three of the ten districts. The chief deficiency is a lack of data concerning the ratio of *folwark* and village lands in 1808 and 1810. Such an estimate, if it existed, would enable us to calculate the number of evictions. We shall consider, therefore, only one distinct category of data, given in the so-called sowing tables. They list separately the amounts of corn used for seed in the villages and on *folwark* grounds. The data are summed up for every county (*powiat*), and for various kinds of crops, even less important ones like millet, buckwheat, hops, and tobacco. One should realize, however, that these sowing tables were composed for fiscal ends, and by the landlords themselves: hence a tendency to diminish the amounts of seed on *folwark* grounds and to exaggerate the amounts for the villages. It is known, besides, that ratios of seed output differed between the larger and smaller exploitations. Therefore a large portion of the data from the sowing tables seems unreliable. They are useful as a source for the history of agriculture, but it is impossible to draw conclusions from them about the surface under cultivation.

More explicit are the data of the 1810 census concerning the population's structure, although it is true that data from three districts are lacking, and these were the three eastern ones, that is, the most backward regions of the country. The population was divided into nineteen categories, eight of them having to do with rural inhabitants. These were the landlords, the tenants, the manor officials, the farmhands (two categories: boys and girls), and finally, three categories of peasants. Each category was again divided into still more numerous subgroups: for example, fourteen subgroups of farmhands, eleven subgroups of peasants. The number of titles is overwhelming. One wonders if the different denominations really corresponded to distinct groups, if their boundaries were not too fluid, and if their names were merely local. Some peculiarities of these statistical tables lead us to suppose that the census instructions were not very accurate or that they were inaccurately applied. And, further, the numerous subdivisions of peasant population were not carried through on a uniform basis. Three different criteria of classification were used simultaneously: the size of the farm, the kind of charges, and the kind of property rights.

For the sake of clarity, we shall pass over these subtleties and divide the peasant population into three main groups: (1) the peasants proper, possessors of holdings theoretically sufficient for their subsistence; (2) the intermediate layer of peasants, who had too little land to live on and were forced to seek supplementary means of subsistence; and (3) the landless peasants.

The first group, in ancient times called *kmiecie*, is now most often called *gospodarze*, a word with many definitions: host, housekeeper, farmer, landlord, and manager. From the point of view of their charges, they can be divided into two categories: the rent payers and the compulsory laborers. There was, of course, an intermediate group, composed of persons performing some compulsory labor and paying some rent. In ancient times, the *kmieć* had a whole *łan*, or *włóka* (41.5 acres), of land and worked on the domain with his own yoke of oxen or pair of horses. As a rule, he employed two or three farmhands, sometimes his sons or sons-in-law, sometimes hirelings. In the course of centuries, the size of the land of a *gospodarz* steadily dwindled. Nevertheless, his characteristic feature was still the possession of oxen or horses and the employment of farmhands.

The second category of peasants is today called *małorolni*, or *little-land-possessors* (small-holders). This is a new, rather general term. In the nineteenth century many characteristic names were in use, showing in a picturesque way the degree of poverty of such people. Thus an *ogrodnik* was one who possessed only a little garden around his house. The *zagrodnik* could boast of a house and farm buildings, but no garden. The *chałupnik* possessed only a *chałupa*, a cabin or cot, without any other farm buildings. The *komornik* did not even have a *chałupa;* he lived in a *komora*, the smaller room of a peasant house belonging to someone else. And at the bottom of the social ladder, we find the *kątnik*, the man who lived with his family in a *kąt*, a corner of somebody else's room. We must, however, stress that these appellations, found in nineteenth-century sources, do not exactly correspond to their original meanings. A *zagrodnik* was usually supposed to be better off than a *chałupnik* or a *komornik*, but these names did not always mean that the person in question had no land and no house, however small, in his possession. The same group, or almost the same, was named *chałupnik* in one region, *komornik* in another; and similarly, the name *komornik* might relate to various categories of peasants, according to different regions. The common features of the whole group were the following: they used exiguous lots of land (not always the same every year); they did not have their own horses and oxen; they performed compulsory labor only as "workers on foot"—and above that, they were expected to perform some obligatory work for hire, because otherwise, they could not support their families.

The third category—the landless peasant (*bezrolni*)—can be divided into two groups: the farmhands, permanently employed (mostly on a year's contract) on a manor farm (*folwark*) or by a full peasant (*gospodarz*); and the journeymen, employed only occasionally, mainly during harvest time. The pay of the journey-men was higher, on a day rate, but it was not assured or regular—and thus they can be regarded as belonging to the lowest level of the social hierarchy in the village.

We should not ascribe to these categories of peasants, at the beginning of the nineteenth century, the same substance and meaning which they acquired later, after emancipation. Poland always had, and has today, well-to-do peasants, small-holders, and landless peasants. The meanings of these appellations today, however, do not correspond to those of 150 years ago. During the capitalist epoch, after the emancipation, the peasant was the owner of his land—an independent farmer, however small—or he belonged to the rural proletariat. He belonged to a class, and he could change his class by acquiring property or by losing it. Not so during the feudal epoch. At that time, the village population formed one class, the peasants, and they were differentiated, not according to property—they had none—but according to the landlord's arrangements. It was convenient for the landlord to have some teams and some foot-laborers and to have in his village a given number of *gospodarze* and *komornicy*, as well as farmhands and journeymen. The group to which one belonged depended, in large measure, upon the landlord's will. The groups were fluid; there were no class barriers between them.

One example will explain the situation. The 1810 census, al-ready quoted, calculated separately under each title the number of family heads, or independent owners, and their family members. Among the rural population, for each family head there were usually three–four family members, that is, wife and children. Farmhands, however, formed an exception. In the seven districts mentioned, 140,000 male farmhands (*parobcy*), that is, family heads, were counted. But these 140,000 farmhands had in all only 50,000 family members. The proportion was still more dras-tic with farm girls (*dziewki*): 80,000 of them, in the seven districts, and only 5,000 family members. As can be guessed, the great majority of these were young unmarried persons, sons and daughters of peasants, who earned their livings as farmhands before they married. After marriage, the landlord allotted each of them a piece of land (a part of his parents' land), charged with new obligations. So the rural proletariat was, at least in part, not a class but a transitory condition.

54

This proletariat was, however, rather numerous. The 1808 census counted 39.7 percent landless peasants in the Bydgoszcz district, 39.7 percent in Płock, and 33.3 percent in Warsaw. In the other districts, and even in Poznan, the rate was under 30 percent. These data concern conditions before any possible evictions actuated by the December Decree. Was the census inaccurate? Of course it was. But it was easier to overlook the roving, landless population than the settled and reliable *gospodarze*. Did the landlords distort the statistics in advance, in order to keep a free hand for future evictions? This is not impossible, but unlikely. As has been said already, most landlords did not envisage—yet— the advantages of evictions. There remains, still, one plausible explanation: the desolation of the countryside as a consequence of war. The northern districts were the most affected by war, and here also the migrations were the most numerous.

A comparison of statistical data from 1808 and 1810 denotes an abrupt fall in the number of independent—that is, propertied— peasants. In the Płock district the rate declined, in the course of two years, from 45.7 percent to 18.6 percent (counting only the family heads); in Kalisz, from 55.5 percent to 20.9 percent; in Warsaw, from 48.1 percent to 34.5 percent. In Płock, the decline was in favor of the landless peasants; elsewhere, in favor of the small-holders. Such data are absolutely improbable. Some evictions could have taken place during the two years, but not on such a scale. The criteria of classification must have changed, paralleling a very probable reduction in the size of holdings.

The 1810 data for the Płock district, counting only the family heads, seem to indicate a far-advanced proletarianization. There were, in fact, only 18.6 percent full-holders, 19.2 percent small-holders and 62.2 percent landless peasants. But we have seen already that the last category was a temporary one. This appears clearly when passing from the counting of family heads to an evaluation of the whole population, family members included. For the same Płock district, there were 34.5 percent full-holders, 26.6 percent small-holders, and 38.9 percent landless peasants. Płock was, of course, an extreme case. Let us take, for comparison, two other districts, also including family members: Krakow—27 percent full, 55 percent small, 18 percent landless peasants; Lublin—75 percent full, 15 percent small, 10 percent landless. In general, these indices point to three diverse types of social structure existing in the same Duchy of Warsaw, in regions not widely separated: the Płock village, the most advanced on the way to proletarianization; the Krakow village, characterized not by proletarianism but by the predominance of small-holders; and the Lublin village, the most traditional in structure, in which the majority of the peasants had independent holdings—there were few small-holders and still fewer peasants without land. These three distinct types of social structure existed for a long period, and their differences became even sharper; some traces of these differences remain to this day.

In 1810, 224,000 full-sized peasant holdings were counted in all, and out of this number only 17,000 were paying rent. Data are lacking for three eastern regions, but since they were still more backward than the others, we may presume that rent-holdings were even more rare there. So the index of rent-paying peasants for the whole country would be, not 7.5 percent, as it reads for the seven districts, but approximately 5 percent. These figures express the first consequences of the December Decree. The adjustment of peasant charges, under the new law, depended on the landlord's convenience—and the great majority of the landlords voted for compulsory labor.

How could a feudal institution such as this have been reconciled with the bourgeois chart, the Napoleonic Code? Various legal concepts were advanced by conservatives, to provide logical bases for the new relations. The peasant was no longer a serf and could not be compelled to perform compulsory labor as a serf. So, it was said, the peasant was now obliged to perform compulsory labor in exchange for the holding given him by the landlord (who had been declared owner of the village land). This explanation made the peasant a temporary leaseholder, but a leaseholder bound by a singularly disadvantageous contract. The contract was oral, with term of duration unspecified, and it was revokable at any time by either party. The lease was to be paid in labor. The trouble was that such a form of contract was absolutely incompatible with the Napoleonic Code. Article 1142 read categorically, "No one can be forced to perform any function. Every unfulfilled promise must be indemnified." Applied to compulsory labor, Article 1142 meant, The landlord is not entitled to enforce compulsory labor. If the peasant has promised to work and does not, he may be sentenced by court to pay an indemnity.

How could Article 1142 be applied to concrete situations? Every peasant would have the right to declare that the he would no longer work on the *folwark* but would pay a fine imposed by the court instead; that is, he could unilaterally convert his compulsory labor into rent. Some peasant communities and some radical lawyers actually invoked this clause, but of course to no avail. Even though recognizing the correctness of the above reasoning, the landlord could always answer: Well, if you do not want to work, I will send you away. The courts, in consequence, adopted the course of simply tacitly admitting that the Napoleonic Code did not cover relations between the landlord and the peasant. This reasoning was correct, in a sense. Since compulsory labor was a feudal institution, it could not be dealt with by means of bourgeois legislation. This amounted to a corroboration of the obvious fact that the abolition of serfdom did not automatically erase all feudal relations.

The consequences of this course were grave, not only because the peasant was deprived of all rights to the soil, but still more because the personal liberty freshly won became in such circumstances illusory, or endangered. In a capitalist society, especially during its earlier stages, it was property, exclusively, which guaranteed liberty. The more so in a feudal society, where lack of property was always associated with dependence. The condition created by the December Decree—compulsory labor without serfdom—was a temporary one. It was bound to evolve in one of two directions: toward a change of compulsory labor or toward a restriction of personal freedom. These tendencies formed the background of a more and more violent class struggle, which eventually led the peasants to full emancipation and to the right of possession of their holdings.

4

THE PRUSSIAN EMANCIPATION

The Duchy of Warsaw achieved a partial reform which freed the
peasants but refused them a right to the soil. Later, the 1815–30
regime in the Congress Kingdom professed, as we shall see, an
apparent neutrality in the contest between peasant and landlord;
an attitude unfailingly playing into the gentry's hands. In the
meantime, the Prussian government began a thorough reform of
the peasant question. It was to be called the Regulation Reform.
Started in 1807, that is, at the same time as the Warsaw reform,
it was developed from 1811 to 1816 and carried through gradually;
it was hastened a little in 1848, because of the revolution, and
brought to an end about 1860. It was a protracted affair, but it
exerted a decisive impact on other central European countries.
It was applied from the start in two Polish provinces, Pomerania
and Silesia, and after 1823 extended to Poznania, Gdansk, and
the Toruń region. Half of present Poland was directly affected by
it.

The relevant literature is vast, statistical material is profuse, and manuscript sources are endless. But a clear, up-to-date synthesis is lacking, because it is difficult to achieve. The story is intricate, and one cannot dismiss the thought that it was made so by design.

The Regulation Reform

The most important feature of the Regulation Reform was that it was an act imposed by the state, in the interest of the ruling Junker class, although it had a taint of belated Enlightened Absolutism. One can consider it an extention of the *Bauernschutz* tradition. But the *Bauernschutz* remained, or at the least became, a dead letter, especially after Frederick II, in regard to evictions. It was to the state's interest not to tolerate evictions, since peasant land paid higher taxes, in comparison with Junker land. But the *Landrat* was a Junker himself, and he seldom opposed the doings of his friends and neighbors. Toward the end of the eighteenth century all social reforms in Prussia came to a standstill. They were discussed, it is true, in bureaucratic circles, and numerous memoirs were composed, by lower officials or by bourgeois, advocating social reforms. Most of these memoirs came from Silesia, and very soon we shall see why. But little or no attention was paid to them until external catastrophe struck.

It was the disaster of Jena, in 1806, which obliged Prussia to take a bolder step. As a result of Napoleon's conquests, serfdom was abolished in 1807 in two provinces bordering on Prussia: Westphalia on the west, and the Duchy of Warsaw on the east. It became absolutely impossible to maintain serfdom in between. It was suppressed, accordingly, beginning with St. Martin's Day, 11 November 1807. The next step was taken in the following year: peasants in state domains were granted full rights to their holdings, although their rent obligations were maintained. More important and more difficult was the application of this step to private estates. One should ask, was their reform hastened not only by political necessity but also by pressure from below? Did the peasants' attitude or insistence contribute to Berlin's decision? On the whole, peasant subjects of the Hohenzollern state were an obedient lot—with, however, one notable exception: Silesia.

This rich and thickly populated province was conquered by Frederick II between 1740 and 1763, and the peasants continued to rebel after that time for half a century. Ferment was brewing in Silesian villages, among both Polish and German peasants (the linguistic border in Silesia ran at that time more or less along the meridian of Wroclaw). Tension was particularly acute in the years 1766–68, 1784–86, 1793–95, and 1798–99. Here and there the peasants would abandon their work and march on the manor or town with scythes and pitchforks. They resisted military coercion, and in the 1790s opposition was particularly marked in the Sudeten foothills, with the insurgents openly admitting that they took their example from the French Revolution. All these risings were local revolts extending, at most, to a few districts, and lacking skilled leadership; it was relatively easy for the troops to deal with them. The very persistence of these revolts, however, convinced some bureaucrats and most liberals that it was high time to introduce reforms.

The question that should be of particular interest to historians is, Why, exactly, did the Silesian peasants so stubbornly resist the Hohenzollern state, in contrast to peasants in other provinces? They had, it is true, come recently under Prussian rule, but not much later than western Pomeranians, and earlier than Royal Prussians. It is a fact that the peasants' charges actually increased in Silesia after the Prussian conquest—fiscal charges, together with conscription and compulsory labor. But one advantage must be considered: the majority of Silesian peasants enjoyed stronger rights to the soil than peasants in other Prussian provinces.

The most common category of peasants east of the Elbe, from the juridical point of view, was called *Lassbauer* in German history (*lassyta*). The term is German, but not the phenomenon. The creation of such a term became a necessity for German officials and jurists, in comparing the rights and duties of a Brandenburg or a Pomeranian peasant with those prevailing in Frizia, Westphalia, or Schlezwig. No such need made itself felt in Poland, inasmuch as all, or almost all, of the Polish peasantry were *Lassbauern*—without knowing it.

The *Lassbauer* was simply a peasant with a weak right to the soil—an adjunct of his master's land, settled for an indeterminate time, without formal contract, without the right to dispose of his holding, and always subject to eviction. One important state-ment: the *Lassbauer* was obliged to discharge his duties (either in rent or in kind or in labor) not "in exchange" for his holding—as under Roman law or in a capitalist society—but as a serf, obliged to serve his master. He had some rights to use his master's woods and pasture (the servitudes), but once again, not "in exchange" for his services, but as a favor of his master. He could, on his death, leave the holding to his son, but not as a right to succession, only (and again) as a favor.

German specialists have discussed for some generations the genesis of *lassitism*. Two theories have been advanced, both of them questionable. One theory holds that the *Lassbauer* was a Slav peasant and that, among Slavs, the peasants lived under poorer conditions than in Old Germany—which is why, east of the Elbe, on former Slav territories, the "weak right" to the soil maintained itself to modern times. This statement is nonsense. The weak right to the soil was an invention of the sixteenth century. In earlier times Slav as well as German peasants en-joyed a stronger right, and still earlier they were free owners of whatever land they took in possession. The other theory attributes the phenomenon of *lassitism* to German conquest. In conquered Slav territories the German knights could impose harsher condi-tions on the peasants than in aboriginal, western German lands. But this again is an absurd statement, since the phenomenon (if not the term) of *lassitism* was not limited to the area of Prussian expansion but reached out farther, embracing the whole of the Polish Commonwealth and parts of Russia and Romania, as far as the Volga and the Black Sea. *Lassitism* was a con-sequence of, and a corollary to, compulsory labor; it appeared only in the framework of the estate and compulsory labor sys-tem, albeit it was not indispensable for the functioning of the latter—as can be seen from Silesia's example. Silesia was a region of manor farms and compulsory labor—but the great majority of the peasants had stronger rights to the soil (some historians hold this fact to be a consequence of former Hapsburg rule, of the influence of neighboring Bohemia, etc.). There were, besides, Silesian districts with a majority of *Lassbauern*, both Polish and German. But it may be that a stronger right to the soil gave the Silesian peasant more assurance, or forwardness, in his fight against compulsory labor.

The last big peasant insurrection burst forth in 1811, in Upper Silesia. Eighty mostly Polish villages rebelled under the pretext that compulsory labor had been canceled by the king but that Junkers and officials had allegedly suppressed the decree. Armed groups of peasants stormed the manors, burned residences and farm buildings or went in search of the hidden Royal Manifesto. The revolt was suppressed; there were about three hundred people arrested. There is some irony behind the fact that Polish and French troops, garrisoned at that time in most important towns and fortresses of Silesia (these were the years of Napoleon's apogee) showed no interest in the class struggle of the Polish peasants and thus passed up the chance of making use of the struggle to hold Prussia in check; there were even instances of Polish officers helping Prussian forces in restoring legal order. It seems, however, that the possible consequences of a foreign interference with Silesian social disturbances might well have influenced the final decision in Berlin. One should not forget that Prussia was feverishly preparing for her war of retaliation against Napoleon, intent upon winning over the masses to the national cause. The fact is that the Royal Regulation Edict was published in September 1811 and became effective on 11 November of the same year.

The edict* specified that the recently freed peasants in private estates could now acquire property rights to their holdings by means of free understandings with their masters. If such understandings could not be reached in the course of two years, the state would step in. In every province, a general committee would be appointed whose function was to regulate (or settle) the new situation of each village and peasant. The regulation set up compensatory standards. All peasant charges of every kind in behalf of the land were to come to an end, as well as the lord's duties in behalf of the peasant. Some of them were enumerated: the peasant's right to the lord's woods and pastures, the lord's duty to assist the peasant in the event of economic ruin, the lord's obligation to administer the village affairs, etc. The edict openly acknowledged the difficulty of establishing an accurate base of comparison between these mutual duties and obligations. Arbitrarily enough, it decided as follows: The peasant's obligations, rent, compulsory labor, etc., should not exceed one-third

* See Appendix, section *C*.

of the total profit of his holding. This clause applied, however, only if the peasant could claim a strong right to his holding. If he were only a *Lassbauer*, his obligations would be evaluated as one-half of his profits. The method of settling the matter was an easy one, but by no means one favorable for the peasant.

Before the Regulation Edict could even begin to be applied, the war broke out, and it lasted until 1815. The Berlin government came back to the matter in entirely changed circumstances, in a pacified and reactionary Europe. It is not surprising that the Junkers brought new pressure to bear on the king and his ministers. A royal declaration, issued in 1816, restricted the edict of five years earlier in two important respects.

1. Not all the peasant holdings could come under regulation— only those which could, after being curtailed in size to one-half or two-thirds, exist as independent, and self-supporting farms. This was taken to mean either farms which were actually performing draft labor or farms which were acknowledged as capable of providing and keeping the needed horses or oxen. As a consequence, all the small-holders were excluded from access to property. In some provinces local laws further barred the way to regulation. Thus in Upper Silesia, a province inhabited almost entirely by Polish peasants, twenty-five *morgi*, or 17.5 acres, was set as the lower limit of regulated holdings. The result was that the overwhelming majority of the peasant population in a typical small-holder region like Upper Silesia was excluded from the new arrangement.

2. Also excluded were *new* holdings, or holdings which had not belonged to the same family for a prescribed length of time. For each province, a different "normal year," that is, a date prior to which a holding could be considered an old one, was fixed. The normal year for Silesia was to be 1763, and for West Prussia 1772. This meant fifty-three and forty-four years, respectively— nearly two generations.

The Regulation Reform was supplemented by two other edicts. One of them (1821) introduced the procedure of *reluition*, or redemption of charges not falling under the regulation proceeding. All sorts of rent agreements based on written contract together with cases of perpetual lease belonged here. It is apparent that only peasants with a strong right to the soil could benefit from the *reluition* procedure. The pertinent charge was

evaluated in capital, and the peasant had to acquit it in installments. Numerous were the instances in which a peasant was liable
to the regulation procedure for one part of his charges and to the
reluition for another. *Reluition* was the more acceptable to the
peasant, because it did not entail the loss of a portion of land; in
Polish provinces, however, it was applied on a much smaller
scale than elsewhere.

Along with regulation, or the conferring of property, and with
reluition, or the redemption of specific charges, a third operation
was initiated in the 1820s—the separation of common grounds.
This procedure chiefly concerned woods, meadows, and pastures,
but also common rights to water and quarries. As a first stage,
the rights of the landlord had to be separated from those of the
village by means of a partition of the grounds or by compensation
in cash. Next, the grounds utilized by the village as a whole were
to be divided among individual peasants. The evaluation involved was rather complicated; it will suffice to remark that it
favored the landlord rather than the peasant, inasmuch as it
took into account only qualifications consigned in written contracts—whereas the servitudes were based for the most part on
traditional usage.

The Prussian reform of 1811–16 at first included only two
Polish provinces, Silesia and Pomerania. A third one came under
Prussian rule in 1815: the Grand Duchy of Poznan (Poznania).
King Frederick William III (1797–1840) announced in his in-
corporating Manifesto that his peasant reforms would be extended as soon as possible to this new possession. The inevitable
consequence of this announcement was that the landlords
started to forcibly evict their peasants so that they could not
avail themselves of the regulation provisions. (It must be remembered that Poznania in the years 1807–15 had belonged to the
Duchy of Warsaw and that the peasants in this province had
been presented with personal freedom, although deprived of a
right to their holdings.) Only in 1819 did the Berlin government
become aware of the situation and proclaim a formal ban on
evictions. Thereupon, the government announced its desire to
learn the opinions of those concerned about the ways and means
of the reform to be introduced. Numerous officials as well as landlords of both nationalities expressed their views in lengthy
memoranda, which showed a fair balance between partisanship

of and resistance to the reform. The adversaries, it is clear, were conservatives. The dividing line of opinion ran, it should be noted, across national differences; there were as many die-hard conservatives as liberal-minded landlords among both the German Junkers and the Polish *szlachta*. Eventually, in 1823, the Regulation Reform was extended to the Grand Duchy with slight modifications, mostly favoring the peasants. In practice, however, the reform took a different course in this province because of the fact that the average size of the holding was smaller in Poznania than in other Prussian provinces. The great majority of the peasants' holdings would have become very small had they been curtailed by one-half. The General Committee was obliged to choose another way: It limited its task to converting compulsory labor into rent, leaving to the future the definitive indemnifying of the landlords. Let us stress at once the essential difference between the earlier rent reforms of the eighteenth century and the one introduced in Poznania in the 1820s. Those earlier attempts were acts of favor by the landlord, who remained the owner of his peasants' holdings. Now, however, the Regulation Reform in Poznania granted the peasant full property rights over his holding; it left him encumbered only with the obligation of paying rent to the former landlord until he should be able to redeem his debt in capital. In this way the reform could extend to a relatively large number of holdings, and in that sense it favored the peasant (the Prussian government had less reason to defend the interests of the Polish *szlachta* than those of the German Junker). In theory, this procedure could have included even the small-holders, but here opposition arose. In 1836, a royal ordinance announced that regulation would not extend in Poznania to holdings smaller than twenty-five *morgi*. It was the same provision which had been applied earlier in Upper Silesia.

Let us now state more precisely the main characteristics of the Prussian reform:

1. It was a gradual one, imposed on Junkers and peasants by the state, but imposed in a way that would not infringe on the rights of, nor hurry the decision of, the Junker side. The fact hidden behind the paragraphs of the edict is that the reform was simply codifying and making easier a process already set in motion. For many decades numerous Junkers had perceived the advantage of switching from compulsory to hired labor, but they

wanted to do it gradually and without being pressed. Different estates, as well as their owners, were not equally ripe for reform, which required special conditions; even after the reform began it was not convenient to break with compulsory labor all at once and irrevocably. The Prussian regulation was just suited to this frame of mind. It did not oblige all the estates to open the procedure at one time. On the contrary, the General Committee worked slowly and set about its task in gradual steps. A landlord could call for faster regulation of his estate or, conversely, let some years pass before coming to a decision. There was also the stipulation that even after regulation the landlord could retain, if he wished, a portion of compulsory labor for up to twelve years. This mainly concerned foot labor; the landlord was often ready to introduce his own draft teams (oxen or horses) but was still in need of compulsory labor at harvest time. Or even if he dispensed with compulsory labor, perhaps he wished to contract for a given quantity of compulsory hire. Or, still another variation: He could let the well-to-do peasants acquire their holdings but change nothing in the small-holders' lot. For the time being, they could perform compulsory labor as before, and later one would see; at a given moment one could always evict the *komornicy* and turn them into farmhands. The royal edicts provided for all these Junker preferences, but on the other hand it discriminated against the peasant; if the regulation moved too quickly for the peasant's need, so much the worse for the peasant!

2. The reform was a partial one, in a twofold sense: first because it involved only some of the peasants (a minority, as we shall see), leaving outside its scope not only the landless peasants but also the small-holders; and second, because it granted the peasants full property rights to only a portion of their holdings. The net result of the reform was the division of the village population into two sharply delimited groups; the proprietors and the proletarians.

3. The reform was carried through at the peasant's expense. He was obliged to reward his landlord for every decrease of his income. The state acted only as a go-between; the costs of the operation were shifted to both parties, and they were often ruinous for the poorer side.

A reform so disadvantageous for the peasantry surprisingly provoked no marked opposition. Numerous complaints, individual and collective, were lodged against regulation; but few villages—less than a dozen in each province—made a peremptory protest. Still more rare (and short-lived) were cases of open opposition against regulation. The chief reason for such passivity on the part of the peasant class seems to be the above-mentioned split of each village into two camps with opposing interests. For centuries it had always been the well-to-do peasant who exercised authority in the village, and he also led in cases of conflict or struggle with the manor. But now these same wealthy and privileged peasants were cooperating with the landlord and profiting from the regulation. The poorest and most injured layer of the peasantry had no tradition of initiative or leadership.

Only later, in the 1840s, when the exploitation of the smallholders reached its peak, when they were threatened by final eviction, did the social ferment arouse the Silesian and Poznanian peasants. These events were directly connected with the 1848 Revolution and will be dealt with later. Now we shall state only that the revolutionary situation and the peasant participation in it forced the Berlin parliament to make some concessions in behalf of the peasants. A law passed in 1850 introduced two important amendments to the regulation procedure. (1) The regulation was extended to all peasant holdings, irrespective of their size—those holdings, of course, which had not already been liquidated. (2) The rent encumbering the regulated holdings was to be bought up through a state bank. The bank was to issue bonds which would clear the landlord's dues, and the peasants would pay off the bonds on an amortization basis. The rent was capitalized at the onerous rate of 4 percent; that is, the capital due the landlord was evaluated at twenty-five times the annual rent.

Consequences of the Reform

Appreciation of the Prussian reform varied with political viewpoint. The landlords, distrustful at first, soon perceived the advantages of the reform and praised it unanimously as a sound and equitable instrument of reconstruction, helpful to both the big estates and the well-to-do peasants. Left-wing polemists, with the Communist Wilhelm Wolff (1809–64) at their head, severely condemned the reform as an immense swindle, a robbery of hundreds of thousands of peasants by the Junkers. A correct interpretation of the net results of the reform is not easy, despite existing statistical data. The General Committee issued a separate report every year for each regency (there were ten of them, east of the Oder and the Neisse). This report enumerated how many peasants had been freed from their charges (from the beginning of the reform) and for what price in land, in capital, and in rent. These summarized figures did not state how many peasants had merely ceded land or how many had been entirely switched to rent. The same figures for a whole regency included data for very different regions. Thus, for example, in the Breslau (Wroclaw) regency, the Oder valley was a region of big, intensively cultivated manor farms employing numerous farmhands. In the same regency, the Sudetenland was a poor and overpopulated region of small-holders who gained additional income from weaving at home. The initial conditions and the results of the regulation must have been entirely different in both these regions.

Another difficulty in using the reports results from their treating separately the three main aspects of the reform. We have separate data concerning regulation, *reluition*, and separation. It is obvious that the figures concerning individuals, land, and money overlap. Let us quote a typical instance, the report of the Königsberg Regency for 1848. It states that from the beginning of the reform to 1848 the committee made the following settlements: (1) Under the heading of regulation, 12,000 holdings measuring 250,000 *hectares*. The average size of a regulated holding was twenty-one *hectares*, or fifty-two acres. No data are given about the amount of land ceded to the landlord. (2) Under the heading of *reluition*, 2,350 holdings (some peasants could hold plots of land subject to both procedures, and they were counted twice). They ceded 30,000 *hectares*, that is, 12.5 *hectares*, or 31 acres, per holding. This time, we do not learn how much land was retained. (3) Under the heading of separation, 43,000 owners, 950,000 *hectares*. In this case all categories of peasants together with the Junkers and other groups of landowners have been lumped together. The 950,000 *hectares* consisted of fields, meadows, woods, bodies of water, etc. There is no way of knowing how much land of any category changed hands under this operation.

Summarized figures give us only a general view of the results. Until 1848, 7,300 *Lassbauern* were regulated in West Prussia;

6,300 in East Prussia; 4,300 in Upper Silesia (*Lassbauern* were a marginal problem in this province); and 26,500 in Poznania, where a much higher percentage of *Lassbauern* was admitted to regulation. Separation of lands was carried through in 64,000 holdings before 1848, and in 97,000 more holdings afterward.

The average size of a regulated holding was sixty-two acres in East Prussia, fifty in West Prussia, thirty-five in Poznania, and only twenty-two in Upper Silesia. As can be seen, in both the Prussian provinces only a small number of relatively wealthy peasants were included in the regulation. In Poznania the reform was applied more broadly, resulting in a lower average size of holding. As for Upper Silesia, this had always been a region of small-holders, and the reform could not change this fact. In West Prussia the regulated peasants were deprived of one-sixteenth of their land, in Poznania of one-seventh, in East Prussia of one-fifth, in Upper Silesia of one-third. The peasant who ceded less land had to pay more money in capital or rent; this was the alternative of the wealthy peasants. The poorer the peasant was, the more land he had to abandon.

Reluition was applied to 3,000 holdings in East Prussia, 5,000 in West Prussia, 17,000 in Poznania, and 18,000 in Upper Silesia. These figures do not include the later and complementary *reluition*, carried through after 1848, and affecting 89,000 holdings in Poznania.

The reports of the General Committee do not take into account private transactions between peasants and landlords, achieved without official mediation but with the same purpose of freeing the peasant from charges. Such private transactions could amount to 10 or 15 percent of the official statistics, as has been established from samples in Silesia.

A more conclusive estimate of the eventual results of the reform can be obtained from a comparison of the agrarian structure of 1800 with that of 1860. Figures for the latter year are good; those for 1800 are less reliable. Under the feudal system it was often difficult to distinguish the possessions of the lord from those of the peasant.

Turning to the Prussian statistics for 1860, we find all land divided into five categories: (*a*) the big property of over 375 acres; (*b*) the middle-sized property (185–375 acres); (*c*) the property of well-to-do peasants (19–185 acres); (*d*) the property of small-holders (2.5–19 acres); (e) the tiny holdings of under 2.5 acres. These divisions are not well chosen. From an economic and social point of view, the land in a capitalist society should be divided into the following categories: (1) the property of landlords who run their estates with hired hands only; (2) the property of wealthy peasants who work their farms themselves with the help of hired hands; (3) the middle-sized property of peasants who do not hire labor but whose farms are sufficient for subsistence; (4) the farms of small-holders who are obliged to earn additional money in order to live on their plots; (5) the plots of proletarians who earn additional income from a tiny patch of garden. The divisions by size among these five groups will vary according to the quality of soil and agricultural techniques used, and the determination of such partitions for given region and time is an arduous task. It is clear that the statistical limits quoted above do not suit the required conditions. The first group—over 375 acres—corresponds to the landlords. But the second (185–375 acres) must include, together with a majority of landlords, some wealthy peasants also. The third group (19–185 acres) consists of wealthy but also of moderately well-to-do peasants; the fourth (2.5–19 acres) of middle- and small-holders. This situation is common when the historian has at his disposal inadequate sources of economic data.

Turning back to the five categories of property, however defective this classification may be, the figures for Prussian Poland in 1860, just after the completion of the reform, are shown in table 1.

Silesia was a highly differentiated province. The fertile Oder valley was a region of big manor farms, with a small sprinkling of large peasant farms of more than fifty acres. Middle-sized peasant farms were more numerous along the Sudeten range. The Junkers possessed almost all the forests. There were about 200,000 peasant owners in Silesia in 1860, but 117,000 of them had less than three acres. Moreover, there were 300,000 proletarians with no land at all. The figures for West Pomerania are still more extreme.

The Prussian reform contrived to establish in the countryside two kinds of capitalist enterprise: the big estate of 500–1,500 acres (and some aristocratic families accumulated more than one estate) and the big peasant farm of about fifty acres. The big estates constituted about half of the total field area, and almost all the forests. Both types of enterprise were vital and productive; both contributed to the rise of agriculture, which transformed these eastern provinces in "Germany's granary." Conservatives and agrarians had many reasons to praise the Prussian reform. The price paid was the eviction of the great majority of the peasant population. Toward the middle of the nineteenth century,

TABLE 1

FARM CLASSIFICATIONS IN PRUSSIAN POLAND IN 1860

	GROUP					TOTAL
	1	2	3	4	5	
No. of farms, in Poznania (000's)	2.6	1	45	38	25	111.6
Percentage of field area.............	57	4	33	5	1	100
Percentage of area in East and West Prussia...........	44	8	44	3	1	100
Percentage of area in Silesia...........	51	4	31	12	2	100

this brutal act of injustice seemed to become a serious source of social unrest. Eventually, this unrest was to be weakened by means of a decrease in the rural population. In Silesia, this decrease contributed to the growth of a big industry in the same province, which was a positive factor. In Poznania and Pomerania, the surplus population emigrated abroad, which was a loss for the nation. We shall observe the later development of these provinces and the interdependence of social and national factors, in their influence on the economic evolution.

5

THE CONGRESS KINGDOM
1815–1830

The Congress of Vienna created a new kingdom of Poland, composed from the major part of the Duchy of Warsaw. This so-called Congress Kingdom was to be united with the Russian Empire. It retained a separate administration and was granted a liberal constitution, including a parliament (*Sejm*) and a Polish army. The Poles were to rule themselves, albeit under the strict supervision of the emperor's brother, Grand Duke Constantine. Many of the constitutional provisions remained a dead letter, which was to lead, fifteen years later, to an armed outbreak against Russia.

The country emerged from the Napoleonic wars with a ruined agriculture. Losses of cattle and horses were particularly heavy. The Russian army of occupation requisitioned the remnants of supplies left over by the French. Losses of life were still more painful: the Polish contingent in 1812 (the largest after the French) amounted to 100,000, and only 18,000 returned. New drafts in 1813 took away still more labor, especially from the countryside.

Abandoned holdings and ruined cottages were to be seen everywhere. And there was a great deal of social unrest in the villages. The peasants asked for alleviation of compulsory labor and taxes so that they could make a new start with their farming.

Poland's fate, meanwhile, was decided by the "dancing" Congress in Vienna. It was expected that central Poland would remain under the Russian scepter and would retain some sort of autonomy. Prince Adam Czartoryski (1770–1861), the czar's friend and chief adviser in Polish matters, was busy with a new constitution and other political arrangements. As chairman of the Civic Committee, an advisory body to the Russian provisional government composed of a score of big landlords, Czartoryski wanted to take stock of the actual state of the agrarian problem. He therefore organized a separate reform committee and ordered it to issue a detailed questionnaire concerning the settling of the peasants' status under the new political conditions. The questionnaire was sent round to prefects and subprefects, the district councils, the county courts, and also to a number of private persons—but whether private or official, the respondents belonged almost exclusively to the proprietary gentry. All the replies have been preserved in the Czartoryski archives, and they constitute a valuable source of information about the gentry's attitude during that period. The response was generally unfavorable to the peasants, and it could not have been otherwise at a moment when a fresh Russian victory announced a switch to conservatism in European politics. Respondents from the eastern and southern provinces represented the most conservative attitude; they criticized the 1807 Constitution and proposed various ways of limiting, if not canceling, the peasant's personal freedom. In any case, they supported the continuation of compulsory labor. Representatives of western and northern districts (later including Poznania) expressed more progressive views, in that they at least seemed reconciled to the emancipation and to the December Decree. They only wanted a free hand in dealing with the peasants (the right to evict them or to commute their charges), with no interference from the state.

This was the point of view of the governing class. The peasants were not asked for their views, although some groups of them tried to raise their voices. In numerous crown (now "national") estates whole peasant communes petitioned the authorities to dispense with compulsory labor and to charge a rent instead. The peasants even proposed that they lease the national farms, divide them among themselves, and pay a higher rent than the present leaseholders. Such proposals were heeded, to some extent. The national domains were in a state of ruin and brought in a negligible income; arrears in rent from the big leaseholders were growing. But it was difficult to reach a firm decision in such a transition period, and so the government contented itself for the moment with appointing another committee, which was to organize the national domains.

As to the private estates, the authorities simply resolved to leave everything unchanged. The 1815 Constitution of the new kingdom of Poland (or Congress Poland) confirmed the personal liberty of the peasants, but it silently passed over their rights to the soil. The December Decree thus remained in force together with the landlord's right of eviction. Some years later, in 1822, the problem of peasant property rights was again raised in the State Council, chiefly at the suggestion of Staszic, but with no result. Staszic had been a steady champion of the peasants during the four-year *Sejm*. He was now a wealthy, important, and respected person, a state councillor and chairman of the Scientific Society, but he could not force through his views on social justice. He tried instead to become a popular benefactor on a small scale. He bought the extensive domains of Hrubieszów in eastern Poland (about ten villages with fertile soil) and divided the estate lands among the peasants, giving them full property rights. He also founded the "Peasant Society," organized along cooperative lines, to which all the peasants would belong and which would superintend the exploitation of forests, waters, and other common ground, as well as set up schools, hospitals, and other social institutions. All this establishment, conceived along modern lines, was consigned to the tutelage of one of the neighboring landlords, whose trusteeship would be hereditary and honorary. This remarkable act of donation, although reduced in more than one respect by subsequent state interference, has managed somehow to survive to the present time and has assured a relative prosperity to the inhabitants of Hrubieszów.

This lonely act of philanthropy did not change the general picture of a disadvantageous position of peasants faced with hostile authorities who unanimously sided with the gentry. The govern-

ment's attitude toward class conflicts between landlords and peasants was ambiguous and, in fact, hypocritical. In any case of
complaint by a peasant or a village commune against a landlord,
the chief of the county or, on a higher level, the Palatinate Commission relegated the plaintiff to the judicial procedure. Administration, so it was said, was supposed to remain neutral in such
cases. The judicial way, however, was long, costly, and uncertain;
it was difficult to obtain justice from a court which was usually
in sympathy with the landlord. This was one side of the government's policy; the other became apparent when the landlord himself appeared as plaintiff—for example, when a peasant refused
compulsory labor or showed disobedience in some other way. For
these cases *secret* government legislation empowered local authorities to lend assistance to the landlord and to enforce obedience in the village. This task was most often carried through by
the military.

There were also instances of *public* legislation which caused a
worsening of the legal conditions of peasant life. One of them concerned local administration on the commune level. In feudal
times, no such administration was needed at all in the countryside. In a private domain, the landlord was master; he maintained
public order and administered the law with no kind of appeal
allowed the peasants. This system was necessarily upset by the
1807 Constitution. The landlord ceased to be master as such; he
was to be replaced by a state official, and the state justice was
to prevail. A reform of this kind, however, was difficult to carry
through, in all its aspects, at one time. The Duchy of Warsaw
had neither candidates for such posts nor the means to pay them.
Choosing the easiest interim way, it decreed that each private
estate would constitute a commune and that the prefect would
appoint the mayor. In 90 percent of the cases, the mayor ap-
pointee was the landlord himself or his steward. This emergency
arrangement was to be modified or settled in peaceful times, after
1815. It was indeed settled in 1818, by a royal decree* which ruled
that the owner of the estate (*dziedzic*) was local mayor (*wójt*) by
law; he could exercise his functions himself or appoint one of his
officials as deputy. The Commission of the Interior reserved for itself only the right to refuse acceptance of, or to depose, a deputy
mayor recognized as incompetent. The mayor's responsibilities

* See Appendix, section *D*.

75

were extensive in both the administrative and the judicial fields. He applied the law in minor criminal cases, prescribing penalties (including short-term arrest or a given amount of thrashing) for any breach of the peace or disorderly conduct. The defendant could, of course, appeal to the County Court—but with little chance of success.

A second instance of public government policy was the decree on rural journeymen, of 1821. It prescribed particularly onerous conditions of contract for the landless peasant employed on a manor farm. He was engaged for a calendar year and could not break his contract except in cases of cruelty, rape, or the like. The master always had the right to fire a farmhand for laziness or disobedience; he was also allowed to apply the so-called house discipline, that is, to beat him. But if the farmhand dared to quit before the year's end, he was brought back by the police, handcuffed if necessary (a similar *Gesindeordnung* was binding in Prussia until 1918).

A third example of public policy concerns national domains. They presented an important problem, since they contained about one million peasants, 5,000 villages, and an area of one million square miles, of which 300,000 square miles were under cultivation, constituting one-fifth of the total tilled area of Congress Poland. Some trials at rent reform had been attempted there in the 1820s, by the Organization Committee mentioned above. But these attempts were opposed as being against the interests of the gentry and particularly of the big leaseholders. The latter were well-connected profiteers who exploited the peasants and cheated the treasury. Their aim was not to give up the national domains, but rather to purchase them cheap, with full property rights. Their goal seemed attained in 1828, when a royal decree announced the sale of all national domains, by whole estates, into private hands. Any peasant rights to the soil were to be disregarded. The measure was justified by the necessity of accumulating large sums for industrial investments; nevertheless, the blatant disregard for the peasants, which would lead to a worsening of their condition, was appalling. It was only as a result of unexpected circumstances that this planned sale was not carried through.

Industrial investments played an important role in Congress Poland, during the period in question. They were encouraged mainly by the energetic finance minister, Prince Ksawery Lubecki (1778–1846). Thanks to state enterprise, state loans, and a policy of protection, a new center of textile industry was born in the Lodz area; foundries and forges were expanded in the southwestern corner of the country. These developments, however, were to influence but very gradually the condition of the peasantry. Until the middle of the century the heavy and textile industries remained mostly in the manufactory stage, and did not absorb much manpower from the countryside (coal mining was one notable exception). On the other hand, Lubecki's policy of industrialization required higher taxes and higher prices for such monopolized articles as salt and tobacco—and these burdens were borne mainly by the peasant masses.

The Congress Kingdom was governed by conservative aristocrats subservient to the emperor's will. The emperor-king was opposed by a large section of the liberal gentry which had its representatives in the *Sejm*. But this liberal opposition had no more understanding of the peasants' problems than the ministers. It will be sufficient to quote two votes of the *Sejm* in 1825, neither resulting from government pressure. One of them was concerned with the purchase of some farms under perpetual lease. According to the Napoleonic Code, the leaseholder had the right to free himself of further charges by paying outright the capitalized value of the rent. A special resolution of the *Sejm* prescribed that this right of purchase would not concern the peasant rent payers who would not be permitted to become full owners of their holdings by their own choice. The second bill passed by the *Sejm* in the same year—an innovation to the Criminal Code in arson cases—drastically sharpened the penalties. Arson was a characteristic form of peasant vengeance.

In 1830, half a year before the November Insurrection, Jan Olrych Szaniecki (1783–1840), one of the few representatives of the radical bourgeoisie, in the *Sejm* (himself a successful lawyer, a nouveau riche, and landowner) proposed a motion making it mandatory that compulsory labor in private estates be converted to rent. There was an indignant outcry on all sides, and the motion was turned down without any debate whatsoever.

Two additional matters ought still to be considered in this connection: the attitude of the peasants themselves and the programs of the revolutionary party. One should also not forget the actual circumstances of the different groups of the peasantry and the evolution of agriculture and its impact on the peasants' charges. The latter question will be dealt with at greater length in a later chapter, covering a longer period of nearly fifty years (1815–60). We shall limit ourselves at present to some general considerations.

The degree of personal freedom actually enjoyed by the peasant during the so-called constitutional period (1815–30) remains for discussion. Some authors wondered if the abolition of serfdom (1807) remained a dead letter. In order to move, the peasant had to procure for himself at his mayor's (that is, his landlord's) office a migration certificate. Such an attestation could be refused in cases of unfulfilled duties. The last provision covered arrears in taxes, in rent, in compulsory labor, as well as breach of contract and unpaid debts—and how few were the peasants who were not in debt! The landlord-mayor had sufficient opportunity to make a peasant's departure difficult. It was not easy, however, to stop him altogether or to compel him to return if he settled elsewhere, even if illegally. The proof lies in a commonly observed and growing mobility of the peasant population, and especially in the growth of such towns as Warsaw and some industrial centers near Lodz.

Another problem was the policy of the landlords with respect to rent reforms and evictions. Statistical data are not especially reliable for the period 1815–30, but the general trend is evident enough. The economic condition of the landlords in the early twenties was very bad. The main cause was the fall of grain prices as a result of the English Corn Laws. Wheat and rye prices lost almost two-thirds of their value between 1818 and 1825, and the drop was still more severe on local markets. The price of a *korzec* (2.5 bushels) of wheat in Gdansk fell from 54 *złoty* to 19 *złoty* between 1818 and 1825. The price of a *korzec* of rye fell from 35 *złoty* to 14 *złoty* over the same period. Landlords were overburdened with debts and near bankruptcy. Not until 1825 did a slight improvement begin. The slump came to an end, and the Land Credit Society was founded. But during the greater part of the period, the economic situation did not favor investments, and still less a marked evolution toward capitalistic farming. We shall speak later of the new trends in agronomy and breeding. They were not linked, as a rule, with rent reform and eviction. Both processes were on their way, they even gained in strength toward the end of the 1820s. But they had not yet achieved the impetus which characterized the next decade.

Let us now return to the activity of the peasants themselves. By comparison with conditions during the preceding brief Napoleonic episode, it seems that the countryside had awakened—the peasants were stepping out with claims of their own. These incidents were neither important nor general; nevertheless, they were symptomatic. They issued almost exclusively from the national domains; at least, that is the impression given by archival records. It may well be that data concerning private estates have been less well preserved for that period. Notwithstanding, it is clear that the "national" peasants were better prepared for the kind of fight now impending than the private peasants. It was, in fact, chiefly a legal activity; many lawsuits were directed against the leaseholders. In former Poland, the crown estates were ruled by the *starosta*, a magnate who held the estate for life and most often passed it on to his son. He cared for it as for his own possessions. But the present leaseholder was a greedy parvenu, set only on quick enrichment—one whom neither interest nor moral scruples prevented from squeezing the peasants dry. Village communities reacted by legal means, appealing to local courts and then to Palatinate authorities, to the ministers in Warsaw, to the viceroy (*namiestnik*), and to the king. When these protests proved to be of no avail, the peasants turned to strikes, that is, to refusal of compulsory labor. Clashes ensued when military force was used for pacification, and arrests were made. It is difficult to speak of a general movement; rather there were separate unconnected activities centered in various estates. In some cases, the stubborn protests of the peasants induced Warsaw authorities to investigate the local complaints, and sometimes shocking abuses came to light and were punished. Much more often, the peasants' endeavors were not sufficiently powerful to overcome the influence of their local oppressors.

One interesting feature of this peasant agitation was the appearance of local leaders. These were most often people from outside the village: unlicensed legal advisers, retired noncommissioned officers, former leaseholders gone bankrupt, discharged private officials—all sorts of outcasts endowed with some education but not included in the established system. Such were the men who drew up the peasants' petitions and often incited them to violence. In the government correspondence they are alluded to as *burzyciele*, a word meaning something between trouble-makers and saboteurs. They were supposed to be mean intriguers and the sole cause of local social ferment. It is a fact that they were making a living from the peasants' lawsuits, but it is also a fact that they enjoyed their confidence and often rendered them important services. Moreover, they risked certain persecution, as alleged perpetrators of every mischief.

The life story of one of these *burzyciele* is worth mention. Kazimierz Deczyński (1800–1838) was the son of a well-to-do peasant in a crown estate of the Kalisz Palatinate. He received some instruction and became a teacher in his native village. The community waged a lawsuit against the leaseholder and petitioned for a commutation of compulsory labor into rent—or still better, for transfer of the lease to the peasants themselves. Deczyński helped them, although reluctantly, while urging moderation. The leaseholder tried to intimidate him and bribe him to desist. Eventually, he arranged with military authorities that Deczyński be drafted into the army and thus removed. As a private, and later a non-commissioned officer, Deczyński was further browbeaten and harassed because of his radical inclinations. Later he participated in the November insurrection and emigrated; nonetheless, even among his fellow officers and patriots he was held in suspicion as a potentially dangerous initiator of social unrest. He left interesting memoirs and was much later portrayed in a well-known Marxist novel, albeit with some exaggeration, as a forerunner of Bolshevism.

The Deczyński episode leads us to two further matters: the attitude of revolutionaries regarding the peasant question, and the November insurrection of 1830–31. Let us state at first that there was a gap of twenty years between the last underground activities of the Jacobin period in the 1790s, and the first attempts at conspiracy after 1815. The new clandestine organizations, composed of students and officers, wanted to oppose the program of restoration. However, they were small numerically and did not aspire to an upheaval in the foreseeable future. Their aim was the defense of nationality, not the fight for independence, and still less social revolution. They sympathized, of course, with the people; they were aware of Kościuszko's last will, of the connection between social reform and national consciousness of the masses. But they had no clear idea of the kind of reform at which to aim, and they did not even try to establish contact with the rural masses. One member of the clandestine Patriotic Society, Jakub Szreder, a lawyer who defended peasants in their suits against leaseholders, remarked once to the chief of the conspiracy, Walerian Łukasiński (1786–1868), that it would be worthwhile to start some propaganda among the peasants. Łukasiński, a sincere patriot and later a national martyr, approved of his viewpoint but insisted that the time had not yet come.

Comments friendly to the peasants and hostile to the magnates and other wrongdoers came out into the open in literary form, especially after the great romantic breakthrough of 1820. An episode in Adam Mickiewicz's *Forefather's Eve* displays the ghastly apparition of the inhuman landlord, tortured forever in afterlife by the souls of his former victims. The peasants did not read Mickiewicz; the aristocracy did and were offended. In one of his ballads the Palatine discovers at night that his wife has a rendezvous with a young and poor gentleman whom she has loved before. The Palatine, with his servant, hides in the garden in order to kill both the wife and her lover. The servant, however, instead shoots the Palatine in the head. Readers in Warsaw salons were asking themselves, Does Mr. Mickiewicz really want to kill us all with the help of our servants? Mickiewicz certainly did not, although he did not sympathize with the Polish aristocracy.

Only in 1830, some months before the insurrection, did Jan Żukowski (d. 1831), a young journalist affiliated with the underground, publish a book entitled *On Pańszczyzna*, containing a direct attack on compulsory labor. The author dwelt not so much on ethical or political arguments against compulsory labor, but rather on economic motives, aiming to convince the landlords that the use of compulsory labor in farming was backward, inefficient, and self-defeating. He openly advocated the recent Prussian reform as the best way to eliminate feudal conditions. (We have seen that it was not such an equitable way after all.) Undoubtedly, Żukowski had the concealed political aim of preparing the gentry for necessary reforms, in view of the expected insurrection. The book was belated and proved ineffective. The insurrection erupted without any social program at all, and with both sides totally unprepared to cope with the demands confronting them in the name of the national cause.

6

THE NOVEMBER INSURRECTION

The Warsaw outbreak of 29 November 1830 aroused a profound reaction in the countryside. The slogan of liberty was understood by the peasants as freedom from compulsory obligations. In many regions they simply ceased to work. This is not what the conspirators had intended. They wanted to fight the czar and reestablish the independence of their country. They were so sure of the gentry's patriotism that they did not even bother to impose a revolutionary government of their own but left the power to the conservatives, who did not want an upheaval. Thus the authority, central and local, remained in the hands, if not of former officials, at least of persons connected with them. The national government, together with the generals, waged a war without much conviction. It was a conservative revolution, as Engels was to label it later, and its leaders did not intend to link it with any social changes. The peasants were advised to remain inactive, and they were threatened with military court, as in time of war.

A singular situation arose. The army, composed mainly of peasants, fought gallantly and with patriotic spirit. But the peasants at home felt deceived; instead of the promised freedom, they were burdened, in consequence of the war, with additional taxes, deliveries in kind, conscription, and compulsory service in the local civic guard. They could not feel enthusiastic about the war for independence. Maurycy Mochnacki (1804–34), the outstanding publicist of the Left, as early as February 1831 posed the momentous question, Why do the masses not rise? And he answered, Because we are ignoring their problems.

The *Sejm*, elected in prerevolutionary days and composed chiefly of the gentry, was slow to understand. In March, however, with the enemy threatening and some of the conservative members prudently stepping aside, the House finally turned to a debate of the peasant question. A motion was introduced by the new minister of finance, Alojzy Biernacki (1778–1854), a liberal landowner from the Kalisz Palatinate, an experienced farmer and a partisan of rent reform. Being in charge of the national domains as minister of finance, he limited himself to proposing a reform of them through a conversion of compulsory labor into rent. He elaborated a conversion table, based not on the number of days of labor but on the quantity and quality of the soil (according to regions). His project was sent to a committee and returned broadened by an additional proposal for a further step: After the rent reform the peasants should be offered the possibility of redeeming their holdings. The operation was to be stretched in time over more than twenty years, involving only a fraction of well-to-do peasants—and, as has been pointed out, only in the national domains. The ensuing discussion, recorded in the *Sejm*'s minutes, was characteristic. A small leftist minority, headed by Szaniecki, already mentioned, advocated a broadening of the proposed law, which should also include private properties, while speeding up the procedure for distributing property. The landlords, of course, should be remunerated for their losses. Much more numerous and more active was the conservative wing, which opposed reform even in the national domains, since such reform would clearly influence the rest of the peasants, who would claim the same concessions. The opposition to the government's motion used hypocritical arguments, invoking the people's welfare, the unprepared-ness of the country, and the doubtful economic consequences of such a hasty change.They succeeded in extending the debate for a few weeks, and then in suspending it with a resolution to await the arrival of a larger number of deputies. The issue, thus dis-missed from the agenda, was not taken up again. The *Sejm* of the insurrection did not have the courage to vote even a partial reform which might encroach upon vested interests.

Unfavorable consequences of this behavior were soon to be felt. Feelings in the countryside continued to deteriorate. So-cial unrest increased; riots directed against the landlords oc-curred in some places and had to be suppressed with military aid. Desertions from the army were also multiplying. In the villages, patriotic propaganda was met with sullen faces. When called to enroll, the peasants were asking, And what about compulsory labor? Or they might say, The landlords started the fighting; they should fight themselves. Thousands of peasants fought in the ranks of the army, but the mass of the people remained indifferent —with unquestionable consequences on the outcome of the struggle.

Among others, the leftist press and the Patriotic Club in War-saw tried to bring pressure to bear on the government in social matters. Arguments against compulsory labor were developed, as well as definite proposals for the granting of title to land to killed, wounded, or particularly deserving soldiers. Sums were also collected to form a fund for the purchase of land for the brav-est soldiers. These were modest and even naïve proposals, and they had no influence on the government's policy. Joachim Le-lewel (1786–1861), the distinguished historian and chief spokes-man for the Polish Left, had no explicit program of social reforms. Together with all patriots, he felt sympathy for the ruling class (*szlachta*); actually, he belonged to it. He was not yet prepared to break with the *szlachta* or to force concessions upon it, even such as he deemed indispensable for the nation's salvation. The lesson from the 1831 defeat would be learned eventually on foreign soil, after emigration. With respect to the conditions of the peas-ant, the November uprising marked a step back, even compared with Kościuszko's partial reform of 1794. One should remember, however, that the main reform of Kościuszko was the suppression of serfdom; serfdom no longer existed in Congress Poland.

Two contrasting opinions are commonly held, in historiography as well as in popular tradition, on this crucial question of the peasants and their attitude in 1831. One theory runs thus: The oppressed peasantry was totally devoid of patriotic sentiments and refused to fight in a war waged by the *szlachta*. Some Marxist writers have developed this idea. The other theory is best expressed in the famous song composed in 1836 by Gustaw Ehrenberg (1814–95), a radical conspirator of the 1830s: "At the battle of Stoczek the peasants were capturing guns, their hands still black from the plough—while in Warsaw the lords were smoking cigars and discussing the problems of rent!" We should not, however, consider these two attitudes—the peasant defending the country on the one hand, and indifferent to the national cause on the other—as totally incompatible. In all European countries, the soldier in those times was of peasant stock, and he was a good and disciplined soldier. If some soldiers deserted and even rebelled, it was because of mistreatment, flogging, underfeeding, and not as the result of a class attitude. Military service, at that time, was a career, even for the private. It lasted many years and necessarily alienated the soldier from his native village. When home on leave, he considered himself superior to his family, and he most likely became a propagator of his army's ideas. The Polish peasant, when at home from the Russian or Austrian army, most often propagated the cult of the emperor. But when serving in the Polish army, he acted and felt as a patriot. As to the peasants suddenly enlisted in 1831, for a campaign the necessity of which they did not perceive and which appeared only as a burden, this was another affair.

When condemning the conservative stubbornness of the *Sejm* in 1831, or the timidity of the Left, which was incapable of developing and still less of enforcing a radical program in agrarian matters, we should be careful not to attribute to the peasant problem an absolute or fatalist meaning. We may assume that the failure to deal with the peasant question had an unfavorable influence on the course of events. It would be a gross simplification to state that the insurrection was defeated *because* it did not satisfy the peasants. It is impossible to prove that radical agrarian reform would have raised the enthusiasm of the masses (while estranging the *szlachta*) and that this enthusiasm would have been enough to assure victory. The historian must remain realistic. The landlords in 1831 could have shown more foresight, of course, and the Polish Left more determination. Some kind of reform could have been voted by the *Sejm*, and it could have had important consequences in the future. We must feel sorry that it did not happen. The maximum degree of reform of which a *Sejm* of gentry might have been capable, out of patriotism, would have been some sort of compromise such as that elaborated by Polish democrats on foreign soil in 1836. That it would have saved the country seems dubious. One thing is certain: The 1831 insurrection disclosed the abyss between the peasants' backing of the national cause and the fact that the major problem was left unresolved—even untouched. This was to foster further ideological developments.

7

PROGRESS OF AGRICULTURE IN
THE FIRST HALF OF THE
NINETEENTH CENTURY

Let us now step back for a while in order to examine, from the
point of view of economic progress in agriculture, the whole period
of Congress Poland, beginning with its foundation in 1815, to
the emancipation reform in the sixties. Changes were important,
and they certainly influenced the parallel sequence of reform and
revolution. It is more difficult to evaluate the effect of these
changes quantitatively. Two different approaches are possible,
the individual and the statistical. In the former, one can examine
archival or published material concerning individual estates or
peasant farms, as, for example, administrative records of some
domains or descriptions of model farms in the agricultural press.
Such material, however valuable, is seldom typical. Well-pre-
served administrative files testify that the given estate was well
run and can hardly be envisaged as a typical example. As for
descriptions in the press, they usually concerned special farms,
whether big or small. Statistics, on the other hand, give us an

average, but they may often be misleading. There exist, of course, statistical data about areas planted, the quantity of crops harvested per acre, the kind and number of agricultural tools and machines, the use of manure and other fertilizers, and chattels and breeding. However, these will be data concerning whole counties (*powiaty*); that is, they will confound information about estates and about peasant holdings. At the time in question, these represented two very different types of agriculture; the estates were progressive, the peasant farms were not. Even among estates in a given county, surprising differences were to be found. Some Russian statistics, it is true, give us separate data for gentry and nongentry farms, but they are not less misleading. Thus, the small holdings (*zaścianki*) belonging to the poorest *szlachta* are intermingled with the gentry farms (in some regions the *zaścianki* comprised up to 25 percent of the tilled area). Furthermore, an estate purchased by a burgher—and often a model one—is classified as *nongentry*. The Austrians arranged their statistics into two categories: the dominical and rustical lands. These corresponded approximately to large- and small-scale culture, although there were some small farms on dominical soil and a small quantity of rustical land belonged to the estates.

Evaluation of the rate of evolution of Polish agriculture in the first half of the nineteenth century varies according to the point of view. A specialist in the economics of the eighteenth century will most likely see interesting manifestations of capitalist farming as early as the Enlightenment period. On the other hand, a historian of the capitalist epoch will undoubtedly say that capitalism in Polish agriculture began only after the emancipation, and even then not at once. Nowadays we take it for granted that every economic reform is accepted but gradually, but what should be more important to the historian—the majority of cases, belonging to a passing epoch, or the more rare examples of pioneering innovations?

From a theoretical point of view, we can accept the thesis that every technical innovation, before it is commonly accepted, passes through the four following phases:

1. The new technique is explained and discussed in the press; it is also experimented with on a small number of leading estates.

2. The technique is adopted as a paying one on some of the best-managed estates.

3. The majority of estates and some of the best peasant farms adopt the new technique.

4. The new technique becomes universal, but the old methods are retained in backward regions or on backward farms.

It was common in nineteenth-century Poland for one or two generations to elapse between the first and the fourth stages of evolution. It does not matter whether we are considering the use of scythes, or the rotation of crops, or beet culture, or fertilizers, or drainage—when speaking of the time and place of appearance of new techniques, one must be careful to specify the phase of evolution which is referred to.

The principal difference between large- and small-scale culture in Poland consisted in the fact that for centuries the estate had produced chiefly for the market whereas the peasant's crops went chiefly for his own use. ("Matthew has harvested, Matthew has eaten" was a common proverb.) Let me emphasize that this was generally, but not exclusively, true. From the beginning of the nineteenth century the peasant's contact with the market broadened steadily (keep in mind, he was a rent payer as a matter of course but discharged labor duties as well). Nevertheless, in the light of total production, especially of the four main cereals (wheat, rye, oats, and barley), the peasant's share of the market was still insignificant. His share was appreciable for flax, hemp, poultry, dairy products, and pigs.

Two important innovations were introduced in the manor economy in the first half of the nineteenth century: potatoes and sheep. The potato was, of course, known since the preceding century, but as a curiosity rather than a variety of vegetable. The peasants did adopt potatoes as a field crop earlier than the domains. In 1810, two-thirds of the potato plantations were on peasant land and only one-third on the landlords'. The proportion changed after 1820, with a rapid growth of production: 3 million bushels in 1822, 23.5 million in 1839, 41 million in 1843. This growth resulted from an expansion of tilled area and not from a rise in yield, which remained low: thirty to forty bushels per acre. There was a difference in the importance of the growth of potato production to the peasant holding and to the manor. For the peasant, potatoes could well mean that he could now get more food from the same plot. This would have been a correct statement if the peasant were owner of the soil—but he was not, and therefore the statement went as follows: Thanks to potatoes, the peasant could get the same quantity of food from a smaller plot. Under the December Decree, the growth of potato production simply enabled the landlord to diminish the average size of the peasant's holding. But the landlord himself was also adopting potatoes, for quite another reason: the British Corn Laws. For centuries, the Polish *szlachta* had been an exporter of wheat. But in 1825 the export of wheat from Gdansk had dwindled to one-half the amount in 1800, and this one-half fetched only one-quarter in cash. The landlords therefore desperately sought new sources of income, and they found two: wool and alcohol.

Wool and Alcohol

The 1820s opened the era of expansion for the Polish textile industry. Local factories were given state protection: loans, customs barriers, orders of cloth for the army. Polish cloth from the new factories in the Lodz area was exported to Russia and China. Hence there was a growing demand for wool and a rise in sheep breeding: 900,000 sheep in 1808, 1.5 million in 1822, 3 million in 1830, 4 million in 1844. This last figure marks the peak of production. In the following years up to 1870, the number of sheep oscillated between 3 and 4 million. This was followed by a period in which the quality of breeding ameliorated, and with it the quality of wool. In 1822, only one-third of the sheep belonged to the merino species; in 1857, the fraction had risen to two-thirds. By that time, 90 per cent of the sheep were bred by the big property owners. Such a rapid expansion of breeding, under the December Decree, brought with it unfavorable consequences for the peasants (in fact, every change did). The landlord needed more and more pastures for his sheep, and so he seized the common grounds. Peasants often complained that the pastures were "wrested" or "torn" from them. This trend was detrimental to the peasants' ability to raise their own cattle.

The second new and important source of income for the landlord was vodka. For centuries Polish *szlachta* had exercised a monopoly in the distilling and selling of liquors on their domains, and the trade was gaining in importance, while vodka was replacing beer or *hydromel*. In the nineteenth century the production of alcohol rose dramatically. The reasons are twofold. First, there was a drop in the export prices for grain; henceforth it was more

profitable to turn grain into alcohol. Second, a technical innovation appeared—the *Pistorius* apparatus, invented in 1817 by a
Berlin engineer. This rather simple device was to increase the
output of alcohol fourfold; it was said that the new plant's cost
could be amortized in less than one year. In the course of ten
years all Polish distilleries adopted the *Pistorius* system. In this
field, as well as in the production of wool, the state favored the
estates. In 1822, Minister Lubecki introduced in all the major
towns a consumption tax on liquors. The tax was collected at the
toll bars, from the goods introduced into the town. A requirement
for the success of such a scheme was the suppression of all distilleries and breweries located *inside* the toll bars. The suppression was equivalent to granting the landlords the privilege of
henceforth being the sole producers of vodka and beer—not only
for the countryside but for the towns as well (by that time most
towns had developed liquor production). Swelled by these in-
ducements, the flood of alcohol rose steadily in Congress Poland,
reaching its peak in 1844 with an output of 11 million gallons.
These are official data, most probably incomplete. Since spirits
were not yet used for technological purposes at that time, and
since there were no opportunities for export, we may assume that
the entire output went down the throats of the Polish population.
This amounted to about three gallons of 100 percent spirits yearly
per head, including women and infants—about six times today's
consumption.

Down to about 1830, vodka was distilled mainly from rye; after
that time, more and more was distilled from potatoes. It seems
that one-quarter of the potato crop went to the distilleries—practically all that remained after local consumption. A part of this
production was sold to the towns, but the great bulk was forced
upon the peasants. This was rendered possible thanks to the
propinacja, a feudal monopoly of the distillation and sale of spirits
on a given estate. *Propinacja* continued despite the suppression of
serfdom. The so-called *propinacja* compulsion (the obligation to
purchase a given quantity of vodka) was now forbidden. However, other abuses remained; for example, the habit of paying the
peasants with inn vouchers. Instead of cash, the farmhand received a scrap of paper with which he could shop at the village
inn, and there was not much to be bought there other than vodka.
The peasant was, of course, forbidden to distill spirits himself or

to bring vodka from outside the domain (he was not forbidden to drink outside the domain when traveling). The peasant, as a rule, was indebted to the innkeeper, who bought his production (poultry, dairy products, etc.), and paid mainly in vodka. The Polish literature traditionally represents the innkeeper as a Jew and charges him with the chief responsibility for the peasant's economic and moral degradation. The innkeepers were mostly Jews both at the beginning and the end of this period, and without interruption in Galicia. In Congress Poland, Jews were forbidden to run inns from 1820 to 1862. Innkeepers during those forty-two years were Christians—causing neither more nor less harm than the Jews—sharing the moral responsibility for village drunkenness with the landlord, who gained most of the profit from the *propinacja.*

In earlier, strictly feudal times, *propinacja* was a device introduced in order to restrict the circulation of money inside the domain. Every penny spent by the landlord in the village, for wages or purchases, eventually returned to him by way of the inn. Some eighteenth-century estate accounts show an accurate balance between the cost of wages and *propinacja* income. Toward the middle of the nineteenth century, the situation changed. The *propinacja* income was considerably higher, providing evidence that the peasant's contacts with the market had grown manifestly. In many estates, the net income from the inn was equal to one-half of gross cash income.

We shall examine later the consequences of the *propinacja* system—the plague of drunkenness and the different attempts to fight it.

The Three-Field System

A more auspicious trend in agriculture was already making itself felt before the November insurrection. The prices of grain were slowly rising in the thirties, and after a brief slump at the beginning of the next decade a violent boom set in, beginning in 1845 with the abolition of the British Corn Laws. Wheat export was rising steadily. It reached its maximum for the nineteenth century in 1857, the year after the Crimean War, when 3.3 million bushels were shipped from Gdansk. In the next ten years the figures oscillated in the vicinity of 2 million bushels—twice the average amount exported in the 1820s, and at more than double the price. No wonder production of corn regained first place in the rural economy. The role of distilleries declined, and the expansion of sheep breeding came to a standstill. A new crop, the white beet, came into existence. The first sugar factory opened in 1827, but production was low during the next decades: 2,000 tons of sugar in 1850; 11,000 in 1865. In 1860, barely 0.25 percent of the tilled area was devoted to white-beet production. Most of the beet plantations were on the estates, but in some regions the peasants were beginning to plant beets as well.

Production of grain was rising rapidly, between 1822 and 1864. Wheat rose from 0.6 million bushels to 3 million, a more than five-fold increase; barley from 1.1 million to 10 million, a ninefold increase. The total output of rye and oats only tripled in the same years. This seems to indicate that at least part of the estates were switching to the more lucrative production of better-paying grain. The birth rate in the Congress Kingdom was low in those years: 3 million people in 1830; 5 million in 1864. Between 1843 and 1856, as a result of bad harvests, epidemics, and wars, there was no population increase at all. The surplus production in these circumstances went abroad. It may also have helped to some degree to raise the standard of life in the cities. On the average, one-fourth of the wheat production was exported; one-third if there were a good harvest.

Were bigger crops accountable for this rise of production? It seems not. Average crops remained low, eight to ten bushels per acre, only half the output in France, not to speak of Great Britain. There were of course, regions and individual estates with much higher output, but they were exceptions. There were two causes for the growth of production: (1) A growth of tilled area. In 1820, only 34 percent of Congress Poland was under the plough. In 1865, it was already 50 percent. Much barren land was brought under cultivation, and many forests were cut down. (2) The reduction of fallow land. While tilled land grew by 50 percent, sown land increased by 111 percent. The traditional three-field system was gradually given up. In 1815, immediately after the Napoleonic wars, 50 percent of the land lay fallow in the ruined country. In 1863, fallow land was reduced to 27 percent. These figures were to start an avid discussion of the origin and progress of a convertible husbandry in Poland.

The three-field system was closely bound up with feudalism;

it functioned as long as manor and village grounds were tilled under common control. However, every regulation reform, and every attempt at an improvement in husbandry, required a separation of manor fields from the peasants' fields. This was also a precondition for the introduction of a rotation of crops. The Prussian reform paved the way for the rotation system in Poznania and Silesia. In Congress Poland analogous regulations were also introduced. These regulations, as well as extensive discussions about the rotation system, caused many authors to conclude that the convertible husbandry was already in effect in a majority of estates before the great reform of the sixties. Another group of specialists take a different view: If the figure for 1863 is 27 percent fallow land, this area must correspond to a threefold larger area operated under the three-field system. This amounts to 81 percent three-field-system land (assuming that there were no two-field-system lands left). We have proof that the rotation system was an exception in 1863. We know, of course, that the villages were more backward economically than the estates. But even if we exclude all village lands and all the small *szlachta* lands from our calculations, we still get 61 percent estate land under the three-field system. This amounts to the statement that until the emancipation of 1864 the majority of landowners were farming in the old manner—especially if we take into account the fact that the elimination of fallow land was not necessarily equivalent to modern convertible husbandry.

The partisans of a more optimistic view of Polish economic progress argue, on the contrary, that if nearly 40 percent of the estates eliminated the fallow lands before 1863, this can be considered distinct progress. In nine counties out of thirty-nine this percentage exceeded fifty, and in three counties it amounted to ninety. We are dealing, then, with both more and less advanced regions. One should also take into account that the above statistical data are taken from the landlord's fiscal declarations. A special tax called "supply contingent" was based on the area of land sown. It is conceivable that these data were often lowered purposely. More accurate assessment gives us the following picture: An actual rotation system, consisting in a reduction of corn to one-half of the tilled area, was in effect in the western parts of Congress Poland, but even there it was an exception. Such innovations were as yet absolutely unknown east of Warsaw. As to the peasants, they often made use of fallow land by planting potatoes in the third field. With the diminution of their holdings, they would not have been able to subsist otherwise.

The primitive condition of agriculture in Congress Poland can also be demonstrated by noting the quotas of different crops. Let us divide them into three groups: the new, increasing crops— potatoes, beets, clover, tobacco, and hops; the traditional group— wheat, rye, oats, barley, and peas; and the declining group— buckwheat and millet. The distribution of area among these three groups of crops was as follows: 8, 83, and 9 percent in 1822; 13, 82, and 5 percent in 1863. Progress was obviously insignificant. In 1840 clover covered one-half of one percent of the tilled area, compared with 3 percent in 1863. These are, of course, average figures. When we exclude village lands, and when we consider some of the important regions in the west, we shall obtain more meaningful data. As for the rise in harvest yields between 1822 and 1863 computed separately for the same three groups of crops, it is estimated to be 134 percent for the new crops, 51 percent for the traditional ones and none at all for the declining ones. The comparison seems to suggest the general trend of evolution.

Let us continue with some further remarks concerning the prog-ress in breeding. Between 1822 and 1861, the number of horses rose 94 percent, and the number of oxen only 40 percent. This indicates that during this period horses were beginning to sup-plant oxen as draft animals but had done so only partially. In 1864 one-third of the horses and one-fifth of the oxen belonged to the estates, and the rest to the peasants. Considering the fact that the estates at that time covered more than half of the tilled area, we must assume that draft labor, although declining, still existed. There were, however, counties in the north and west where the estates did own 50–70 percent of the horses as early as 1842— proof that compulsory draft labor was suppressed here. As for cattle, 60 percent of them belonged to peasants in 1842. On the estates, there was no large-scale dairy production to speak of. Only toward the middle of the century did the more enterprising landlords begin to attach some value to dairy products. Most often this production was organized on a lease basis. A small entrepreneur, a Jew as a rule, purchased the dairy production of the estate barn wholesale, paying in advance a yearly sum, so much per cow, and delivering the milk to the market. Such a system, of course, did not induce the landlord to improve breeding and feeding for higher yields. Polish cattle were of poor quality, and Warsaw slaughterhouses regularly imported oxen from the Ukraine steppes of a variety specially bred for butchering. Large properties specialized chiefly in sheep-breeding. Some purebred Arabian and full-blooded English studs, owned by aristocrats and also by the state, acquired international renown, but this was a nobleman's fancy, without any serious influence on the breeding standards of the native horses.

Private Regulations and Evictions

Against the background of slow but steady progress in agriculture, let us now examine the policy of the government and the activity of the landlords with respect to the peasants. The government had changed since the failure of the insurrection; the 1815 Constitution had been rescinded and the country found itself under the iron rule of the viceroy (*namiestnik*) Ivan Paskevich (1782–1856). Only for a brief moment, during the last weeks of the 1831 campaign, did Paskevich attempt an appeal to the Polish peasants to rise against the gentry. This policy was dropped in the aftermath of victory, and the new regime was to become an ultraconservative one. In practice, it continued the tradition of the 1815–30 years: no state intervention in cases of peasant complaints; intervention on behalf of the landlord in cases of peasant unrest. A large number of Russian generals and civilian dignitaries had been liberally awarded national estates after the insurrection. In this way the people in power became local latifundists who were sympathetic to the Polish aristocracy. As a result, under the December Decree still in effect, the landlords were entirely free to dispose of their estates as they wished, using the very effective threat of eviction with no fear of state interference.

In contrast with the early twenties, the present boom in industry and agriculture encouraged an increase in production, more intense husbandry, and consequently a gradual diminution of compulsory labor. The tendency toward regulation was the same in Congress Poland as in Poznania. The name itself was soon borrowed from neighboring Prussia, and in the thirties and forties the Congress gentry advocated more and more the imposition of regulations patterned after the Prussian example. There were important differences between the regulations in the two provinces. (1) The Congress regulations were not sponsored by the state as were those in Poznania; they belonged entirely to the domain of private enterprise. (2) The Congress regulations did not confer upon the peasants title to property. But the scheme was pretty much the same as in Prussia: a small number of peasants (those with larger holdings, or those considered better farmers) were now freed from labor duties with their obligations converted to rent. The majority had their holdings reduced and were no longer required to perform draft labor, but only foot services. Some peasants were evicted and either driven away from the country or transformed into farmhands. The grounds thus freed were either added to the estate or distributed among the rent-paying peasants. Most often, such a regulation was accompanied by a total reshaping of the village. Estate and village lands were separated, new and integrated holdings were surveyed for the rent payers, and new houses were erected, with the common result that the peasants were shifted to poorer land or were obliged to clear barren land. Often the landlord brought in foreign colonists, usually Germans, who paid him an entrance fee and higher rent, and the former inhabitants were driven away. All these changes occurred on the basis of free contract, but with the peasant totally helpless and powerless. Entire villages are said to have disappeared in the course of one or two decades. The process bore a striking resemblance to contemporaneous evictions in England and Ireland, and it is a fact that numerous Polish landlords were at that time fervent anglophiles.

Private regulations were not, as a matter of fact, a mass movement. They were more common in the more developed western and northern regions than in the south and the east; and latifundists were more prone to impose regulations than the middle gentry—not only because aristocrats were better read in agricultural literature but because they stood to gain more as a result of a rent reform than the owners of single estates. It was the same problem of eliminating the go-between costs of a tenant or steward which, as we have already observed, was faced in the eighteenth century.

The biggest latifundist of Congress Poland was the state. The national domains included 1.12 million acres, over one-fourth of the total area of the country. A large fraction—475,000 acres—

had just been granted to about 200 high Russian officials. They were entailed with the proviso that they could not pass into Polish hands. The czar himself recommended that the inhabitants of these domains be converted into rent payers in order to reduce the friction between this new Russian aristocracy and the peasants. An instruction was actually issued in 1841 and carried through in the next decade. The village grounds were separated and divided into reasonably large and well-shaped holdings, with rents that were not too onerous. The remaining estates were forced to shift to wage-labor, although a sufficient number of small-holders was left to provide the landlord with foot services and compulsory hire. The same instruction was also extended to the remaining national estates, although here the change proceeded more slowly and was still in its early stages in the fifties. Generally speaking, the rent-paying peasants on national estates were granted economic independence, although not ownership, with relatively good conditions; much better, in any case, than those under the contemporary Kisselev reforms on the state domains in Russia proper. The negative side of the Polish state regulations was the fact that the peasants as a rule were deprived of the servitudes.

An exception among national domains was the so-called mining estates. They were situated in the southwest region of the country, in proximity to iron, copper, and lead mines and foundries belonging to the state. They were formally allocated in the 1820s to these business enterprises, then intended to be developed, as a source of free labor. The peasants in these domains were to discharge their services as unskilled workers in the mines and foundries, mostly as woodcutters (the foundries were still operated with charcoal) and as conveyors of raw materials and manufactured goods. This antiquated system was still in effect, in most of the state-owned heavy industry. It was hard to induce conservative officials in the mining estates to get rid of compulsory labor. In vain did the peasants protest and demand to be assimilated with other national domains, long since converted to rent.

Private latifundia did not await the example of the state to start rent reforms. By far the biggest of them was the Zamoyski entail, covering most of Zamość County in southeast Poland. It numbered 100 estates and about 100,000 inhabitants. The estates were leased and brought but small income; the region was backward, far from trade routes and markets, and a natural economy still prevailed. Thorough regulation seemed totally impracticable, but Count Zamoyski devised a shortcut. In 1833, the so-called ransom (*okup*) was introduced. Every peasant in the latifundium was entitled to pay this ransom instead of his labor duties, at the rate of one *zloty* (seven cents) per draft day, payable for a quarter in advance. He was then freed from labor obligations, with the exception of twelve days yearly of road labor. If he refused to pay, he automatically returned to compulsory labor in the next term. At first, the Zamoyski administration induced the peasants to use the new system by persuasion. Later, when the results were not as swift as had been expected, the threat of eviction was applied. In the course of ten years, 90 percent of the peasants adopted the ransom system, but a large fraction of them suffered eviction and had their land integrated into larger holdings. In the late forties, when the country was swept by a revolutionary wave, the Zamoyski peasants began to refuse to pay, but the revolt was crushed with military help. The reform was certainly profitable for the Zamoyski family. The effect on the peasants was questionable. The conversion of labor into ransom was by formula, and some peasants were overburdened. In a year of bad harvests, they could experience real difficulties in accumulating money for the next installment; the land was fertile enough, but local prices were low because of the distance of markets.

Other members of the Zamoyski family, owning less extensive domains in the Lublin and Podlasie regions, undertook more careful regulation reforms which were linked with a reshaping and integration of holdings and a more careful evaluation of the amount of rent to be paid by each peasant. The key problem in these reforms, especially in the eastern region, was the shifting of the estates to wage labor. It was difficult to find tenants ready to lease an estate without labor duties, since such an enterprise presupposed more agricultural skill and more accounting than average leaseholders were accustomed to. Count Andrzej Zamoyski (1800–1874), a cadet of the family, leased without compulsory labor two estates of his family's entail and managed them as a model to show that the new system was viable and profitable. He also imported a number of experienced farmers from as far away as Scotland, and leased them some of his own estates without any labor services. These examples, however, could exert influence but slowly. Some latifundists, among others Marquis Alexander Wielopolski (1803–77), entertained the idea of a complete liquidation of the estates, of dividing them among rent payers. The landlord would then become an absentee, as was common in England. He would be able to devote himself to political or cultural activities. Ideas of this kind did not come to fruition, to begin with because they were contrary to Polish *szlachta* tradition. Even among the Polish nobility, absenteeism was relatively rare. There were, in addition, more serious objections to such a system in Poland. (1) Rents would be more difficult to collect if the estates disappeared, because the peasant would not fear a return to compulsory labor. (2) The extension of peasant holdings could become dangerous for the landlords, since the actual possession of land might serve as a basis for granting title to property; this could happen in the event of a revolution or a government reform.

The net result of private regulations in Congress Poland will be examined later, inasmuch as other events, revolutionary in character, also influenced the Polish countryside toward the middle of the century.

8

THE DEMOCRATIC PROPAGANDA

We now approach an important turn in Poland's history, when the feudal system based on compulsory labor faced a crisis. Economic factors were at work, as we have seen, to discredit compulsory labor. The boom in agriculture encouraged a rising percentage of the landowners to try more intensive methods of production, requiring improved tools, skilled staff, and hired labor. We have observed, however, that this tendency was far from a sweeping one in Congress Poland, and it was almost nonexistent in Galicia. Unlike the landlords in the Prussian-ruled provinces, the majority of the landlords in central and southern Poland were still reluctant to get rid of compulsory labor. During the 1840s, however, two other factors began to come into play: first, the propaganda of Polish democrats, and second, the revolutionary activity of the peasants themselves.

Programs in Emigration

The new programs in agrarian matters all arose from emigration. The 8,000–9,000 Poles who left the country after the defeat of

1831 and settled mostly in France were for the most part officers (privates and noncommissioned officers had been forced to accept the czar's amnesty). These officers were mostly of gentry origin, but in a majority of cases it was an impoverished or altogether landless gentry. There were, of course, a number of aristocrats headed by Prince Czartoryski who retained some wealth. However, the bulk of the emigrants had no resources left and either had to earn their livings or live on meager subsidies paid by foreign governments. The subsidized emigrants did not have much money, but enough leisure to concentrate on politics. As is true in every political emigration, they were convinced that retaliation would come soon—as the result of a war or a revolution—which would bring them back to their country, arms in hand.

As a rule, open discussions of the causes of the last disaster occupy a prominent place in every emigrant's life. All circumstances of the November insurrection were discussed extensively in France by Polish exiles, and the agrarian problem was given much attention in the debate. Political strife raged during the thirties; every party assigned responsibility for the defeat to its opponents. For example, the Left accused the aristocrats of having brought the country to ruin out of class selfishness. Nothing, they said, was done for the peasants; the countryside remained indifferent, and the campaign was lost! This argument was instrumental in bringing to the attention of numerous emigrants the importance of a program of reform. If there had not been a conflict within the emigrant groups, it is doubtful that the Polish Left would have arrived so quickly at such radical solutions.

The leaders of the Warsaw Patriotic Club rallied in Paris under Lelewel's direction and formed the National Committee, which was to seek an alliance with revolutionary forces in western Europe. Lelewel, elected chairman, was chiefly bent on winning to his side officers from the lower gentry who formed the bulk of the emigrants and who until now had been little interested in politics. When urged by his radical followers to formulate a program of social reforms, Lelewel played for time, anxious not to antagonize the majority of his countrymen. Early in 1832, a minority in the National Committee broke with Lelewel and founded the Polish Democratic Society. Its first principle was to unite people around a common program, which should define the necessary means of reestablishing Poland and the principles upon which Poland was to be organized in the future.

The views on this principle held by the founders of the society were far from unanimous. Their inauguration manifesto announced that all Poles are free and equal, that all peasants have a right to their soil, and what is more, everybody has an equal right to use the soil and its fruits. The statement was fairly vague. Some of the leaders of the society tried to give it a more radical meaning. On the second anniversary of the insurrection (29 November 1832), Tadeusz Krępowiecki (1798–1847) made a public speech in Paris before a group of French sympathizers of the Polish cause. He said that the revolution had failed because the patriots had joined with the *szlachta*. Only the peasants could bring Poland salvation. The next revolution would be a social one, waged in alliance with the peasants against the gentry. Krępowiecki openly advocated a repetition of the Ukrainian-Polish class wars, of the seventeenth and eighteenth centuries. This speech caused a scandal; public opinion condemned this "washing dirty Polish linen in public." The speaker was forced to secede from the Polish Democratic Society. However, he found adherents and was to initiate a new tendency in Polish political life.

The next few years, down to 1836, saw the simultaneous elaboration of all the major programs which were to dominate the political scene until the final emancipation of the peasants. The relevant discussions were apparently theoretical; fighting waged in a void. Actually, all these programs were to crystallize in a mutual interdependence, and their authors worked with their minds directed toward the country, taking into account the needs and aspirations of the people remaining at home. There was only one point of difference: the conservatives chiefly considered the interests of the propertied classes, whereas the radical wing thought to gain the support of the peasants.

The right wing of the emigrants, headed by Adam Czartoryski, did not include the ultraconservatives, who preferred to serve the czar rather than to abandon any of their privileges. The Czartoryski party hoped to regain Poland's independence, with the help of the Western powers, by means of a European war. Poland would become a constitutional monarchy on the French pattern, with Adam I as king. An evolution toward capitalism was deemed necessary. Such concepts were to bring former conservatives together with the liberal center on the basis of a commutation of compulsory labor into rent. Such a reform, however, soon appeared insufficient from the standpoint of the radical opinions of the emigrants. As early as 1833, Czartoryski came to the conclusion that the peasants should receive full property rights to the land they tilled for themselves and that the reform should be conducted according to the Prussian pattern; that is, only well-to-do peasants should become proprietors, and the landlords would be fully reimbursed by the peasants themselves. It is characteristic that Czartoryski thought it wise to impart these ideas to only a restricted circle of collaborators. The scheme was to remain a party secret. Not until ten years later, under the impact of democratic propaganda, were Czartoryski's agents in Poland invited to advocate a grant of property (*uwłaszczenie*)—a program still considered inopportune by most of the wealthy *szlachta*.

The central groups of the emigrants still followed Lelewel, a fervent democrat and a friend of the peasant cause but a vacillating politician not inclined to radical steps. In 1833, Lelewel, challenged by the orators of the Polish Democratic Society, publicly admitted that compulsory labor was an abomination that should be suppressed, particularly on moral grounds. But at the same time he raised further questions. How to carry out such a reform? What setbacks would it cause in the economic and political fields? Would not the *szlachta* be estranged, the agriculture ruined? Would the peasants be won over at once, or would the czar or the Austrian emperor perhaps outbid the Polish patriots? These were sensible enough reflections; but it must be remarked that a politician who takes no risks is likely to get nowhere. This happened to Lelewel's camp. They were to form a fluctuating centrist group, inwardly inclined to the democratic side but shrinking before the task of formulating positive programs.

The Polish Democratic Society was by far the most important group of emigrants, not so much because of the number of members as because of its organization, its clearly formulated program, and its later influence on the country. The program itself was the result of exhaustive discussions led by members of the society grouped in so-called sections in every French or English locality where Polish emigrants were to be found. The sections communicated continuously by mail, exchanging views and formulating opinions about successive drafts of the proposed articles of faith. Important issues were put to a vote, and individuals or sections that refused to accept agreed-upon views were removed from the membership rolls. Eventually, a manifesto was composed by Wiktor Heltman (1796–1878), introduced to the sections, voted and signed by all members, and published in December 1836 as the *definitive* creed of the society. This was the so-called Great Manifesto (as compared to the much shorter inaugurative text of 1832), named also the Poitiers Manifesto after the seat of the society's Central Committee (*Centralizacja*). The manifesto discussed at length conditions in Poland, the chances of a resumption of the war for independence, and the constitutional principles of a future democratic Poland. We shall be concerned here only with the manifesto's approach to the peasant question—one of its most important concerns.

The program in question called for compromise. Between 1832 and 1836 the leaders of the society managed to eliminate dissenters from its ranks: persons inclined to seek an accommodation with the gentry, as well as radicals who, like Krępowiecki, preached suppression of gentry-owned estates. The main argument ran as follows: Poland can (and may) regain independence through an insurrection backed by the whole nation. The peasants will participate in such a fight if they are assured not only of equal rights as citizens but also of their economic welfare. Therefore, the national government will proclaim, on the first day of the insurrection, that all peasants farming a plot of land will receive title to the property without any payment whatsoever (be it in labor, in kind, or in money) to their landlords, and with no indemnity of any other kind. The landlords will be asked to agree to this distribution in the name of justice and in behalf of the national cause. If someone dares oppose the decisions of the insurgent power, he will be ruthlessly suppressed; individual interests will be sacrificed to the bliss and happiness of the millions.

In short, the Poitiers Manifesto proposed the gratuitous enfranchisement (*uwłaszczenie*) of all peasants holding even the smallest piece of land. This seemed at first sight a clear enough proposition, and one which would interest a large majority of the peasants. Not all of them, of course; the landless peasants were not mentioned. Nothing was said, also, about the estates and their prospective subdivision. Silence on this point implied that the estates would be permitted to exist in future democratic Poland. It should be noted that the retention of the estates and the failure to provide for the landless peasants were directly connected. If a big estate was to subsist, a rural proletariat was required in the neighborhood to serve as farmhands. Conversely, if landless peasants were to be enfranchised, some part at least of the land owned by the gentry must be given to them. Clearly, it was not by accident that this crucial point was not mentioned in the manifesto. As has been said, the program was a compromise and could unite all voters only with some deception. It seems clear that even among the society leaders the fulfillment of the manifesto was not viewed identically. There was a liberal wing in Poitiers which thought that Poland would evolve into a bourgeois and capitalist society, with both big and small farms run in the same way, with gentry and peasants united under the national flag. There was also a radical wing which secretly considered the proposed enfranchisement as only the first step of a further social revolution; that for the time being the help of the patriotic elements of the gentry was essential, but later the *Sejm* would decide whether more land should be distributed among the peasants. Reflections of this kind, given no publicity, were nevertheless to influence the democratic propaganda directed toward both landlords and toward peasants.

Despite its double meanings, the manifesto of 1836 must be considered a big step in the direction of social reform, and not only by Polish standards. It should be remembered that until that time, except during the French Revolution, all agrarian reforms in central and eastern Europe were the acts of monarchal power. For example, the Prussian *Bauernschutz*, Joseph II's *Urbarialreform*, Napoleon's constitution, and the regulation in Prussia were all acts directed from above for improving the state of agriculture and thereby securing the peasants' gratitude for the throne. The year 1836 was a milestone, when a clear program was formulated by an organization ready to act, to arouse a social upheaval from below in order to stir the peasants to a revolution against the established powers. The revolutionaries were outbidding the governments; the Poitiers Manifesto promised more than was granted the peasants under the Prussian regulation system. Soon we shall see that carrying through of this revolutionary program was not an easy matter. Nevertheless, it was to exert a tremendous influence on the course of events—on the landlords, the peasants, and the governments, both in Poland and elsewhere. These events of 1836 should be considered the first signs of an era in which the agrarian question became the major issue of a revolutionary movement—an era by no means at an end today.

It has already been mentioned that the Polish Democratic Society with its manifesto did not represent the extreme left wing of Polish emigrants. There was a still more radical faction headed by Krępowiecki and numbering not more than a dozen people. In 1836 it was to find a larger audience.

The czar's amnesty, proclaimed in 1831, granted full pardon to all Polish "rebels" who would submit to authority, with the exception of the most guilty leaders. When Polish soldiers put down their arms on the Prussian and Austrian borders, the two governments arranged with St. Petersburg to allow the officers to depart for France, while the rank and file were turned over to the Russians. Most of these Polish soldiers were forced into the czarist army and sent to fight in far-off lands against the Kirghizes or Tcherkesses. Soldiers resisting extradition were forced into it by the Prussian army. Black hussars charged defenseless crowds, volleys were fired and blood was shed; the Western press gave voice to indignation. Eventually the Prussian authorities sentenced some hundreds of recalcitrant Poles to one or two years of hard labor for public disorder. They served these penalties in the fortresses of Grudziądz and Gdansk; then in 1834 they were put aboard three ships bound for the United States. They protested, however, anxious not to be separated from their country by the immensity of the Atlantic. They persuaded the ship authorities to allow them to disembark while still in Europe. The passengers of one ship found their way to France; those of the second were eventually enlisted in the Foreign Legion in Algiers. The third ship discharged about three hundred ex-soldiers in Portsmouth. The British authorities placed at their disposal some unused barracks and later assigned them a pitifully small allowance. Different political groups took interest in these new emigrants of plebeian (mostly peasant) stock. A section of the Polish Democratic Society was soon founded in Portsmouth, but Krępowiecki, Dziewicki, and Worcell, its radical opponents, succeeded best in gaining the confidence of the Portsmouth community.

Soon the Portsmouth section protested against proposals of an enfranchisement devised in Poitiers which would give land to some peasants and refuse it to others. In 1835 the schism was total. The Portsmouth group declared that they were separating themselves from the rest of the emigration. They formed instead their own commune (*gromada*) Grudziądz, named after the Prussian fortress where they had suffered for the national cause. Following their example, another commune was formed in St. Hélier on the island of Jersey. This group was composed of a small number of intellectuals and called itself *Gromada Humań*, a name which recalled the peasant uprising of 1768 in the Ukraine.

Both communes rejected the program of the Polish Democratic Society, claiming that it did not satisfy the needs of the people inasmuch as it substituted the privilege of money for the ancient privilege of birth. The Poitiers democrats aimed at a compromise with the gentry, but no such compromise was possible. All the land belonged to the people. Was this communism? A pamphlet by Stanisław Worcell (1799–1857), publicly approved by the commune, declared that property was a historical category, that its character changed with the passage of time, and that it would disappear in a better society. Such utopian-socialist views were widespread in western Europe in the 1830s. The commune did not dream, however, of common management of big estates on the Soviet model of today. They imagined that the government of the people would distribute land (for individual use) for a lifetime to members of the community capable of manual work. The basic features of their program were the abolition of the gentry's property rights and the assumption of power by the people.

With such views, the communes remained isolated among the exiles and did not succeed in establishing continuous contact with the homeland despite the fact that their publications did influence left-wing democrats there. Owing to their isolation, the communes became less active as the years passed. Their most prominent members, Krępowiecki and Worcell, withdrew, and this dwindling refugee group became a kind of political sect with a growing inclination to mysticism. The slogans it had uttered, however, were revived later in the underground movement at home.

Conspiracy in the Countryside

Among the four groups of Polish emigrants listed above, only two were capable of presenting their programs to the country. The Czartoryski party addressed itself to the wealthy stratum of landlords, with mixed success. Who could be reached by democratic propaganda? It found, of course, ready support in the towns among the students, the intelligentsia, the craftsmen, and the workmen. But the key problems to be solved were in the countryside; one would have to persuade the peasants if a popular insurrection were to be risked at all. This was not easy. The peasant community remained a group impenetrable to foreign influence. Centuries of feudal oppression had resulted in isolating the peasants from the rest of society. Those who were not peasants were either oppressors (the landlord, the overseer) or aliens (the official, the local Jew, the traveling townsman). One obeyed oppressors as long as it seemed impossible to fight them; but aliens were not to be trusted. An alien was easily distinguished, by his dress, his dialect, his demeanor, his smooth hands. One showed him respect but did not engage him in conversation. There were, of course, the priests, who enjoyed immense influence —but outside the scope of class differences. The peasant obeyed the priest when told to attend mass, to fast during Lent, to make pilgrimage. It would have been useless, however to urge him to stop stealing lumber from the landlord's forest or to work efficiently on a compulsory-labor day.

As a means of influencing the countryside, a democrat had the choice of two expedients. One of them was easy—the way of the manor (*dwór*). The Polish *szlachta* was hospitable and patriotic. It welcomed with pleasure any guest from the outside world and was ready to hide him from the police. The landlord was the mayor (*wójt*). He could issue a false passport, and he could play host for even a year or two. One was almost entirely safe in the manor, in a tenant's, steward's, or an overseer's cottage (*dworek*) —but he was, so to speak, trapped in an environment hostile to the peasants and so was unable to speak with them freely and gain their confidence.

The other way was to masquerade as a peasant among the peasants. This was not only much more difficult for a member of the intelligentsia; it was also more risky. A gentleman (*pan*) rode, a man (*czlowiek*) walked, and a wandering stranger excited suspicion; he was asked for his passport and his conversations were controlled. He could actually gain the confidence of the village only when siding with the village against the manor. In most cases he was picked up by the *wójt* before he could persuade the peasants to give him shelter and assistance. Therefore, most democratic emissaries did not even try agitation "from below." Their idea was not to incite the people against the *szlachta* but to unite all the children of Mother Poland in a fight against her oppressors. It seemed to them that they could persuade the *szlachta* to adopt the Poitiers theses; then in turn the *szlachta*, for the sake of the national cause, would mitigate their demeanor toward the peasants and would spread the patriotic propaganda. With such illusions (and a false passport) would an emissary arrive from France to a friendly manor, playing the role of a distant relative, a teacher, or a bookkeeper, but soon he would be imbued with the atmosphere of the manor and come to believe that the peasants were not yet capable of patriotic feelings, that the dissemination of patriotic propaganda was a long-range affair, and that, above all, it should not be carried out by strangers. Heltman, the author of the first draft of the Poitiers Manifesto and a sincere democrat, spent more than two years as an emissary in different parts of Poland. He himself acknowledged that only once during that time did he have a serious conversation with a peasant.

The Central Committee of the Democratic Society, since 1840 functioning in Versailles, established its first clandestine contacts with Poznan and Warsaw. Galicia, for the time being and for reasons to be explained, was ignored. Patriotic activities in Poznania were relatively easy; the Prussian regime was not unduly harsh, and censorship was somewhat relaxed. The wealthy gentry, for one thing, was not categorically opposed to democratic ideas, in their Poitiers variant. Compulsory labor had already been suppressed in the province, and the peasants enfranchised; the democrats did not feel they should demand from the *szlachta* any new sacrifices. As for the small-holders, who were excluded from regulation and obliged to perform some compulsory labor, they were considered of secondary importance. The gentry was ready to support the democratic propaganda—funds were collected, journals published, and agents appointed in every county. The province was to be prepared for the insurrection, which it was thought would not come for many years.

Things went otherwise in Congress Poland, under the harsh rule of Paskevich. Tiny conspiring circles were unable to survive more than a couple of months. Every year, dozens of young patriots were sentenced to Siberia. Opposition to the Versailles leadership, was growing, and it was necessary, in order to hasten the beginning of revolution, to devise methods of winning over the peasants quickly. Three persons should be mentioned in this connection: Kamieński, Dembowski, and Sciegienny.

Henryk Kamieński (1813–66) was a wealthy landlord from the Lublin Palatinate, a self-taught intellectual and a master technician in the art of clandestine activity. He was absolutely convinced that the promise of enfranchisement along Poitiers lines would be sufficient to assure the participation of *szlachta* and peasants alike in the movement. No conspiracy was needed, just mass agitation, conducted not by the landlords themselves but by their officials. At a given signal all peasants would seize their scythes, pitchforks, and axes, and the "people's war" (*wojna ludowa*) would overwhelm the Russian military. One provision was essential: everywhere, peasants should be promised land with full property rights. Any opposition from a landlord would endanger the revolutionary cause, and the penalty for such opposition would be death. Such ideas, widely circulated in clandestine literature, caused some panic among the gentry; Kamieński was accused of preparing a slaughter of the *szlachta*. Later he justified himself by saying that he had proposed the death penalty only in a premonitory way, in the hope that the revolutionary powers would not be compelled to practice it. Kamieński himself did not take part in any agitation among peasants and was arrested three months before the outbreak of the insurrection.

His cousin, Edward Dembowski (1821–46), was an extremely gifted young intellectual who began a literary career at twenty-two and died a hero's death at twenty-five. In his brief life, he wrote many books, reviews, and editorials on philosophy, literature, and economics. Within the narrow bounds set by censorship he managed to advocate a social revolution and abolition of private property and to condemn liberal half-measures. He emphatically dissociated himself from old Polish aristocratic tradition. One of his favorite slogans was "*Szlachta* are not Polish; only the people are Polish." Dembowski exerted much influence over left-wing conspiratorial groups in Warsaw and Poznan. Later, in 1845, he worked as a revolutionary agitator in Galicia.

Piotr Sciegienny (1800–1890) was a peasant's son and a village parson. He campaigned among the peasants for a number of years, rousing in them a national and revolutionary spirit. He distributed an apocryphal "Letter by Pope Gregory XVI" which called upon the peasants to rise against the landlords and put an end to class exploitation. He also urged the common people of Poland and the Russian troops to join hands and fight together against the Polish *szlachta* and the Muscovite czar. Sciegienny's followers included peasants from his native village, younger priests, and private officials. He was also in contact with the national underground movement. He was arrested in 1844, just when he was ready to launch a mass campaign, the forerunner of armed upheaval. As a popular agitator, he was to remain an exceptional figure for a long time, at least in Congress Poland. In the Poznan province, however, there existed an underground group called the "Plebeians," composed of craftsmen, students, and intelligentsia, which was influenced to some extent by Dembowski. They propagandized, not without success, among the peasants in the immediate neighborhood of Poznan. Their propaganda was more national than social-revolutionary in tone.

The different programs framed by emigrants all failed to meet the demands of a planned uprising. Czartoryski encouraged his aristocratic supporters to gradually introduce rent reforms. They did so, with the usual consequences for the great majority of the peasants. The Poitiers Manifesto was unanimously accepted by the Polish middle classes, but it was ignored by the gentry and remained almost unknown to the peasants. More radical proposals inspired by the Portsmouth communes found few supporters in the countryside, and their unusual recommendations succeeded only in arousing apprehension among the propertied classes. The bulk of the population, with most at stake in what was about to happen, remained totally unprepared to accept the revolutionary gospel.

9

THE PEASANT RISING OF
1846 IN GALICIA

The attempt at an insurrection, with the Poitiers Manifesto as
guiding principle, ended in 1846 in a disastrous failure. Never
have Polish patriots been so shamefully discredited. The Galician
massacre arose from local circumstances. We have not been concerned with Galicia since the time of Joseph II and his reforms.
Indeed, not much happened in the interval. Galicia remained
the most backward of Polish provinces. Its agriculture was
blocked by customs barriers from the natural outlet, the Vistula.
There was no industry to speak of, and the Austrian bureaucracy
did not care for the welfare of this distant province. A natural
economy still prevailed in the countryside, together with the
three-field system. It was said that the peasants, out of ignorance,
burned heaps of dried manure in the open—nobody told them
how to use it. The peasants were still serfs, their status being inferior to that of peasants in Congress Poland; but, on the other
hand, they were protected, at least in theory, against eviction.

Compulsory labor also continued, although in a moderate form. Rent reforms were made so difficult by official regulations that nobody cared to adopt them. The bureaucratic control of peasants' rights proved inefficient. With the growth of village population the peasants wanted to divide their holdings—a measure forbidden by authority. The landlord approved illegal partitions of holdings, but at the same time he increased labor duties, also illegally. The soil yielded less and burdens rose. There was the right to file suit before the *Kreis*, against the oppressive landlord. These lawsuits helped the peasantry organize, but they also embittered relations between village and manor without ever solving any problem under dispute.

One telling example is the case of Jakub Szela (1787–1866), the leader of the 1846 peasant rebellion. He was a small-holder from Smarzowa, a village in the Tarnów district. As was required by law, the community elected him a plenipotentiary in their suit against the landlord Bogusz. The dispute originated in 1803, and it dealt with "pregravations," that is, labor exacted in greater quantity than was due. In 1822 Szela filed a suit in the name of the village. The *Kreis* resolution was passed in 1830, and it admitted in part the peasants' claim. Bogusz adroitly challenged, not the merits of the suit, but Szela's competence as plenipotentiary. Maybe the village would have gained by giving in on the personal issue, but Smarzowa stood firm and Szela's role became a matter of principle. The community leader went on foot to Lvov to plead his cause. In 1841, he was confirmed as plenipotentiary by the governor-general. Bogusz appealed to Vienna; Szela's confirmation came back from the capital in 1844. Once more, Bogusz filed a request for a stay—the dispute was not yet resolved in 1846 on the day of the catastrophe. In the meantime, Bogusz continued extorting the increased amounts of compulsory labor. He also found more than one occasion to penalize Szela with arrest and flogging by virtue of his power as local police officer. No wonder a local disagreement about the number of days of labor was transformed, in the course of years, into a stubborn war, full of hatred.

Numerous sources testify that a deadlock had developed between the gentry and peasants in Galicia, arising from hate born of immemorial grievances but also of ignorance (there were no schools in the countryside). Another example is that of a young lady who settled in Galicia after her marriage in the 1830s and, full of Christian feeling, wanted to help both poor and rich by distributing food and medicine. She soon learned that the women and children, who accepted the medicine with thanks, did not use it; they actually suspected the illustrious countess of trying to poison them! This was the state of things when democratic emissaries came, urging the peasants to revolt.

We have seen that this propaganda seldom reached the peasants themselves and, when directed toward "enlightened" classes, tried to avoid all anti-*szlachta* overtones, stressing instead the need for voluntary concessions in the peasants' behalf, out of patriotic feelings. These activities indeed influenced the propertied classes; they felt obliged to try some reforms in order to prevent a radical upheaval.

After the partitions, Galicia was provided with a *Sejm* which was convened in Lvov every year in September, for one week only. It was not an elected house, inasmuch as all landlords belonging to the *szlachta* had the right to attend. This antiquated body had practically no power; it could, however, address petitions to the emperor. A group of more enlightened landlords resolved to interest the *Sejm* in the peasant question. Beginning with 1842, various motions were proposed. Some members wanted to obtain for the landlords the right of regulation and eviction, following the Congress Poland example. Others spoke of gradual rent reform. Debate dragged on, every motion was first censored by the governor-general, and then sent to Vienna, whence a dilatory reply would come only the following year. Eventually, in 1845, the *Sejm* resolved to elect a committee which was to frame a program of agrarian reform. The country was then swarming with democratic emissaries; an insurrection seemed at hand. Not wanting to be outbidden, the *Sejm* included instructions that the committee was to consider, among other things, the problem of making the peasants owners of their holdings. Appointment of the committee was never ratified in Vienna, and it never did meet. The net result of the *Sejm*'s proceedings was stories in the countryside that the noble lords had again discussed compulsory labor but had done nothing for the peasants.

The other program concerning the peasants coming from the propertied classes was the temperance movement sponsored by the church. Let us refer to what was said in chapter 7 about the rise in vodka production in the 1820s. The results were a steady fall of alcohol prices and a widespread plague of drunkenness. Around 1840, a half-pint of 50 percent vodka was sold for two *kopeks*, the price of a pound of bread or five pounds of potatoes or one-third pound of meat. The cost of one calorie consumed in the form of vodka was one-fortieth the cost of the same calorie eaten as bread. The drunkenness was a result of poverty no less than of ignorance or vice. Memoirs tell us of unconscious peasants lying in the mud on village streets. Statistics record hundreds of deaths caused by intoxication; for instance, drunkards frozen to death in the snow. Such images were not a Polish peculiarity; they are well known in other countries at a similar level of evolution, such as England or Ireland at an earlier period, and Russia at a later.

A campaign against the alcohol plague was undertaken by the church in many countries—by numerous Protestant churches in America; by the Roman Catholic church in Ireland. The Irish model of temperance fraternities, introduced by Father Matthew, began to spread in Germany. It reached Poland first in Upper Silesia, where Father Jan Ficek (1790–1862), parson at Piekary, was a fiery protagonist of the movement. From Silesia in 1844, it propagated toward Poznania, Galicia, and Congress Poland. Its success was overwhelming. Whenever a parish priest invited his flock to join the fraternity, thousands of men foreswore drink, while their names were entered in the Golden Fraternity book. Hymns and litanies were sung, indulgences were promised, and the majority of male adults solemnly promised not to drink any more. (Sometimes the oath took in only strong liquor.) In the course of some months, 500,000 people joined in Upper Silesia, and 800,000 in western Galicia. The inns stood empty or were closed; the *propinacja* income fell to nothing. The initiative of the priests met with such a response because it coincided with an awakening consciousness of the masses. In peasant eyes, the temperance slogans imparted a flash of hope. In parting with vodka and with the landlord's inn, the peasant seemed to throw down the whole of his yoke. And it was true that the temperance movement ran against the *szlachta*'s interests. Some of the gentry backed temperance out of philanthropy or out of conscience or by calculation. (Did not a sober farmhand work better than a drunkard? Was not vodka a danger in time of revolution?) But other landlords protested to bishops and government offices. The Austrian government did nothing to hamper the movement. Pas-kevich in Congress Poland suspected, not without reason, that the temperance movement had some links with democratic agi-tation. Sciegienny, among others, was a temperance advocate, and temperance sermons could easily lead to anti-*szlachta* pro-nouncements. The fraternities were actually forbidden in Con-gress Poland. Instead the government undertook another policy for fighting alcoholism. A ukase in 1844 introduced a progressive tax on the production of alcohol. Some distilleries and inns were ordered shut, and minimum vodka prices were introduced. Some of these regulations were evaded, as often happens; nevertheless, the production of alcohol in Congress Poland sank 50 percent in the next few years (the potato disease was partially responsible). As for Prussian Poland, the government bought up the *propi-nacja* from the landlords with tax funds (1845) on an amortized basis.

The temperance movement, even when not officially forbidden, did not solve the drunkenness problem, and still less other social problems of the time. The revolution of 1846 signaled a termina-tion of the oath. The peasants, having resumed drinking, were inclined to think that having once perjured themselves they freed themselves of all other divine and human commandments as well. It was an illusion of the peasants and of the clergy that some sermons followed by a common oath would heal all the country's evils as by magic. Drunkenness was a social fact, and it could recede only when other social factors changed. It was to recede, as a matter of fact, with the disappearance of compulsory labor, with the improvement of general well-being, of thrift, of educa-tion.

Let us turn back to Galicia in 1845. This province witnessed a remarkable clandestine activity during the 1830s. Most of the democratic circles, however, were uncovered and their members arrested and sentenced; from 1841 there was no democratic move-ment to speak of. But in 1845, when insurrectionary propaganda was already well under way in Poznan and Warsaw, the Versailles emissaries felt obliged to include Galicia in their schemes. Some energetic agitators—Dembowski among others—were sent into the country. The propaganda in the countryside now seemed the vital issue. "Popular apostles" were recruited, instructed, and sent out, mostly from the ranks of craft apprentices or private servants. New texts were composed, some of them by Dembowski himself, to be copied by hand or, still better, learned by heart. One of the most active of these apostles was Julian Goslar, the grandson of a peasant, the son of a village police officer (*mandatarius*). Goslar was a student, a poet, and a revolutionary. His appeal to the peasants was circulated in central Galicia in the fall of 1845. It promised the peasants full possession of their holdings, as a result of a national insurrection in which they should take part. Compulsory labor was condemned vehemently, but the Austrians, rather than the *szlachta*, were stigmatized for it. The peasants were called to arms, but certainly not against the *szlachta*.

For many months, rumors of varying origin were prevalent in Galician villages about the imminent end of serfdom and compulsory labor. Landlords debated the problem in Lvov, priests alluded to it in their temperance sermons, unknown agitators flitted about the country exciting the peasants with more or less vague allusions, and the Austrian bureaucrats felt obliged to assure the peasants that the emperor would surely devise a reward for such peasants as would show themselves faithful and worthy. But meanwhile, daily labor was exacted, the old oppression continued, and new disasters befell the country: floods, bad harvests, potato disease. According to the press of the time, hundreds of thousands of people were hungry in central Galicia, and neither the state nor the *szlachta* was able to help them. Tension increased, great events were looked for, the future of the country was at stake. In some communes, more energetic leaders decided spontaneously to arm themselves to be ready for any opportunity. As early as the spring of 1845, small armed bands of peasants were arresting travelers on the highways and harassing them under the pretense of seeking "rebels."

Mainly because of the unrest of the peasants, Polish democrats decided not to put off the insurrection, although preparations were far from complete. Social conflict was brewing; it could explode at any moment. The only way to master the current was to canalize it—to guide it against the foreign enemy, to exploit it for the national cause. This was the point of view of a large number of the middle gentry who now joined the movement. They were partly moved by patriotic feeling, partly by tactical reasoning (one ought to remain in control of the movement);

some were also intimidated by threats of gallows for the traitors. When given commands in the future revolutionary army, these *szlachta* conspirators promised more or less sincerely to abolish compulsory labor on fateful D Day. They protested most energetically, however, against any propaganda waged from below by unknown agitators. They felt that such propaganda could well promote an anti-*szlachta* tendency. And thus Goslar was categorically forbidden to pursue his wandering about the country, whereas Dembowski was sent away to Lvov to organize students and craftsmen, a task considered comparatively harmless. As a consequence, the peasants were not told in advance what the insurrection was to be about nor what it would change in the peasant's lot. Kamieński's concept of a sudden summoning of the peasants to a "popular war" was now discarded. Ludwik Mierosławski (1814–78), member of the Democratic Central Board, arrived from Versailles to assume the post of commander-in-chief. He also distrusted the peasants' "anarchist" inclinations. According to him, the insurrection should develop in two stages. First, a handful of picked conspirators would attack the local garrison and occupy the capital of the county. Only then, when the new authority was installed and had taken over, would the time come to issue an appeal to the peasants, to proclaim the decrees of the national government, and to draft the peasants into the regular army and into the framework of military discipline. This scheme, though dictated by prudence, entailed a terrible risk. By withholding the necessary explanation of the aims of the insurrection, the leaders, distrustful of their future soldiers, were suddenly to face them as adversaries.

We shall not enter into details. Some of the right-wing conspirators were so frightened of what was about to happen that they denounced the plot to the Prussian and Austrian police, preferring to enter jail before rather than after the catastrophe. Preventive arrests made a simultaneous upheaval almost impossible. With all its might, the conservative *szlachta* attempted to prevent the more impatient elements from carrying out the orders of the insurrectionary powers. As a result, only in a dozen places did piteous attempts at armed insurrection take place, and the insurgents were either dispersed or they disbanded of their own free will after a few hours, except in Krakow, where the insurrection held out for eleven days. A national government was formed, and in Krakow on 22 February a proclamation was issued.* It is notable in that it went a little further in its prescriptions than the Poitiers Manifesto. It proclaimed that all distinctions of class or creed would be abolished, that all forms of feudal charges, including *pańszczyzna* and rent, would be canceled, that all peasant holdings would pass into full ownership of the peasants, and, furthermore, that landless peasants who enlisted in the national army would receive a grant of land from the national estates after the war. Further proclamations, inspired by Dembowski, went even further, suggesting that the national government intended to better the lot of all landless peasants by assigning a homestead to each of them. These were of course emergency moves, and an opportunity to fulfill such promises was never to come. What is more interesting is how the peasants reacted to these proposals.

In the immediate vicinity of Krakow they reacted favorably, and this attitude should be explained. By a decision of the Congress of Vienna in 1815, the town of Krakow, together with a district of about four hundred and fifty square miles, was declared a neutral free city. This territory had belonged, since 1809, to the Duchy of Warsaw, where serfdom had been abolished and the December Decree introduced. However, in later years, the condition of the peasants in this small territory evolved more favorably than in Congress Poland. One reason is that a free city was forbidden to have armed forces, with the exception of a small militia. The propertied classes were therefore unable to hold the peasants in check and were obliged to compromise. A fair number of the estates in the Krakow district belonged to the state, the church, the university, or other institutions. All these estates were now divided among the peasants, and compulsory labor was commuted into rent. The example proved contagious, so that most of the private landowners in the district felt compelled to follow with rent reforms. In 1846 the peasants in the Krakow region, although not the owners of their holdings, had not performed labor duties for almost a generation. They were small independent farmers burdened with rent, but since the soil was rich and market conditions were advantageous they prospered, and educational standards improved together with the public welfare. Here patriotic

* See Appendix, section *E*.

propaganda fell on receptive ground, the peasants cheerfully backing the national government and enlisting in the insurrectionary army. This example radiated to some extent to the neighboring Galician communes, which seemed, if not too eagerly, to follow the orders of the new Krakow authorities.

This was not the case in Galicia proper, however. In the environs of Tarnów, the insurgents prepared for an assault on the town. The Austrian *Kreishauptmann*, Breinl, panicstricken because he had only a small garrison, sent emissaries to neighboring villages promising peasants the emperor's favor if they would help disarm the rebels. For some days the peasants had been arming themselves of their own accord. Strange rumors circulated that the *szlachta* were arming with the aim of slaughtering the peasants! It cannot be ascertained where this tale arose. The resulting panic was instrumental in arousing the rural masses. It is not clear how these peasants would have behaved if the assault on Tarnów had succeeded (some peasants were enrolled in the insurgent detachments), because the attempt was dropped. The conspirators were too few in number, and the movements of the different detachments were not synchronized; some of them lost their way in a raging snowstorm and the remainder simply gave up the attempt. The peasants saw that their old foes were doomed, and they rushed at them in order to get rid of their masters. In the night of 18 February groups of peasants attacked scattered insurgents in some places, disarmed them and drove them, bound and unconscious from beatings, to Tarnów. The *Kreishauptmann* was very frightened. He tried to temper the crowds gone wild, afraid they would attack him too; he flattered them and distributed money—tips, as he later explained. Breinl was accused of having promised and paid blood money—five or ten guldens for a nobleman's head. This cannot be proved, but money distributed to the peasants for the delivery of wounded and maltreated rebels was sufficient proof that this time the government did not oppose the peasants in settling their old accounts with the gentry.

In the course of the next three days all the manors in the Tarnów district were plundered and most of their male inhabitants massacred. Persons having nothing to do with the revolutionary plots were massacred as well as gentlemen respected for their democratic convictions and their mild handling of peasants. A crowd, having achieved a pogrom at one manor, went to the next one, setting an example for the other villages and even encouraging their neighbors to follow suit. In some cases villagers invited the outsiders to slaughter their masters; they preferred to leave the bloodshed to unknown persons. In the neighborhood of Tarnów, only a few aristocratic residences expressly protected by Breinl escaped loss. In the next days the movement spread to other districts, but the farther from Tarnów, the milder was the course of the revolt—there was more plunder and less bloodshed. The course of events seemed independent of the attitude of the authorities. Some officials encouraged the peasants directly, especially in Bochnia, where they were induced to combat the Krakow insurrection. Others remained passive and helpless. Still others energetically opposed the peasants' excesses. In the course of one week, about four hundred manors were plundered, and 1,200 persons killed, among them about two hundred landowners or members of landlords' families. The rest were mostly officials from the gentry. Women were spared, and Jews left unmolested. Fewer than ten priests perished, and those in exceptional circumstances. Some priests tried to stop the massacres but mostly without success.

The disaster lay in the fact that the peasant masses, expected to back the struggle for independence, turned not against the Austrian government (the chief guardian of the feudal regime) but against their immediate oppressors, the *szlachta*. At one blow, they destroyed the democratic movement, just as it offered them the promises of liberation. At Gdów, the peasant crowds, allied with the Austrians, took part in an encounter with Krakow insurgents and massacred the prisoners. Krakow capitulated without fighting, frightened by the threat of a peasant pogrom.

Was there any possibility, in 1846, of uniting the two movements—the democratic trend, aiming to liberate Poland; and the spontaneous antifeudal movement, directed against the *szlachta?* Dembowski did strive fervently for such an agrarian revolution. He composed and circulated leaflets, sent emissaries, and offered to meet the peasants at the head of a peaceful religious procession. And the peasant movement did, at times, seem to take on an anti-Austrian cast. Some of the peasant detachments in the southern sub-Carpathian region tore down the Austrian eagles from public buildings and were later dispersed by the military. In Chochołów in the High Tatras, the mountaineers were swayed by the example of school teacher and organist Jan Andrusikiewicz (1815–50), a fervent patriot and friend of Goslar's, into arming themselves for Poland and against the Austrians (it is true that most latifundists in the Tatra region sided with the government). The Chochołów mountaineers were dispersed the next day after a skirmish in which Andrusikiewicz fell severely wounded. Dembowski was killed on 26 February in an encounter with Austrians on the outskirts of Krakow.

The democratic insurrection was crushed, and the peasant movement entered a new phase. The pogroms spread over seven out of eighteen districts. Now peasants ceased to perform compulsory labor throughout the province and also in Ukrainian eastern Galicia. The movement was taking a markedly anti-Austrian turn, and it also found a chief in the person of Jakub Szela. The previously mentioned leader of the Smarzova commune organized the massacre of the Bogusz family in cold blood and then tried to bring order amidst the chaos. He organized a peasant militia, installed new mayors, issued orders, signed furloughs and other permits, sent mounted emissaries, gave advice to other communes, and was generally admired and obeyed throughout a radius of twenty miles. His policy was to refuse *pańszczyzna* and to enter into an agreement with the government for rent reform. He did not explicitly demand ownership of the land, and still less a subdivision of the estates—although within his zone of influence no landlord dared to appear, and the peasants undertook the spring planting by themselves.

The Vienna government was profoundly annoyed by what had happened. The Western press savagely accused Metternich of having fomented the massacre, and there was danger that the peasants' disobedience might spread to other Hapsburg provinces. Order had to be restored. First, an imperial proclamation was issued which thanked the peasants for their loyalty and attachment to the throne. It ended with an appeal to abstain from any disorder and to return to their normal duties. Next, upon a concentration of major military forces, compulsory labor was reimposed on the peasants with the help of infantry columns which marched from village to village and administered severe thrashings in cases of disobedience. Szela was interned in Tarnów and some months later sent under escort to Bukovina, where he was granted a new large holding and where he spent the rest of his life. During the summer of 1846, the province returned to "normal," although local centers of resistance did persist for the next two years. The peasants had tried to throw down their yoke with the help of a foreign government. They were betrayed and forced back into servitude. Metternich seemed triumphant, but it was a Pyrrhic victory.

For long years, Polish national tradition has contended that the Galician massacres were treacherously organized by the Austrian bureaucracy and that the ignorant peasant was "the blind sword in Satan's hand," as we read in the poem, by Kornel Ujejski (1823–97). The thesis does not stand up. The peasants had their own grievances against the Polish *szlachta*, and certainly they did not revolt out of love for Emperor Ferdinand. The massacre served to severely discredit Metternich's regime. Not only was he obliged to resort to the help of wild peasant gangs in order to control an insignificant revolt, but he disgraced himself in the eyes of all European nobility by his indirect endorsement of the jacquerie. From Lombardy to Transylvania, the gentry now knew that it could not count on the government's help for the maintenance of the social order, and so it was advisable to ally with the revolutionary party. When two years later, in March 1848, Metternich had to flee Vienna without any support from members of his own class, his behavior during the Galician massacres was one of the explaining factors. Now the most urgent thing to be done in the face of a new revolution, if one were not to be massacred by his serfs, as in Galicia, was to put an end as quickly as possible to feudal exploitation. Not only within the limits of the Hapsburg monarchy but also in neighboring countries, from Romania and the Ukraine to Germany and Italy, the fear of "Galician scenes" obliged landowners and governments to precipitate reforms. Galician peasants might have lost their game, but the European peasantry most certainly profited by the loss.

The year 1846 saw a complete defeat of the Polish cause. The conservatives were now more than ever confirmed in their abhorrence of all insurrectionary means of regaining independence. Some of them, such as Alexander Wielopolski, proclaimed that it would be sensible to renounce independence once and for all in order to safeguard "the quiet country life," that is, the old feudal order. The democrats had been not only decimated in their last attempt; they had also lost face. The inference deduced in Versailles from the last events was that next time careful agitation directed at the peasants themselves would be indispensable before an outbreak. Leaflets and brochures to this effect were immediately prepared and published. More than ever, they warned the peasants not to fall into the enemy's trap, not to lift a fractricidal hand against the *szlachta*. For many decades, the democrats were haunted by the specter of 1846. The fear of a new social war, fatal to the national cause, would paralyze them in moments of decision. As for the peasants, they must have realized that they had been grossly cheated by Austria. But they were isolated from the rest of society by a lake of blood, and the term *robbery (rabacja)* conveniently expressed the conservative feeling, "Do not trust the peasants, do not grant them any political rights." Peasant children, in the course of three generations, were taught at school that Szela was a bandit and a traitor, but in utmost secrecy, the Galician countryside worshiped his memory. Two wars and two revolutions were necessary to overcome this prejudice.

Historians argue even today whether the catastrophe was inevitable and whether the peasant rebellion should be condemned. A thesis has been advanced that under the feudal system, with serfdom and compulsory labor still in effect, a regular feature was the myth of the good monarch. The serf had to have some hope, and thus he was willing to believe that the "White Father czar" or the benevolent emperor in Vienna cherished his subjects who were oppressed by the landlords and the officials. According to this concept, the peasant serf could not be induced to revolt against the sovereign—neither by the local landlord nor by a conspirator from outside. At most he could be deceived for a while by a revolutionary manifesto falsely attributed to the czar or the pope. Such assertions can be corroborated by numerous pathetic examples from Poland, Russia, or Italy. Examples to the contrary, such as the Chochołow case, are not conclusive enough. Nevertheless, it seems objectionable to exclude categorically the possibility that a better-organized movement would have yielded better results. One more remark: If compulsory labor were indeed a serious obstacle to an understanding between the democrats and the peasant masses, then everything which speeded the liquidation of compulsory labor and the emancipation of the peasants also paved the way for nationalist propaganda among the peasants in the future. This emancipation was a necessary, and what is more a sufficient, condition for a greater diffusion of national consciousness. This was no grandiloquent slogan, but a statement repeatedly confirmed by history. As early as 1848, events give evidence confirming this thesis. Whereas the fateful rebellion of the Galician peasants evidently hastened the emancipation patents of 1848 and made them more complete and more radical, it can be also affirmed with some degree of validity that the 1846 *rabacja* contributed, although indirectly and at long range, to the cause of national revival.

10

1848

Insurrection in Poznania

In 1848, the European revolution struck (although it did not overthrow) two of the partitioning powers, Austria and Prussia. In
March, street fighting broke out in Vienna and Berlin, compelling
the two monarchs to make liberal concessions: freedom of speech
and association, convocation of parliaments, and promises of con-
stitutions. The monarchies were not abolished, but their restric-
tive powers were crippled for a time. Two parts of partitioned
Poland, Poznania and Galicia, acquired a short-lived freedom of
movement. Russia had not been touched by the revolutionary
blight, and the Congress Kingdom was not able to move. This
immobility of central Poland sealed the fate of any possible national insurrection. All the Polish incidents of 1848 were local,
limited to one province. Whereas the Polish problem remained a
European one, a Poznanian or Galician problem was an internal
Prussian or Austrian matter. None of these provinces had any
chance of becoming independent. Their temporary freedom was

illusory. It lasted only as long as the revolution progressed in Berlin or Vienna, seven weeks in the first case and seven months in the second.

It goes without saying that the agrarian question was one of the factors which interfered most with the initiative of the Polish patriots. The situations were dissimilar in the two provinces.

In Poznania the regulation reform had already been carried through at least on all the major peasant holdings. The well-to-do peasantry had become property owners. They still paid rent, and some of them were in difficult straits, but on the whole they became a socially stabilized group, and this circumstance generated in the mind of the *szlachta* a sentiment of false security which emboldened them when facing the Prussian power. Nevertheless, the agrarian problem was far from settled. A large majority of peasants had not been included under the regulations. These were not only the landless farmhands and day laborers, but above all the small-holders (*komornicy*), each on a tiny plot of land, subject to some labor duties, owing some compulsory hire, and constantly threatened by eviction. These small-holders remained a source of social unrest; they passionately coveted more land and full ownership. In 1846–47 rumors of events in Galicia, coupled with a bad harvest, the potato disease, and ensuing hunger, were the cause of some local riots. The *szlachta* seemed to see Communist agitators everywhere. Eventually the disorders subsided. The Polish patriots, including some liberal-minded landlords, thought it would be expedient to direct the small-holders' aspirations against the Germans. It was the Prussian regulation which had wronged the small-holders, and the progressing German colonization also threatened their future. A national insurrection under propitious conditions would perhaps divert the danger of social conflict.

On 20 March 1848, at the first news of the Berlin revolution, a national committee was formed in Poznan. Putting to good use the temporary inaction of the Prussian administration, the agents of the committee managed to control most of the province while enlisting volunteers in a national army. The slogan was, Let us proceed against czarist Russia in an alliance with liberated Germany! All landlords joined the movement, anxious not to be left out, but to remain in control and to prevent any Galician scenes. At first, their fears seemed baseless. The Prussian bureaucrats were no less afraid of "Galician scenes" and abstained from any provocations. Then the enthusiasm became general. Whereas at first the regulated peasantry remained expectant, numerous small-holders volunteered in the Polish forces. The Poznan committee felt compelled to issue some proclamations to the peasants. They insisted on liberty and equality, confirmed the abolition of compulsory labor, and vaguely promised further benefactions in the interest of resurgent Poland. Isolated landowners donated some of their rents to the peasants or remitted part of the rents. Officially, nothing was said about the rights of landless peasants.

The illusion that the Prussian government would allow the Poles to arm themselves and that it would wage a war against Russia lasted only a couple of weeks. Very soon, a bargain was proposed from Berlin: The Poles may retain some kind of provincial autonomy, but they must disarm and restore the legal order. The right wing of the committee eagerly adhered to the proposals—most landlords were already frightened that the just-armed scythemen might turn their arms against them. Mierosławski, the democratic commander-in-chief, vacillated. He was aware of the chance to give the signal for war, for a national revolution, but such a movement would surely attack the *szlachta*, and Mierosławski, as he clearly put it himself, did not want to become a second Szela. He enforced a compromise which left him a small force of about four thousand men and consented to disarm the rest. The peasant crowd shouted "Treason!" and it was an effort to quiet them and persuade them to go home. Pressed by necessity, the national committee issued in print a new promise of three *morgi* (two acres) of land to every peasant volunteer. This boon was intended to be distributed out of expected donations by patriotic landowners. They never materialized. The committee began to argue: Does the promise of three *morgi* concern all landless peasants who volunteered in the national forces, or those who had been sent home, or, on the contrary, those who remained in the camp? A fortnight later, the insurrection collapsed, and the Poznanian *szlachta* felt released from all promises to the peasants.

Mierosławski's forces were posted in four camps on the border of Congress Poland. Meanwhile, in the remaining parts of the province, Prussian military forces were restoring order in such a brutal manner that general indignation was aroused. This time, spontaneous resistance was opposed not only by the small-holders but by the well-to-do peasants as well. A wave of national war seemed to sweep over the country. Mierosławski, however, did not take advantage of it, and only when he himself was menaced by a Prussian attack did he appeal to the peasants to mass. He was not interested in peasant guerillas.

On 29 April the Prussian army began offensive operations against the small Polish forces. Mierosławski scored some resounding successes, but his forces were soon dissolved. The *szlachta* did their utmost to disband the army. They were more than ever afraid of an insurrection which would lead to defeat and to confiscation of estates and, in the less likely event of victory, to social revolution. Mierosławski was forced to dismiss his supporters and was captured by the Prussians soon after. Some democratic leaders tried to continue a partisan war, but the guerilla detachments were soon dispersed. By the middle of May, the province was pacified.

From a military point of view, the Poznan insurrection proved a failure. From the political and moral view, it could almost be considered a triumph. The big surprise both for the Germans and the Poles proved to be the attitude of the peasants; their volunteering under national banners, their gallant fight at Miłosław and Sokołowo, the hatred they openly showed to the Germans, and also their readiness to vote Polish in the first elections to parliament in Berlin. Two years after the Galician *rabacja*, this was a comfort to Polish hearts and a source of hope for the future.

The reason lay simply enough in the already carried-out regulation. The abolition of compulsory labor lifted the barrier which had rendered impossible any understanding between patriots and peasant masses. It did not, of course, suppress social frictions, but these now seemed a secondary matter in face of the great upsurge of nationalist antagonisms.

National strife in Poznania was to be exploited on both sides. This proved to be uniform behavior of right-wing parties. Soon after the defeat, a Polish league was founded by a group of liberal leaders—landlords, priests, and intelligentsia—a mass organization following the English and Irish models which aimed to centralize all national activity in Prussian Poland. The league was short-lived; it was soon to be interdicted by the Prussians. It was, however, the first example of further legal activity in which popular masses were harnessed under the leadership of landlords and priests for the defense of language, creed, and land. As early as 1848, the influence of the league extended beyond the borders of Poznania, gaining firm ground in western Prussia, and also reaching out to Mazuria and Upper Silesia.

Awakening in Upper Silesia

Silesia did not experience the 1848 revolution less deeply, but class played a bigger part here than in Poznania. The southern and mostly Polish part of the province was endowed with immense natural riches, and a big industrial basin had been developing rapidly since the end of the eighteenth century. But the surrounding countryside had poor soil, the peasant holdings were small, and most of the villagers had been excluded from regulation. The year before, in 1847, a series of disasters overwhelmed the population: the potato disease, hunger, and a fever epidemic. Whole villages were stricken, and casualties were numbered by the thousands. A doctor from Berlin who came to the rescue later told the press that in one village he had found whole families starving, although a notice was posted on the mayor's house that food would be distributed in the adjacent town. Unfortunately, the poster was printed in German, nobody read German in the village, and nobody had bothered to translate the announcement into Polish. The tale is grim; it illustrates the double disadvantage of the Silesian population, handicapped both as paupers and as Poles.

The news of the Berlin revolution was the signal for a wave of peasant disorders, the first on such a scale for nearly forty years. Most of the Silesian countryside rose up, the movement reaching as far as southern Poznania. The communes refused to pay rents and other feudal duties. Groups of peasants came to the manors, threatening the landowners, demanding that they give up their game privileges, make restitution of rights to the forests, restore property to evicted peasants, and even give new holdings to the landless population. Many Junkers, intimidated by the crowds, made oral or written promises. This peasant movement was spontaneous and unorganized. The authorities, confused by the revolution, were helpless. Instead, the liberal bourgeoisie took the matter in hand. The bourgeois were not happy about the peasant troubles, and their national guards were instrumental in pacifying the country. They tried to explain to the peasants that the new regime, particularly the national assembly to be convoked in Berlin, would redress all the popular wrongs. The people should behave quietly; their votes would settle everything.

The argument seemed sensible, and the peasant disorders subsided. The elections took place in May. They were general (with the exclusion of women), but a two-grade procedure was adopted which favored the more enlightened bourgeois candidates. The results of the elections in Upper Silesia were characteristic. The Polish peasants did not trust anybody, neither Junkers nor bourgeois intelligentsia; they elected mostly peasants and some priests. These peasant deputies, appearing in Berlin in their rustic attire, and with practically no knowledge of German, excited public surprise and even scorn. They were of course unable to play any role in the debates. Nevertheless, they were aware enough of their class interests to back the Left in all votes concerning social reforms. They also supported Father Józef Szafranek (1804–74) from Bytom, who moved to reestablish the Polish language in the courts and the administration of Upper Silesia. The only peasant elected to the German Assembly at Frankfurt was also an Upper Silesian, Krystian Minkus. He sided with the radicals and gained notoriety by publishing letters in the Silesian press addressed to his countrymen, in which he urged the peasants to stand firmly by their rights and even to use force against the Junkers, if necessary.

Both German parliaments in 1848 ended in disillusionment. In May 1849, a new revolutionary war broke out in southern and western Germany. Peasant disorders flared again in Upper Silesia, not so widespread as the year before but more violent in character. This time they were pacified by military force, and martial law was proclaimed in the province. The revolution was quelled, and liberal concessions were canceled. Only in agrarian matters did the government feel compelled to make some concessions. Between 1848 and 1850, partly by act of parliament and partly by decree, the regulation edicts were amended. The small-holders were admitted to ownership of their plots of land, the rents and other obligations were somewhat reduced, and a redemption procedure was arranged in order to liberate the peasants from the remainder of their duties. The peasant upheavals of 1848, in which Silesia took a big part, had not been in vain after all. One incidental remark in connection with this agrarian legislation: The Polish Club in the Berlin parliament voted against the granting of property to the small-holders. Class interest came before national duty; the Poznanian landlords felt no obligation to support Polish peasants against German Junkers.

Emancipation in Galicia

In the Prussian state, the revolution of 1848 brought the end and fulfillment of the Regulation Reform initiated at an earlier time. In Austria, the same year marked the beginning of a new era in the peasants' life which was to bring them emancipation and grant them property (*uwłaszczenie*).

Two years after 1846, Galicia was still in a state comparable to a hangover. The propertied classes had not yet recovered from their fright. They knew that something ought to be done about compulsory labor, and without losing time; still, they did not want to pay too high a price for their security. Negotiations dragged on in Lvov and Vienna between Austrian officials and representatives of the Polish gentry concerning the modes of commuting or redeeming compulsory labor. No workable solution was reached. Most leading patriots were still in prison, unrest was brewing in the countryside, and renewed cases of refusal of labor were reported every week. The peasants would have been still more active were it not for a new calamity: The potato disease, hunger, and a fever epidemic took a still heavier toll of lives in Galicia than in Silesia. The death toll for 1847 in Galicia was 250,000 higher than the average of the fifteen preceding years. The "hunger years" lasted until about 1855, and they especially made themselves felt in the mountain regions. A peasant, in his memoirs, recalled his childhood experience of one Christmas Eve, when his father brought on a sieve a dozen potatoes to be cooked as a special treat. There would be no more potatoes until the next harvest, only weed salad and hot water seasoned with flour. The masses were crippled with hunger but were nonetheless angry and unresponsive to any calls from the upper classes.

At the first news of an outbreak in Vienna, a meeting of landowners and bourgeois liberals in Lvov composed a petition to the emperor containing a list of standard 1848 propositions (amnesty, civil rights, etc.) coupled with nationalist claims for the use of the

Polish language in schools, offices, and the courts. One item proposed the complete abolition of compulsory labor and other duties which the Galician landowners intended to impose on their former serfs. The address did not decree any social reforms; it only begged the emperor to settle the matter. The Polish propertied classes were unwilling to antagonize the government, even a defeated one. Meanwhile, Governor Franz Stadion, a shrewd politician, warned Vienna that something ought to be done about the peasant question and without delay. Particularly, it was imperative not to leave the initiative to the Polish *szlachta*.

Three weeks later, a group of democratic leaders arrived in Krakow from Versailles and formed a national committee. They wanted to take advantage of the revolution and to renew the insurrectionary movement, this time with a more effective approach to the peasants. According to the Poitiers Manifesto, they were supposed to proclaim the immediate abolition of compulsory labor in the name of the national government. They did not dare, however, to make such a move, since it could endanger the *szlachta*. They proposed instead that the *szlachta* abolish labor duties of their own accord. This act of renunciation would reconcile peasants and landlords and thus open the door to a national front directed against Austria and Russia. An appeal to the landlords was composed and printed, renunciation formulas were distributed throughout the country, and the date of the people's spontaneous liberation was fixed for Easter, 23 April.

This scheme was bound to fail, although not exactly because of the *szlachta*'s class egoism. The labor problem was indeed more complex than was imagined by democrats in Versailles or at home. According to the reformers, if the estate was to survive emancipation, the landlords would have to retain some paid manpower as a substitute for compulsory labor. This could be accomplished by two means: either by granting the landlords compensation in cash for lost benefits (this had been the Prussian way), or by securing them a guaranteed amount of cheap labor. How was this feasible? Every landlord knew exactly how: by suppressing the servitudes together with labor duties. The peasant could not subsist without fuel, timber, and pasture. If the manor forests were closed to him, he would remain in a servile position with respect to his former master. He would be obliged to take some work on the estate, and of course, without being able to negotiate terms.

Thus, indemnification of the landlords or cancellation of servitudes was an indispensable condition; otherwise, the estate would collapse. But voluntary abolition of compulsory labor, as proposed by the democrats, was incompatible with both schemes. You could not abolish compulsory labor *and* beg for compensation—either of the peasants or of the state. Neither could you appear to be the peasants' benefactor while expelling them from the forests. Here lay the crucial reason why the great majority of the landlords felt unable to subscribe to this momentous act, however much they might be moved by patriotism or by fear of the peasants. Less than one hundred out of about five thousand gave up compulsory labor of their own will and without delay.

Maybe their example would have forced the rest of the *szlachta* to act, especially since the peasants had ceased to work nearly everywhere. But the Austrian government was not to remain inactive. Governor Stadion pressed the Court of Vienna to forestall the Poles and to proclaim emancipation. The fateful decision threatened to be delayed, and so he took a bold step, and on Saturday, 22 April, he issued a proclamation stating that the emperor had canceled all labor duties and that indemnity would be paid to the landlords from government funds. Servitudes, on the other hand, would be retained. Thus the peasants would be placated, the landlords satisfied, and the government's authority strengthened. Vienna ratified Stadion's decision ex post facto; the emperor's patent was published some weeks later, back-dated 17 April.*

Actually, labor duties had been suppressed in Galicia by European revolution and by the peasants' resistance. But it was the Austrian government which gained the political profit. The villagers were to owe their land to the emperor and not to the Polish *szlachta* or to the Polish democrats.

The attitude of the peasants was revealed explicitly two months later, in the course of elections to the parliament in Vienna. These elections were to run, as in Germany, with a general franchise and on a two-step basis. The same symptom could be observed in Galicia as in Upper Silesia. The peasants did not want any *szlachta*, or intelligentsia, or even any German official deputies. The Polish patriots were in despair; the votes of the ignorant peasants would submerge the national candidates. It turned out,

* See Appendix, section *F*.

however, that the danger could be avoided. More than ever, the peasants were suspicious of any revolutionary novelty and also of elections. It was enough to put into their heads that the signing of an election protocol, even with three crosses, would entail dangerous consequences or, still worse, would anger the emperor, and the electors would abstain from voting. In the absence of peasants, the remaining handful of intelligentsia would now elect their national candidate. Thanks to this not-too-democratic subterfuge, these first Galician elections had a satisfactory outcome on the whole. For a total of 100 seats, there were only thirty-one peasants elected in Galicia—seventeen Poles and fourteen Ukrainians. Most of the Polish peasants were elected in the class-conscious middle-Galician districts, where civil war had raged in 1846. Except for some priests, only peasants were elected here.

The peasant deputies, who were unable to speak German, were not of much use in parliament in Vienna. Since the Polish national party, which was composed of landlords and intelligentisia, sided with the left-wing opposition, in political matters the Galician peasants often voted on the conservative government's side. But when the agrarian problem was placed on the parliament's agenda, a change occurred. Stadion's proclamation of April concerned only Galicia, but it was bound to influence other provinces. Kudlich, the Czech deputy, moved to enact a law for the peasant's emancipation in the whole monarchy. The most important issue was whether the landowners should be entitled to indemnification or not. In this matter the Galician peasants disagreed, with the government, which advocated the indemnification principle. Ivan Kapuszczak, the Ukrainian deputy, made a sensational speech which he probably learned by heart and delivered in broken German. He said, among other things, "We have worked too long, under the menace of the whip, for the Polish lords. Are the blows and the wounds we have received equivalent to the proposed indemnification?" In the decisive vote on the indemnification question, most of the Polish landowners changed sides and voted with the government, whereas the peasants voted unanimously with the Left. Indemnification was adopted by a small majority. The law was published under the emperor's name on 7 September 1848.

The Austrian revolution was to collapse shortly thereafter. Vienna was stormed in October by imperial troops. On 2 November, Lvov was bombed and martial law was proclaimed in Galicia. In March 1849, parliament was dissolved and a constitution granted by the new emperor, Franz Joseph, which was never to come into force. Freedom of the press and association was suppressed and the police regime reinstalled. Of all the achievements of 1848, only one remained in Austria: the emancipation of the peasants. The victorious reactionary party did not dare to revoke this act. There were indeed attempts to limit or to evade the new law. The Polish gentry in Galicia begged the new governor, Agenor Gołuchowski (a conservative Polish aristocrat), to restrain the peasants who refused to work, even with pay, and who treated the forests as their own property, grazing and felling lumber at will. The problem of hired labor was a difficult one in Galicia. There were few landless peasants in this province, thanks to the former ban on evictions. Most of the peasants were smallholders, now included in the emancipation scheme. Could one compel them to work, even for hire? After having consulted Vienna, Gołuchowski replied in the negative. He acted more energetically on the other issue of the servitudes, promising military assistance to the gentry in cases of willful forest devastation.

The law of 7 September was not precise; many details were to be settled later, after protracted negotiations between the government and the landowners. This delay proved disadvantageous to the peasants. The revolutionary atmosphere was forgotten, and reaction set in everywhere in Europe; hence many of the details which were settled in the later fifties were detrimental to the peasants. Of course, the main features of emancipation achieved during the revolution could not be changed. In contrast to the Prussian reform, peasants holding the smallest plots of land, whether rustical or dominical, were to immediately become full owners of these holdings. As has just been said, there were few landless peasants in Galicia, and thus the large majority would receive land. They were not obliged to pay for it; theoretically, they received the land free, as a gift of the emperor. The landlords were to be indemnified, not for the suppressed serfdom, but for the canceled duties. In theory again, it was up to the Vienna government to pay. In practice, this debt became the province's burden. Since *pańszczyzna* was heavier in Galicia than elsewhere, the indemnification was to be higher, and other provinces were not inclined to support the charges in Galicia. Meticulously, the number of canceled days of labor was calculated on every estate and evaluated according to a graduated scale. This value was then multiplied by twenty to arrive at the total amount of indemnity. Of the total sum, one-third was deducted, and this sum represented the landlord's charges in respect to the peasant. The remaining two-thirds was to be paid off in bonds guaranteed by the provincial treasury. Some accounts were paid to the landlords in the middle fifties; the bonds were issued in 1857. They could be sold, but their value was low, and most of the owners, pressed by need, were to lose another 30 percent on the transaction. The purchasers were mostly small German capitalists, and they were to share with the Polish *szlachta* the profits of the operation.

Who was to pay? In order to cover the interest on the bonds and the amortization, an additional indemnification tax was imposed on the province in the form of a percentage addition to any other taxes. This additional tax was to be collected for more than thirty years. In the beginning it amounted to about 70 percent of the taxes. Later, with economic progress and hence a rise in national income, the rate declined to about 30 percent (the principal amount of course remained unchanged). But again, who was paying for this indemnification? Every taxpayer: the *szlachcic*, who had been indemnified and was thus deprived of some part of his due; the burgher, who had nothing to do with the matter but was to participate in the landlord's remuneration; and finally, the peasant, who had been assured he would receive his land free from the emperor but was later obliged to pay for it over a thirty-year period in the form of taxes (perhaps not the full value, but certainly some part of it). The promise of a gratuitous grant proved false—or at least only partially true. The ransom was to be paid by the peasants after all, if only on a partial and camouflaged basis.

The wrong done to the peasants was to appear still more conspicuously on the other issue, the servitudes. Both the Stadion proclamation in April and the parliament law in September had maintained the servitudes, that is, the rights of the peasants to woods and pastures. The exact evaluation of the amount of these rights was left to further regulations; they were not issued until 1858, and then in an entirely changed political situation, in which the Vienna government was seeking the support of the Polish aristocracy. It was decided then that all peasant claims would be examined and settled by judiciary procedure. Special commissions were instituted for the purpose of examining the peasants' claims. These courts fell mostly under the gentry's influence, and the peasants were to lose the large majority of their lawsuits. The landlords, accordingly, were to gain in the long run on both counts. Not only did they receive indemnification (reduced, it is true), but they were relieved of servitudes as well. The *propinacja* monopoly was also left intact; it was not to be liquidated for many decades.

The net result of Galician emancipation can be expressed by two figures: the landlords retained in their hands 43 percent of the arable land and 90 percent of the forests. The reform, carried by the revolutionary spirit, gave some land to nearly every peasant. But most of the peasants received too little for subsistence. Two-thirds of the new holdings were under ten *morgi*, or fourteen acres, and this situation was to be aggravated still further through family partitions. Most of the villagers were unable to live off their own land, especially since they were to be deprived of their rights to forests and pastures. This was equivalent to their remaining economically dependent on the manor.

11

THE CRISIS OF THE FEUDAL
SYSTEM IN CONGRESS POLAND

The story of the peasants' emancipation in the third province of
Poland, the Congress Kingdom, begins with the year 1846. The
national insurrection had also been planned against Russia, and
in some parts of the territory the democrats made appeals to
the peasants, with varying results. Then came the outbreak in
Galicia, and thrilling news came across the border of peasants
having put an end to their oppression. The landlords were frightened. How would the Russian government react? But Nicholaus I
felt too strong to be obliged to woo the peasants' support; he
thought he could force them to behave. He came to Warsaw, and
even to the frontier of the Krakow district, where he addressed
a huge peasant crowd, saying, "I am your only benefactor; you
may rely on me—but I shan't support any disorder." As a matter
of fact, he perceived the necessity for some concessions to the
rural masses. On his return to Warsaw he asked the opinion of
ministerial bureaus and signed a ukase on 7 June 1846 against

the advice of Paskevich and other Russian dignitaries. The ukase*
was intended to hold back the menace of a peasant uprising by
neutralizing some of the most striking abuses by the gentry. At
the same time, it did not infringe on the rights of the gentry such
as the ownership of land or the functioning of compulsory labor,
since an end to these privileges would endanger the feudal regime
in Russia proper. The most important provisions of the ukase
were the following:

1. Evictions were banned. The landlord was forbidden to drive
a peasant from his holding as long as he acquitted himself of his
duties. Every holding abandoned for whatever reason was to be
assigned to another peasant after at most two years.

2. The peasants' prestations were not to be wilfully altered.
The administration would record them in order to avoid any
ambiguity in the future.

3. In case of conflict with the landlords, the peasants on private
estates would have the right to appeal not only to the courts, as
before, but also to administrative officials.

4. The government would elaborate a procedure for commuting compulsory labor into rent on private estates.

There was one important flaw in this act. It expressly stated
that it exclusively concerned holdings of not less than three *morgi*
(four acres). A large portion of small-holders were thus excluded
from its benefits.

As can be seen, the ukase granted the peasants what has been
called a stronger right to the soil, modeled, on the whole, on the
Austrian Josephinist pattern. It did not confer title of ownership,
and it postponed the reform of labor duties to the indeterminate
future. Nevertheless, it was the first intervention of the state in
the peasants' conditions on private estates since the December
Decree of 1807, and it was to influence the future evolution of the
agrarian problem. An analogous measure was introduced simultaneously in the western guberniyas; that is, the former eastern
provinces of the Polish Commonwealth. The Russian government
ordered the drawing up of inventories which were to include the
duties of every individual peasant. The inventories were supposed
to prevent the harmful tendency of raising the peasants' duties.
Measures of this kind were issued only in provinces contiguous

* See Appendix, section *G*.

to inflammable Galicia and inhabited by Polish landowners. The czarist government was not yet prepared to impose such regulations in Russia proper. The inventories remained a dead letter in the Ukraine and Lithuania.

This was not the case in Congress Poland, where the government seriously meant to enforce the new ukase. It is true that its publication was deferred until after the harvest, but at that time the Commission of the Interior published a list of 121 charges besides labor duties which were customarily imposed on the peasants. This list included extra labor extorted at times when field work piled up, various transportation duties, watch duties, and tributes in kind (poultry, eggs, berries, nuts, yarn, and the like). All such prestations, if not expressly stipulated in amount, were now declared illegal. The commission further ordered that a prestation table be made up for every village; this table would list all peasants farming more than three *morgi*, stating the amount of their land, the character of their servitudes (in forests and pastures), and all the prestations in labor, cash, or kind. These tables would form the basis of future official decisions in cases of conflict between landlords and peasants. (National domains were not included in this procedure. The 1846 ukase did not concern itself with them.) Accordingly, the prestation tables were drawn up in 1846, but with all data supplied by the landowners and ratified by an official board which seldom questioned their authenticity. In many cases the peasant's charges were entered as higher, and the landlord's duties (servitudes, etc.) as lower, than was really so. This was harmful to the peasants, but at least for the future it offered them a guarantee of definite contracts.

The peasants reacted to the ukase with a spontaneous refusal to perform labor duties or to pay rent. They interpreted the czar's will in the broadest and most favorable sense. The resistance was most widespread in the southern guberniyas, which bordered on Galicia. It was the first really important mass movement of peasants on private domains; until that time, the peasants on the national domains had always led such movements. The resistance was broken by the cossacks, only to be renewed the next year on a smaller scale and suppressed again—this time with the help of much flogging. Notice that although the Russian authorities themselves indulged in official flogging, they forbade the use of sticks against compulsory-labor workers. As for hired farmhands, they could be thrashed as before.

It has often been said that the ukase of 1846 was a hypocritical half-reform which did not better the peasants' lot in any essential matter. It is true that the official protection extended to the peasants was not particularly effective. The "peasant sections" set up in every gubernial office and in the Commission of the Interior in Warsaw were, in most cases, more favorably inclined toward the peasants than were the courts, but they were hampered by official procedure and their decisions were slow. A sign that the ukase was helping the peasants in some ways was the animosity exhibited toward it by the gentry. Conservative landlords grumbled that with this state control they ceased to be masters in their own homes. Liberals argued that the ukase was a step backward in comparison with the Napoleonic Code; that in place of the equality principle for all citizens it revived a peasant caste and conferred upon it special privileges. The liberals also protested that the ukase should not cancel formal, authenticated contracts. If a landlord had agreed with a group of villagers that for a given time—let us say fifteen or twenty-five years—they would pay him a specified rent, he should not lose the right to evict these peasants when the term elapsed, or to sign a new contract with modified conditions. After much negotiation, this view was confirmed by the Commission of the Interior, and privately regulated estates were acknowledged as not being governed by the ukase if the agreements involved were duly notarized.

Independently of such discussions, the ukase influenced the evolution of the countryside in several respects. The provision that all rent reforms henceforth must undergo official ratification acted as a brake on private regulations. Between 1846 and 1858 only an insignificant number of rent reforms were actually ratified by the peasant section, but this was not due to deliberate postponement of these matters or to inertia on the part of officials. The cause lay elsewhere. The peasants now knew that they could not be evicted any longer and that no new duties could be forced upon them. They were now able to bargain. They often refused to enter into negotiations because, hoping that the ukase was only a first step, they feared to commit themselves and thus lose the right to further benefits to be bestowed by the czar. In such cases the landlord often gave up if he could not win his conditions.

It is not true that rent reforms ceased altogether after 1846. The process continued, even though the authorities were not notified of all the changes. It seems that on the whole the peasants were now getting better conditions.

The other consequence of the ukase concerned the small-holders who farmed less than three *morgi*. Since they were now denied official protection, their eviction was accelerated, and this category seemed to disappear altogether during the following decade. This did not actually happen. Small-holders still existed, under another name and in changed circumstances. The ukase of 1846 taught the landlords that it was dangerous to leave a specific plot of land in the peasants' hands; the state could always declare that the peasant had some right (or even full title) to this land. It seemed more sensible to loosen the ties of the small-holders with the land. Many landlords arranged to give each small-holder another patch of land every year, so that, in the event of a reform or revolution, he would not be able to lay claim to any definite holding. Other systems were also used, such as permitting the small-holder to harvest a given number of sheaves or a given fraction of the crop from a field—again in order not to establish a tighter connection between the peasants and the land.

A further instrument of pressure used against the peasants concerned the forests and pastures. Mention has already been made of the servitudes and their influence on the agrarian policy in Galicia. The problem was similar in the Congress Kingdom. Liberal landowners openly avowed that the most efficient method of securing ample and cheap manpower, after the disappearance of compulsory labor, would be to eliminate the servitudes. (If the peasant lost his rights to free grazing, free fuel, and free timber in the landlord's forests, he would be forced into submission.) Reflections of this kind were mostly coupled with the principle of safeguarding the forests from devastation—the servitudes were an obstacle to the introduction of modern forestry. This is undoubtedly true, but the concern about forestry was specious in most cases. Servitudes were often denied to the peasants before 1864, but forestry plans were seldom introduced. The state was the biggest forest owner in the country, and it set the *szlachta* a bad example. As early as the mid-twenties, the government limited and then denied altogether all peasant claims to the national

144

forests. But these measures had nothing to do with care of trees, although some attempts at planned exploitation of forests were made. After canceling the servitudes, the Forest Department issued a table of charges for the use of the recently closed forests. In addition, it specified how much each inhabitant of national estates should pay for fuel and grazing. If he claimed not to care about it, he was of course suspected of stealing fuel and timber. The liquidation of the servitudes in the national forests was thus obviously fiscal in motivation. Most private owners did not feel this way, but they were glad to furnish their villagers with fuel and grazing commodities under *odrobek* conditions (i.e., to be paid back in work).

Let us now consider the results of this policy of the landowners, in relation to the general economic trend of the country. We have the relatively abundant statistical data collected by the government in 1860, in connection with the proposals for agrarian reform. These data can be considered valid for 1859. They show a decline in the use of compulsory labor and an increase in the number of landless peasants. This process was most advanced in the northwest regions and relatively slow in the southeast. The figures for the whole country showed that 56 percent of all peasant holdings larger than three *morgi* were already commuted to rent. In the national estates the figure was 91 percent; in the private ones, 41 percent. Local differences were substantial: in only nine counties out of thirty-nine did rent definitely predominate. In ten counties one could speak of a balance. Elsewhere, compulsory labor still prevailed, and in three counties there were less than 10 percent rent payers (in private estates).

The other figures, concerning peasants without land, are even more significant. There were, according to official statistics, one million landless peasants in 1827, 1,168,000 in 1846, 1,339,000 in 1859. The last number corresponds to about 40 percent of the agrarian population (30 percent on national estates and 45 percent on private ones). In seven counties more than 60 percent of the peasants were landless. The accuracy of these data has been challenged in recent times. In 1864, when beginning to carry through the granting of land (*uwłaszczenie*), the Russian government found much more compulsory labor and many fewer peasants without land than the data for 1859 indicated. It seems that the data collected by the mayors—that is, the landlords—often counted whole groups of small-holders among the landless peasants. This was most certainly true for all small-holders who did not come under, or were presumed not to come under, the ukase of 1846—for example, all those who had less than three *morgi*. But even for other groups of the rural population, it often was not clear how to distinguish between a small-holder obliged to work for wages on the estate and a farmhand working for wages and in addition using a patch of land. It was only natural that such dubious cases were classified by the landlords according to their interests.

There is one additional argument favoring the thesis that the 1.3 million landless peasants were not rural proletarians in the full sense of the term. With 40 percent of the villagers landless in a country with a slowly advancing industry, there should have been an abundance or a surplus of manpower in agriculture. Instead, from the newspapers, and more especially from the economic journals of the time one gains the contrary impression of a constant and even dramatic lack of manpower. Without cessation the landowners lamented that the peasants did not want to work, that there were not enough candidates for farm work, and that candidates presenting themselves set impossible conditions. Moreover, landowners were anxious to secure supernumerary manpower at haying and harvest time. Bureaus were organized to supply seasonal mowers from Galicia (the Tatras mountaineers were renowned as excellent field workers), and many a landowner was ready to pay double in order to have the harvest done on time. There is no doubt, therefore, that a shortage of rural manpower existed at home, notwithstanding the 1.3 million so-called proletarians. It is true that these poor peasants were not especially eager to work on the local estate for board and room only and almost no cash, while being mistreated and beaten by overseers. It seems that the farmhand preferred to work for a well-to-do peasant, who might be more exacting but who worked along with him and treated him as an equal, even eating his meals with him. Other openings turned up as well for the landless population. The building of highways and railroads required much unskilled manpower which, however poorly paid, was paid better than that on the estate. One must also take into account the relatively low birth rate and the military draft, which took the soundest boys away from the countryside. All these factors undoubtedly played a role in the conditions leading to complaints by the big property owners about the difficulties with manpower. Two other factors are yet to be considered, one economic, the other psychological. First, proletarians who were completely detached from the land were still not especially numerous in the countryside; most of them retained some link with one holding or another. Second, the average landowner did not consider the local villager a free worker with whom one should make a contract (as was done with mowers from Galicia). No, the local villager was the former serf, traditionally meant to obey, a creature not supposed to negotiate his conditions of work.

One more question: Was this differentiation of the villagers into those who did and those who did not possess land a definite one, in the sense it acquired in the later capitalist era? That is, was the village in central Poland in the middle of the nineteenth century already divided into contrasting and separate classes? We have posed the same question concerning the beginning of the century and have decided that the answer is no. We give the same answer now, albeit with some hesitation. Until the enfranchisement, the landlord still retained the power to influence the social stratification of the village. He might decide, for instance, that Maciek would have his holding commuted to rent, while Wojtek would be evicted and changed into a farmhand. And both Maciek and Wojtek would accept this determination of their fates by the *pan dziedzic* ("Mr. Heir") without question as long as he legally remained the owner of their fathers' lands (*ojczyzna*). Rural parish books also seem to show that intermarriages between children of well-to-do peasants and farmhands still occurred before 1864, at least in the more backward Lublin region. This was not to be seen in the next generation.

How did the countryside react to the new policy of the landowners? The opposition to compulsory labor was crushed in 1847, but the unrest recurred in the following year and was one of the reasons why most landowners were absolutely opposed to any participation in the 1848 revolution despite the chances for armed help from abroad. During the fifties, the peasant resistance, although less widespread, attained in many cases a degree of stubbornness unheard of till now.

The national domains were, for the most part, already regulated. In the remaining few, where compulsory labor was still in effect, the peasant communities petitioned for reform and often went on strike in order to enforce their demands. Conflicts recurred in the mining estates of the Kielce region, and in many cases order was restored by military force. But also on regulated estates, one ground for conflict remained, namely, the servitudes. The peasants refused to pay for the use of the forests and felled trees illegally, despite forest guards, lawsuits, fines, and jail sentences. Forestry officials reported that the peasants were stealing much more timber than they needed for their own use; that whole villages were engaged in trading in stolen wood or in manufacturing wooden household implements out of stolen materials. Fighting these clandestine depredations was to no avail, and the maintenance of a forest guard cost more than the timber recovered from the villagers was worth. Scuffles and fusillades between foresters and "forest embezzlers" or poachers were a daily (or rather nightly) routine.

Much more important, however, was the activity of the peasants on private estates. We are better informed about it after 1846, because most of the conflicts were then recorded by the Peasant Section in the Committee of the Interior. These were neither general nor very widespread; just local affairs, but nevertheless protracted and stubborn. A score of them have been studied in detail, using archival sources. They were handled in a legal manner, without threats to, or assaults on, the landlords. It does not seem that there were more than one or two such cases per county at one time. But some of these conflicts lasted many years, and some ended with concessions by the landlord. Their frequency was a steady cause of concern for the ruling class.

The great majority of these contests had to do with the still-persisting compulsory labor. The peasants wanted to get the same advantages which had been granted to the neighboring villages which were regulated. The most effective means of enforcing rent reform was to refuse labor duties. More often than not, the community began by protesting the prestation table. Either the table was wrong, because the landlord had falsified it, or if it was right, the landlord was claimed to exact more than was authorized in the table. Complaints about the beating of workers or about the limiting of servitudes were usually added to the petitions. Official investigations dragged on with no result, until the community decided to stop work altogether. Such strikes were of course forbidden, and the landlord would ask for military help. The practice since the beginning of the nineteenth century was called *military execution*, and it was used for collecting tax arrears. On the request of the civil authority, the military commander installed a given number of soldiers in the house of the delinquent taxpayer or other culprit. The host thus punished was obliged to entertain his "executor," to give him his best bed, to feed him, to provide him with vodka and tobacco, and to pay him a few kopecks extra per day. The "executor" was supposed to behave in such a way as to become as burdensome as possible. This enforced hospitality lasted until the tax arrears were paid; and if one soldier proved ineffective a second was added after a few days, or a third. The same method of harassment was now adopted against disobedient peasants. Twenty or 50 or 100 cossacks were installed in a village where labor duties had been refused. If routine intimidation and bullying of the peasants were not enough, then came the second stage—a public thrashing of the chief culprits. The third stage consisted in evicting the refractory peasants from their holdings. But even this last method did not always prove sufficient.

The most drastic example of such a fight of the peasants against their landlords and the civil and military authorities who were supporting them was the case of Garnek. This was a big estate of seven villages (about three hundred families) in Piotrków County on the Silesian border, owned by a man named Grodzicki. In 1844, a year of threatening revolution, Grodzicki had agreed to commute compulsory labor into rent, but he was careful to insert a sly paragraph in his contract which would enable him to return to compulsory labor if he found it convenient. He took this step in 1850, notwithstanding the community's protests. Complaints to authorities proved to no avail; eventually the peasants went on strike. The military "execution" (at first 3 cossacks, then 6, 50, 140) did not break their resistance, and the authorities felt compelled to suggest some concessions on the part of the landlord. Regulations were issued on the mode of accounting for compulsory labor—but still to no avail. The peasants argued that the local authorities had been bribed by the *szlachta*. Accordingly, the viceroy sent one of his generals to assure the community that it was the czar's will that they should return to work. Soon the peasants were whispering that the general was only a dressed-up Polish *szlachcic*. Next a delegation of peasants was sent from Garnek to Warsaw; they were received in the royal castle, and Prince Gortschakov himself admonished them to be sensible. They listened humbly, but after having returned home they told their comrades that they had participated in still another masquerade. This time the Russians became angry. A number of recalcitrant peasants were sent to the Warsaw Citadel and their holdings were put up at auction (nobody dared to make a bid, however). Part of the population abandoned the village, another returned to work after ten years of fighting, but in 1860 there were still eighty families refusing to work. By 1861, with compulsory labor soon to be canceled, it could be said that the peasants of Garnek had won their fight after all. One of the most astonishing features of the story is that the Polish democratic press of the emigration, ordinarily so eager to denounce all sorts of Russian abuses as well as the *szlachta*'s collusion with the Russians, this time did not breathe a word about the events in Garnek. It was as if all social conflicts in the countryside were taboo and not to be mentioned lest they disturb the myth of national solidarity directed against the oppressor.

The social conflict, however, was a fact. The Garnek case may have been an exception in the degree of mutual rancor it aroused, but similar moods were to be found elsewhere. Numerous were the cases in which peasants—drunk or sober—threatened to resort to "Galician" methods. Many landlords felt as if they resided on a volcano, and most of them felt the necessity for total abolition of compulsory labor in order to prevent an awful outburst. On comparing the Prussian and the Austrian methods of reform, the landlords of course preferred the former. The crucial problem, in the eyes of the *szlachta*, was how to get rid of *pańszczyzna* without the intervention of the czarist government.

Diehard apologists for compulsory labor were few among the Polish *szlachta*, especially by comparison with the number in contemporary Russia. You could not find a defense of it in print; at most there were some sentimental reflections saying that in the past compulsory labor had been a justified, sensible, and on the whole innocuous institution. Now of course it had to go.

Compulsory labor was represented as a waste of time and energy. The peasant who cheated at compulsory labor was to be urged on with a stick—but a stick seemed to have become a dangerous weapon. If the peasants were now to become independent, the reform, in the view of liberal-minded landowners, should protect the interests of the big property owners. If one were compelled to cede some land to the peasants, let it be as little as possible, as late as possible, and at the highest possible price.

There was, of course, the well-tried method of rent reform for getting rid of compulsory labor. Most latifundists advocated it still. They argued that the commuting of labor duties into rent (*oczynszowanie*) would leave intact the squire's right of property and would be less onerous for the peasant; it would compel the peasants to work and thereby eliminate the lazy or otherwise unfit elements of the population, with a consequent benefit to the economy and to morals. On the other hand, *oczynszowanie* was considered less suitable for the middle gentry, and, moreover, it was argued that it would not cut the bonds of interdependence between village and manor. The peasant would not be satisfied with rent reform; he would claim a decrease or a remission of rent, and social friction would continue. The only way out was to cut the Gordian knot once and for all by making the peasant full owner. In truth, title to property was not worth much for the moment; the most sensible course was to sell the property to the peasant while it was still possible.

The action of transforming the peasant into full owner of his holding was called *uwłaszczenie*. This term, accepted by historians, is unknown outside Poland and defies translation. In other central and eastern European countries the peasant became owner of the land at the time of his emancipation from serfdom. (The process was called *Bauernreform* or *Bauernbefreiung* in German and *Razkreposhtchenyie* in Russian.) In Congress Poland *uwłaszczenie* was still to be carried out more than fifty years after the emancipation. What is more, it was an ambiguous term. The Polish landlords understood *uwłaszczenie* as a sale of the holding (or, more exactly, the sale of title to the property) to the peasant. The Russian government was to give title to property free, while indemnifying the gentry. The Polish democrats, referring to the Poitiers Manifesto, announced that *uwłaszczenie* would be enacted by the national government during the insurrection. Some left-wing émigré writers maintained that the peasants, shamefully oppressed for centuries, had lawful rights to the soil; that they ought to be installed as owners without charge; that any action which imposed redemptive charges on the peasants should not be called *uwłaszczenie* ("appropriation") but rather *wywłaszczenie* ("expropriation").

To 1861, such opinions voiced in leaflets from Paris or London by émigrés influenced but little the liberal opinion in the country. The most enlightened representative of this view was Thomas Potocki, a wealthy landowner belonging to a well-known aristocratic family, and the outstanding brain of the Conservative party. As early as 1851, Potocki, writing under the pen name Krzyżtopór, exposed his own scheme for *uwłaszczenie*. In 1858 he gave a more popular version of it in a much-read book entitled *The Carlsbad Matinées*. In this book a group of Polish visitors to this well-known health resort conducted Socratic dialogues on the agrarian question. Each of them represented a different point of view. The marshal was a diehard conservative of the eastern borders. The counsellor represented the point of view of the government. The doctor was a radical, and the rector brought out the moral viewpoint and the interests of the church. Finally, the colonel, a former participant in the 1831 insurrection, was the voice of the author, gradually persuading his collocutors and exposing his general concepts.

Krzyżtopór's argument ran thus: True conservatism does not consist in stubbornly defending outlived institutions, but in preventing social upheavals through moderate reforms. Social equilibrium is best preserved by distribution of property, and the landowners ought to be interested in providing peasants the means for access to property. This should be done without harm to anyone, by amortization through a bank. The price of the holding should be set at a low level, and a given percentage should be forwarded not to the landlord but to the commune fund. The communal government played an important role in Potocki's scheme: it should be on an elective basis, but controlled by the landlord and by the parish priest. The commune would be responsible for the villagers' obligations, and schools, roads, and medical care would be established and paid for out of the communal fund. Sources of friction between village and manor would be eliminated. The landlord would be indemnified in bonds which he could sell if he had to invest capital in his estate. The bank would collect the quarterly installments from the peasants and put up their holdings for auction when necessary. Krzyżtopór's proposal found many adherents. The landlords' attitude in this regard was more liberal in Poland than in Russia. The scheme assured the landowner an indemnity and seemed to offer an alternative to the more radical democratic solution. The plan had a weakness, however. In order to establish a bank, government consent was necessary. The liberal landowners could enforce this reform only through collaboration with the government, and this would lose them support of patriotic opinion.

12

THE INSURRECTION OF 1863

For a long time the idea of *uwłaszczenie* in Congress Poland was academic. In 1857, however, the question was officially raised in Russia. Both contemporary writers and later historians often attributed the initiative for the Russian reform to the Polish *szlachta*. It is a fact that the Polish landowners in Lithuania (a province more advanced from an economic point of view and with closer connections with foreign markets than most of central Russia) were more aware of the anachronism of compulsory labor, than were the Russian *pomeshtchiki*. The evolution of other Polish provinces also had an impact on Lithuania. The landowners in these northwestern provinces were not philanthropists. They advocated abolition of serfdom, not the granting of land to the peasants. Nevertheless, when, after the Crimean War, Czar Alexander II realized the necessity for agrarian reform, and when he needed a show of initiative by the big property owners, he took advantage of the Poles' attitude. Governor-General

Nazimov persuaded the Lithuanian landowners to petition the czar for a change in agrarian relations. This became the formal starting point of the famous "Nazimov Rescript" and the ensuing discussion which led to the Russian reform of 19 February 1861.

The genesis of that reform does not concern us here. Let us examine the attitude of the Polish *szlachta* in Lithuania and the Ukraine during the protracted debates of the provincial committees on the scope and means of emancipation. In the empire, the landowners were divided between the diehard adversaries of any kind of reform and the seemingly more liberal partisans of an arrangement which would oblige the peasant to pay a heavy price for his freedom without leaving him any means of subsistence. In Lithuania and the Ukraine the line of demarcation was different. There were no defenders of serfdom. Opinions were divided on the issue of whether the peasant should be freed with land or without it. Liberal propaganda insisted on a show of generosity from patriotic motives: Lithuanian and Ukrainian peasants ought to be convinced of the good will of the Poles. Motions to this effect were defeated in most provinces, in some cases by a narrow majority, and the final resolutions of the committees in the former Polish provinces were not very sympathetic to the peasants' fate.

The debates on the reform in Russia indicated unmistakably that an end would be put to compulsory labor in Congress Poland as well. All the political parties were anxious to outdo the czarist government by favoring some form of initiative; but whereas the landowners envisaged reform as a way to economic progress or a means of preventing a social upheaval, the democratic intelligentsia wanted to use reform as a lever in the expected fight for independence. Meanwhile the Warsaw authorities temporized. In 1858, new regulations were issued concerning rent reforms on private estates, but they were too complicated to be of any practical use. In February 1861, the newly founded Agronomic Society held a session in Warsaw. It was presided over by Count Andrew Zamoyski, the leader of the Polish moderate party, and attracted most of the country's landowners. The society was ready to come out with a program of agrarian reform in order to forestall the impending czarist ukase and to foster favorable public opinion. According to Zamoyski's plan, the society would vote a program of general rent reform. In the meantime street demonstrations forced the society to take an additional step; on 25 February a resolution was passed providing that after conversion to rent the peasants would acquire title to their holdings on an indemnification basis. This proposal of *uwłaszczenie* was not particularly generous, since the peasants were supposed to redeem all their obligations. Nevertheless, it was a significant suggestion, and the members of the society hastened to propagate it by means of circulars, posters, and announcements made from the pulpit in the village churches. It seemed important to persuade the peasants that the *szlachta* was their benefactor, so that the government would not be able to use the rural masses against the gentry, as had happened in 1846 in Galicia.

The resolution of the Agronomic Society almost coincided with two other events: the first clash of street demonstrators with the armed forces in Warsaw (27 February), which compelled the government to advocate a policy of concessions, and the Russian emancipation ukase (3 March, New Style, published some weeks later). The provisions of the latter reform did not apply to Congress Poland, and they granted the Russian peasants few advantages that the Polish peasants did not already have. Nevertheless, the Russian ukase was considered, not altogether without reason, a portent of change in Poland proper. At the same time, the clergy announced that compulsory labor would be suppressed, and news of the Warsaw disorders was taken as a sign that the established authorities were giving way. As a result, a large number of the peasants on whom labor duties were imposed went on strike at the beginning of April.

This significant event had a quiet course. Entire villages ceased work, without any acts of violence or any attempts to seize the landowners' property. Official reports have confirmed that more than 20 percent of the peasants obligated to labor duties took part in the movement. In many regions this percentage was much higher, and, in any event, these figures are probably too low. Not only the full-holders (*gospodarze*) but also the small-holders (*komornicy*) went on strike. The rent payers on private or national estates followed suit, ceasing to pay rent or petitioning for a lowering of their obligations. Some cases of refusal to pay taxes were also noted. The landowners panicked and fled the countryside with their families—they were awaiting a repetition of the Galician troubles of 1846. Some of the gentry begged for help from the Russian military, but most of the Russian detachments were now concentrated in towns because of the Polish patriotic movement. Cases of military pacification of the countryside were neither general nor very efficient. As for the Polish democrats, they also tried to influence the peasants. Numerous agitators circulated in the countryside. Most of them tried to persuade the country folk that the *szlachta*'s intentions were for the best; that the czar and his officials alone were responsible for the persistence of compulsory labor; that the peasants ought to side with the *szlachta* because in the future everybody in Poland would be free and equal and the peasants would get title to their holdings from the national government. Parallel to this agitation, and in the same interests, there were other incidents involving unknown agitators who sided with the peasants in their struggle against the manors and against compulsory labor. Some of these propagandists were accused of being provocateurs in the Russian service, but such charges seem to have been unfounded. It is much more likely that they were radically inspired participants of the patriotic movement, acting in small groups in their own behalf. Since they could not rely on help from the landowners or the clergy, many of them hid in the forests—hence their surname, "forest men." Some of them, in the Podlasie region among others, succeeded in gaining some influence over the peasants and later in inducing them into active participation in the insurrection.

The czarist government was busy at that time suppressing similar agrarian troubles in central Russia, and also in its western provinces. As for Congress Poland, Alexander II pursued a conservative policy, trying to win over the Polish propertied classes against the revolutionary movement. This was the purpose of appointing Marquis Wielopolski to a governmental post in March 1861. Wielopolski saw that the countryside could be pacified only with a promise that compulsory labor would be suppressed—and that the peasants had to be pacified at once if the country were to avoid an insurrection on a national scale or a massacre on the Galician order. Accordingly, he persuaded the other dignitaries in Warsaw to promulgate the end of compulsory labor. This was not to mean *uwłaszczenie*, but only a temporary commutation to payments in money. Wielopolski also felt obliged to take into account the interests of his fellow landowners. After some consultation it was agreed that the new arrangements would not take effect until after the harvest.

On 16 May 1861 the new ukase was published. It specified that beginning on 1 October all peasants falling under the previous ukase of 1846 (that is, those possessing at least three *morgi*) would have to make a declaration if they wanted to commute their labor charges into a temporary "ransom" (*okup*). The term was borrowed from the reform of the Zamoyski entail in the 1830s. The amount of the ransom was to be calculated on a differential scale which took into account the quality of the soil and the market facilities. The ransom was to be paid in advance, and the peasant who once accepted this arrangement could not revert to compulsory labor. The ukase was emphatically declared to be only a temporary measure, pending thorough and definitive rent reform.

The first results of the official proclamation seemed satisfactory. By the end of May, most of the refractory villages returned to work, although cases of disobedience occurred during the summer in a number of counties. On 1 October more than 95 percent—and in many regions 100 percent—of the peasants involved accepted the ransom. We can consider this plebiscite an unambiguous indication of the peasants' sentiments. This date of 1861 October 1 marks the end of compulsory labor in Polish territories. But while the peasants were emphatically opposed to compulsory labor, they were not at all enthusiastic about the ransom, and for an obvious reason. It was calculated by formula from the number of days of labor. This number varied considerably as a result of differing policies of different landowners. In neighboring villages, and even in the same village, one peasant owed more days than another with an equal holding. It was one thing to extort an excessive number of days of labor from some of the peasants; it was another matter to oblige them to pay more than they could afford. The ransom rates per acre varied drastically even in the same locality. Numerous peasants begged for reduction of their ransom or simply refused to pay; most of them hoped that resistance would assure them better conditions.

At that time (October 1861), Wielopolski had left the government, and Russian officials seriously disagreed over the course to follow. The Commission of Justice followed the strictly legal line; when the peasant did not pay the ransom, he was sued and his debt collected by an executive officer. In hundreds of villages, cows, pigs, sheepskins, and featherbeds of refractory peasants were put up for auction, which led to a further growth of social friction. The Commission of the Interior argued that the ransom ukase ought to be revised to base the payment not on the number of days of labor but on the income from the holding. Some of the Russian commanders tried to pacify the peasants by persuading them that if they remained quiet and loyal the czar would grant them full title to their land. Such propaganda was denounced in the Polish press as dangerous demagogy. During the first half of 1862, unrest in the villages was far from being eliminated.

In June of the same year, Wielopolski returned to power as chief of the civil government. He now had a new scheme for settling the peasant question. It was published on 4 June, in the czar's name, as the so-called Ex Officio Rent Ukase. Wielopolski was, as a matter of fact, an opponent of *uwłaszczenie*. He considered rent reform a maximum concession to the peasants and understood it in the most narrow sense. Rent reforms had been advocated for decades, but not every landowner had been eager to introduce them, and, especially in later years, peasants had also been slow to accept them, preferring to await better conditions. Now a definitive settling of the matter was deemed necessary, and so the government extended the Ex Officio Rent Ukase to all holdings in which rent reform was not yet operating. This concerned, primarily, the peasant holdings subject to the previously mentioned "ransom ukase." In every county, rent delegations were to be appointed by the local self-government, which was composed of landowners. These delegations, together with the county officials, would evaluate the amount of rent due from every holding, taking into account not only the actual ransom, but also the probable income and the financial standing of each peasant. This procedure would have been proper, had not its application been left to official bodies composed mainly of landlords. Other provisions were even less favorable to the peasants. For example, most of the small-holders were explicitly excluded from the benefits of the ukase; and the landlord was to retain certain rights on the village grounds: the rights of hunting, of exploiting minerals, of running inns. On the other hand, all servitudes, that is, the peasants' rights to the landlord's forests, were to be canceled if they were not expressly granted by written agreement (which was rarely the case). The most important defect of Wielopolski's scheme, however, lay in the fact that it did not concede the point most coveted by the peasants: the granting of property. The ukase alluded to it only in the vaguest manner, saying that *uwłaszczenie* would follow at a later period, with the peasants helped to purchase their rent contracts by means of bank loans. It was equivalent to saying to the peasants that only their sons would become full owners of their holdings. No wonder the peasants showed no enthusiasm for the Ex Officio scheme, and were not eager to cooperate with the newly appointed rent delegations.

Wielopolski's idea of siding with czarist Russia in return for limited autonomy for Congress Poland attracted only a handful of followers. Most of the propertied classes—the White party, composed of the landowners and bourgeoisie—readily accepted Wielopolski's social propositions, such as the Ex Officio Rent Ukase, but not its political implications. The Whites did not dare provoke public opinion by siding with a partitioning power; they followed, instead, a policy of legal opposition and of gradual "organic" economic and cultural improvements. At best, in this period of international tension, they were awaiting help from western Europe. That is to say, neither the czarist government nor the Polish propertied class was inclined to gratify at that time the peasants' most ardent desires. This conjuncture opened vast possibilities to the Revolutionary (or Red) party, which had been preparing, since the fall of 1861, a new war for independence.

The clandestine Central National Committee established in Warsaw in June 1862 was not eager to propose an agrarian program of its own. In theory, such a program had been set forth in the Poitiers Manifesto of 1836 and in the provisions of the national government in Krakow in 1846. The Reds never attempted to disown these traditions, but they were aware of the present difficulties: A radical agitation would most certainly estrange the *szlachta* and would possibly provoke a social outburst fatal to the national cause. Accordingly, their patriotic propaganda merely urged both peasants and landowners to come to mutual understanding and good will, to a natural fraternity inspired by patriotism. The landlords were to pursue the rent reform on conditions acceptable to the peasants; and the latter were to seek agreement with their "elder brothers" (the gentry) and not to threaten their lives or property. The propaganda seldom espoused more radical views. A clandestine periodical leaflet published in Byelorussian under the title *"Muzhitskaya Pravda"* ("The Peasant Truth") sharply attacked the czarist reform of 1861 and urged the peasants to conquer the land they were to own, in a national insurrection together with the Poles. The leaflet was written by Constantine Kalinowski (1838–64), the chief of the Red wing in Wilno. Kalinowski is now regarded as the national Byelorussian hero, although he was of Polish (and gentry) origin and never dreamed of separating Byelorussia from Poland.

Only in August 1862 was the Warsaw Central National Committee compelled to formulate its stand on the agrarian question. While engaged in agitation in the countryside, Red agents were often asked the question, What can the peasants expect from a national insurrection and a future democratic Poland? Pressed by necessity, the Central National Committee issued a proclamation to the peasants in which they were promised full equality before the law, the abolition of monopolies on salt and tobacco, lower taxes, shorter military service, broader educational facilities for their children, and full title to their holdings for all peasants using some land (this as a free gift on the part of the national government). The same government would also indemnify the landowners for their losses. This formula was a compromise between the traditions of the Poitiers Manifesto (which was silent on the indemnification matter) and the expectations of the propertied classes. The proclamation did not enter into details; it was silent on the problem of the landless peasants as well as that of the servitudes, and its authors were prone to forget that an indemnification of the landowners (on the Galician model) could only mean new taxes, which the peasants, among others, were to support.

The aim of the August proclamation was to conciliate the two antagonistic forces which were facing each other in the Polish countryside. Both the peasants and the landlords wanted *uwłaszczenie*, but they interpreted it in different ways. The landlords were willing to cede, for money, some of the land to some of the peasants—certainly if no rights to the forests were included. The peasants, on the other hand, wanted to get their land free, with no decrease, and with rights to the forests unchallenged; they also wanted all the land from which they had been evicted since 1846. They would probably back the power which would be ready to support, and would be able to carry through, such claims. The czarist government was still committed to the support of the landlords' interests. The Central National Committee promised the peasants more than the government, although not everything they wished. The crucial question was, Would the committee be able to realize such wishes?

In October 1862, an extraordinary draft was announced by the Russian army, for which the recruits were to be picked from among the politically undesirable element. Declared free from the draft were the landlords, the peasants in possession of any holding, and the farmhands steadily employed on a *folwark* or on a peasant holding. Subject to the draft were the townspeople, the manor officials, the petty *szlachta* (*zaścianki*), and all kinds of loose journeymen who formed a good part of the village population. In the strongly proletarianized Plock province, these landless peasants became seriously alarmed over their impending fate, and they violently opposed all registration measures and medical control for enlistment. Here lay a chance of gaining the support of the lower strata of the village population, by inciting them to oppose the draft, but the Red organization was hesitant about enlisting direct support from the peasants. Many local organizers were anxious lest a too-broad propaganda endanger the conspiracy before its time, or lest it assume a too-radical attitude against the *szlachta*. Most of the leaflets directed toward the peasants before the outbreak of armed insurrection played a patriotic or a religious tune; they recalled the memory of Kościuszko and the brave scytheman Głowacki; they did not transcend the limits of the Central National Committee's promises.

On 22 January 1863, the Central National Committee gave the signal for a general insurrection against the Russians. The time was ill-chosen; Red leaders had been forced to act because of the threatening conscription of their party members. The committee assumed the title of Provisional National Government and, along with a manifesto inviting the nation to fight, issued two important decrees.* The first declared that all peasants now farming any amount of land, never mind by what right, would immediately become full owners of their holdings and would retain all the rights or privileges involved. All former charges due

* See Appendix, section *H*.

the landlords, such as compulsory labor, ransom, rent, and the like, would be suppressed immediately. The landowners would be indemnified later out of government funds. The second decree declared that every landless citizen who volunteered in the national army would receive, after the war and on application, three *morgi* (four acres) of land from the national domains, free and with full title. The same would apply to the widow and children of an insurgent killed on the battlefield. The decrees of 22 January went further in two respects than the August proclamation. First, they expressly mentioned that the new *uwłaszcze-nie* would embrace not only the holdings but also the rights and privileges attached to them, and this included the servitudes. The peasant was not to be deprived of his rights to the forests. Second, mention was made of the landless peasants, who would also be entitled to *uwłaszczenie* if they chose to participate in the struggle.

The impact of the decrees depended on the ability of the organization to inform the countryside as soon as possible of these provisions, and on its ability thereafter to enforce them. The Provisional National Government attached the utmost importance to this problem. All insurrectionary detachment commanders were instructed to gather the inhabitants of each locality they were occupying or passing through and to read them the decrees and leave printed copies of them. A protocol of the proclamation was to be drawn in three copies, one to be given to the mayor (as representative of the landlords), one to the rector, and the last to be sent to the national chief of the county (*powiat*). The landlord was to be instructed not to collect any dues from the peasants and not to enforce labor duties under threat of the severest penalty. The peasants, on the other hand, were to be admonished to abstain from all infringement on private property, while obeying the new national officials and supporting the insurrection.

The effect of these proclamations was not and could not be immediate. Only a small number of peasants were drawn in advance into the conspiracy. The first armed encounters of the insurgents were not a great success, and only after a week or two did larger insurgent detachments come into being in some parts of the country, of a size capable of impressing the population. It must also be emphasized that the decrees could not bring dramatic change, since compulsory labor had already been suppressed

nearly everywhere for sixteen months, and the January installments of ransom and rent had already been paid in most instances.
The decrees amounted merely to a promise, which would materialize or not depending on the sincerity of the insurgents and on
their successes. Both seemed dubious, in the eyes of the peasants.
Only in a few regions did major groups of peasant volunteers
join the national ranks on the first night, 22 January. Many of
the peasants reacted to the outbreak of the insurrection in another
way: They tried to take advantage of the situation by getting
rid of their immediate adversaries, that is, the landowners. In
some regions of the southern part of the country, manors were
attacked by peasant crowds and the landlords or their officials
taken into custody and delivered to the county jail as enemies of
the emperor; property was damaged occasionally. Such behavior
was imitative of the Galician events of 1846, and this example
would certainly have spread had the insurgents been as feeble
and irresolute as in Galicia or had the authorities incited the
peasants to such misdeeds, even indirectly. Such was not the
case. The legal authorities, headed by Wielopolski, were most
anxious not to let the situation evolve toward a social upheaval.
Backed by the Russian armed forces, they efficiently suppressed
the peasant excesses. Frequently, when peasants brought to town
a number of bound prisoners, the latter were liberated with
apologies, while their escort was flogged or arrested. The peasants
actually attacked the wrong adversary. It is true that the great
majority of the landowners was averse to the insurrection and
that the White leaders openly opposed it. But the insurgents, on
the other hand, also restrained the peasant outbursts and branded
them as Russian provocation. All these factors combined contributed to dampening the revolutionary fire, and by the end of
February the countryside could be considered under control. It
was paradoxical that in the same situation both the czarist army
and the national guerrilla were combating the danger of a social
revolution.

The would-be peasant rebellion of 1863 had, nevertheless, one
very important political consequence: It sped up the radical turn
in the White party's attitude. The big landowners simply could
not run the risk of being considered antinational in a moment of
social tension. If they too openly opposed the insurrection, the
Reds might well unleash the rural masses against them. Sugges-

tions of the kind were voiced on the extreme left wing, and some landlords had already been put to death for collaboration with the czarist commandment. Other factors, which were connected with foreign policy, also played a role in the White party's about-face, but its fear of a common front of Reds and peasantry is considered the strongest reason in contemporary thinking. In February and March 1863 the Whites crossed over to the side of the insurrection; at the same time they succeeded in markedly influencing the direction of the movement. The secret Provisional National Government was changed in ways which gave the ascendancy to sympathizers of the White program; and the local national administrations on the Palatinate and county levels were left in the hands of landowners or moderately disposed clergymen.

From early spring to late fall 1863, that is, during the period of the most intense guerrilla warfare, the policy of the National Government (the word *Provisional* was dropped after May 1863) in peasant questions was consequently shaped in a spirit of compromise between the moderate wing of the Red and the progressive wing of the White parties. The adopted slogan was "National unity in the fight for independence." The principle of *uwłaszczenie*, as settled by the decrees of 22 January, was solemnly and repeatedly affirmed. Landowners were advised not to collect rent or ransom, even if the villagers were willing to pay; in instances of disobedience, the landlord was often sentenced by the national authorities to public flogging before the assembled village community. But this was also the limit which these authorities did not dare to overstep. No steps were taken to confer on the peasants the formal ownership of their holdings. Nor was any attempt made to distribute to the peasants the land of open enemies of the insurrection (even of the Russian entail owners). Timid proposals for summoning peasants to a more active role in the movement and conferring on them confidential posts in the national administration on the communal level, and even a higher level, were overruled or postponed. In guerrilla detachments most peasants were armed only with scythes and committed to fatigue duties, while the actual fighting was done by the rifleman companies composed of townfolk or intelligentsia.

Two further examples illustrate the characteristic behavior of the national authorities. The *uwłaszczenie* was a complex problem, and the January decrees had settled only the general lines. Many side questions and individual cases were to be decided. What groups of peasants and what kinds of land were to be covered by the *uwłaszczenie* principle? Which claims to servitudes should be considered valid? How should other peasant dues such as compulsory hire be handled? In all cases which seemed not to be expressly determined by the January decrees, the national authorities, which were composed on the local level mostly of the wealthy gentry, decided against the peasants. This was also true in settling all kinds of conflicts between landlords and farmhands on the *folwark*, conflicts bound to emerge in those critical times; and in dealing with peasants accused of illegally invading the forests and felling timber for their present or future needs. In numerous instances, the peasants could have acquired the feeling that the national government was not an entirely democratic one—that it was inclined, as of old, to side with the *szlachta*.

The other problem was a still more delicate one. In every civil war, the insurgent government tries to secure the nation's obedience not only by patriotic slogans and acts of social justice but also by means of threats or actual violence. Cases of collaboration with the enemy, and particularly of spying on the guerrillas, must be severely punished. Under the 1863 conditions this led to summary executions of actual or alleged enemies. Hundreds of peasants were hung by the national gendarmerie in 1863—and though many of these cases might have been justified by actual guilt, one cannot avoid the suspicion that many insurgent commanders were more eager to condemn and execute peasants or Jews than members of the privileged classes, even when their guilt was manifest. Dozens of peasants were hung not on charge of treason but because of attacks on the landowners' property, and examples have been quoted in which the landlord informed against villagers considered troublemakers and had them hung on the charge of spying. The dreadful abuses inseparable from civil war hit the peasants more heavily than any other class.

What, in such circumstances, was the actual attitude of the peasants toward the insurrection? Thousands and thousands of facts have been extracted by historians from archival and printed sources, and every possible thesis assumed in advance can be supported by overwhelming and reliable evidence: that the peasants enthusiastically supported the insurrection; were barely in favor of it; were cowed into submission; were totally indifferent (either out of ignorance or calculation); were trying to remain neutral; or were savagely opposed to the national fight, for more or less specific reasons. Each theory can be proved by adequately selected and perfectly authentic sources, or by a skillful equipoise of accents which suggests to the reader (and to the author himself) a comforting conviction of objectivity. One thing is obvious about the attitude of the peasants in 1863: it varied greatly over time, depending on the development of a series of factors.

The first to be discussed is the impact of *uwłaszczenie*. On 1 April 1863, the second quarterly payment of rent and ransom fell due. It was not paid, and there was no attempt to exact it (with only minor exceptions). Thus the peasants in Congress Poland could feel free at last from their feudal burden. And they knew they had been freed by the insurrection—a fact important not so much because of the gratitude it inspired as because it was proof of the insurrection's authority and power. The peasants were not necessarily persuaded of the insurrection's victory, but they did see that the conflict might have a positive influence on their interests, especially if it should endure. This accounts for a visible change in the peasants' attitude beginning with spring 1863, from distrust or hostility to expectant neutrality or more or less open benevolence.

On the other hand, the peasants, together with the rest of the population, were bearing all the horrors of civil war: the fighting, fires, and lootings; the misuses of both adversaries; the contradictory orders from the Polish and Russian sides, both supported by threats and blindly dispensed repressions. Numerous peasant groups were drawn into the struggle, partly under pressure, partly of their own accord out of a spirit of adventure or under the influence of the priests. The religious element played an important role in the eastern parts of Congress Poland, where the adherents of the Greek-Uniate rites felt endangered by official Orthodoxy. In western Lithuania the insurrection assumed a predominantly popular, national-Lithuanian character: the well-to-do peasants were revolting not only against czarism but against their masters, who were mostly of Russian and Balto-German origin. Peasant volunteers in insurgent detachments often belonged to the wealthier, formerly regulated strata, from the national domains or from the Zamoyski entail. The Kurpie region on the East Prussian border, well known for its bellicose and patriotic traditions, also furnished many volunteers. Numerous peasants were active in the national gendarmerie, in the same detachments which were enforcing obedience on the rural population. But it can generally be assumed that the bulk of the population was simply trying to survive without incurring the anger of either of the fighting sides unless absolutely necessary. Let us state further that all Russian attempts at organizing or arming the Polish peasants against the insurgents proved ineffective. In some regions, village guards were formed by the Russian authorities, but they mostly remained inactive or even passed their arms on to the insurgents. The German colonists, however, were an exception; most of them collaborated with the Russian forces.

The attitude of the rural population had a decisive influence on the fate of the guerrilla in any given region. The Ukrainian peasants, traditionally anti-Polish, opposed the insurrection and took part in the disarming of the small Polish detachments. Hence the struggle in the Kiev province came to an end in a matter of days. The Byelorussian peasant in the Polesie region remained passive but hostile in face of the Polish movement; and consequently even such energetic commanders as Roginski and Traugutt were unable to hold out for more than a week or two. The benevolent neutrality of the population was an indispensable condition for the guerrilla's survival; in areas where the population really identified itself with the movement, it had a real chance to last and even to achieve success. This occurred in, among other places, the Holy Cross Mountains, where some thousands of insurgents survived the hard winter of 1863/64 and could not be dislodged despite Russian efforts.

This last development is related to the next phase of the war. By autumn 1863, hopes of foreign armed intervention had all but vanished; the czarist regime's reprisals, ever more cruel, were becoming more efficient; and the now disenchanted propertied classes were beginning to withdraw from the movement. Thus in its last and declining period the movement was to assume again a more radical character. The National Government, now headed by Romuald Traugutt (1826–64), decided upon a more direct approach to the peasants. A government decree signed on 27 December 1863 prescribed new and severe penalties—including death—for all offenses against the insurrectionary *uwłaszczenie*.

All guilty landowners or their officials would be tried by special courts, including assessors chosen from among the peasants. Local commanders were also instructed to base the organization, now deserted by the gentry, on the popular elements. General Józef Hauke-Bosak (1834–71), now in command of the insurgent forces in the southwest, carried out these principles with much success. One of his actions was to raid the forest offices in the national estates. Account books of forest depredations were publicly burnt, under the eyes of the villagers, thus demonstrating that the national authorities were siding with the peasants on the important issue of forest servitudes. Bosak actually gained much popularity among the peasants of the Sandomir region. In the last months of the insurrection, guerilla detachments, where they still existed, as in the Lublin and Podlasie regions, were almost exclusively composed of peasants and often had peasant commanders as well. After a year of struggle the insurrection, which had begun its fight without the peasants, was ending as a popular movement.

It was ending nevertheless, and the decisive blow delivered by Russia was connected again with the agrarian question. The trump card of the January insurrection—the *uwłaszczenie* decrees—was now reversed against it, as the czarist government adopted their chief provisions.

13

THE RUSSIAN REFORM IN CONGRESS POLAND

The contrast between czarist Russian and national Polish conditions of *uwłaszczenie* was nowhere more striking than in the western (formerly Polish) provinces of the empire. Lithuanian, Byelorussian, and Ukrainian peasants had suffered drastic evictions in the last years preceding 1861, and the reform of that year proved to be particularly disadvantageous for them. As a result, peasants in these guberniyas almost unanimously refused to accept the *ustavnyie hramoty*, or village charts which fixed the rights and obligations of each peasant under the new ukase. The Polish decrees of 22 January extended to these territories east of the Bug River and offered the peasants markedly better conditions. The Petersburg government was quick in grasping the issue. As early as 16 February 1863, it was decided that in order to "save" Lithuania from the Polish danger, conditions of *uwłaszczenie* must be significantly improved. The new ukase was published 1 March, Old Style; 13 March, New Style. It ordered (1) that the *ustavnyie hramoty* be verified and corrected in the five Lithuanian provinces; (2) that all compulsory labor be discontinued at once; (3) that the redeeming procedure be shortened and made compulsory; (4) that the value of the peasants' charges be reduced by 20 percent. New Russian officials were sent into the countryside as agents of "Little Father the Czar," who was to liberate the peasants from the yoke of the Polish *szlachta*. The peasants naturally presented to these protectors their complaints against the landlords who had been stripping them of land since 1857, even after the debates on emancipation had started. Muravieff, the new governor-general in Vilno, supported these claims with the argument that small-holders and landless peasants had been the pillars of the insurrection and that granting land to the peasants would strengthen the conservative element in the countryside. As a result of the verification of the *hramoty* the area granted to the peasants was augmented by 12–19 percent, according to the guberniya. In the Minsk guberniya, where the peasants had been exceptionally badly treated in the previous years, the correction figure was even higher: 41 percent. In some counties (*uiezdy*) the amount of the peasants' land was doubled. A narrower analysis shows us that the verification procedure did not amount in most cases to an actual assignment of estate lands to the peasants. Rather it obviated future evictions which would befall the peasants were the former ukase fully enforced. Nevertheless, it can be affirmed that the Polish insurrection forced the Russian government to give back to the Lithuanian and Byelorussian peasants some of the land which had been snatched away from them by the Polish *szlachta*. As to the amount of peasant charges, they were reduced to one-third, on the average, and in some regions even to one-fifth of their former value. The chief purpose of this measure was the undermining of the large landowners, who constituted the chief support of Polonism in these provinces.

Two months later, when the insurrection extended to the Ukraine, a similar modification of the reform of 1861 was introduced by ukase in the three southwestern guberniyas. These moves by the czarist government confirmed the Byelorussian and Ukrainian peasants in their indifference to, if not hostility against, the insurrection (the Lithuanian peasants were an exception, for reasons given above).

As for the Congress Kingdom, Czar Alexander II was much

more reluctant to abandon his policy of seeking the support of the Polish propertied classes (and of backing their interests). Only in July 1863 was Wielopolski released from his functions. By August the czar had resolved to change his previous agrarian policy. In September, Nikolai Milyutin was sent to Warsaw on a reconnoitering mission. He was a liberal-minded bureaucrat who had formerly advocated a more pro-peasant version of the Russian reform. Milyutin came back to Petersburg two months later and gave his opinion bluntly: "The Polish peasants are following the National Government because it has given them full title to land. The only way of curbing the rebellion is to appease the peasants, and this can only be done by granting them what they have already gained from the insurrection." The czar's approval of this point of view followed in December, and the new ukases on *uwłaszczenie* were eventually signed on 19 February/2 March 1864. There were actually four of them. The first outlined the general principles of *uwłaszczenie*.* It declared that all peasants using even the smallest holdings would become full owners. All holdings illegally taken from them since 1846 would be returned to them. All unfarmed land belonging by right to the peasants would be divided among the landless population. Patches of land allocated to innkeepers and millers, as well as to farmhands and foresters, were excluded from the operation; they were to remain with the *folwark*. The peasants were to receive their titles of property free, as a gift of the czar, although a land tax was to be imposed which was not to exceed two-thirds of the hitherto paid rent or ransom.

The second ukase assigned an indemnification to the landowners for the losses suffered. A liquidation committee was established in Warsaw. Its agents were to calculate the charges of every peasant. Various deductions were provided for; the final amount was to be capitalized by 6 percent, that is, the multiplier $16\frac{2}{3}$ was applied in order to fix the capital sum to be paid. This multiplier was less advantageous for the landowners than those used in Prussian Poland and Galicia, twenty-five and twenty, respectively. The indemnification was to be paid to private owners in "liquidation bonds" guaranteed by the state. They would be redeemed in the course of the next decades; their interest and amortization would be paid out of the land tax imposed on the peasants.

* See Appendix, section *I*.

The third ukase was concerned with the commune self-government. The previous system, government of the commune by the mayor, an agent of the landlord, was now abolished. In its place, a new two-grade administration was introduced. On the lower level was the "small commune" (*gromada*) composed exclusively of peasants. Above was the "large commune" (*gmina*) composed of several *gromadas*, with the inclusion of adjoining estates and other nonpeasant settlements. The *gromada* was headed by a *soltys*, the *gmina* by a mayor (*wójt*), both elected by the assembly from which, however, landless inhabitants and small-holders with less than three *morgi* were excluded.

The fourth and last ukase organized a whole hierarchy of offices which were to carry through the *uwłaszczenie:* a "Polish committee" in Petersburg, an "organizing committee" in Warsaw, and numerous local committees, one for every two to three counties (*powiaty*).

On the whole, the Russian *uwłaszczenie* was relatively close to the Austrian system. But the important thing was that it followed, at least on the surface, the lines of the national decrees of 22 January: the title of property granted to all the peasants; an indemnification for the landowners; a promise of land to some of the landless. The political aim of the reform was to win over the peasants for czarist Russia, and this aim determined the scope of the reform itself. Polish democrats demonstrated that, in spite of defeat, they had attained one of their major objectives, forcing the czar to confirm their own scheme of *uwłaszczenie* and thus assuring full land ownership to a larger number of peasants and under relatively better conditions than anywhere else in central and eastern Europe. This "Polish" *uwłaszczenie* was to be introduced in all the provinces where the insurrection itself had been active, not only in Congress Poland but also in the adjoining Lithuanian, Byelorussian, and Ukrainian guberniyas. This achievement, as we shall see, was to foster important political consequences in the near future.

The reform was at first a marked success for the Russian government, in that it achieved its objective of undermining the insurrection. The great majority of the peasants now had their eyes fixed on the realization of the reform in their own villages; they wanted to be on hand and on good terms with the Russian authorities. Guerrilla warfare was soon abandoned; only groups which had no way of returning to their villages continued the fight until summer 1864. The insurrection was doomed, but another fight was starting, centering on the mode of application of the new legislation.

According to Milyutin's plan, it was to be introduced by a new set of Russian officials, brought in for that purpose from the empire. Some of these were radicals by conviction who tried their best to undermine the stand of the big property owners and to provide the peasants with as much land as possible. But the leaders of the Organizing Committee considered their work primarily political and were soon to stifle the more radical course. The new viceroy, Count Fedor Berg, was a strong conservative who sympathized with the Polish aristocracy. The reform, undertaken with much zeal and determination, was soon to dwindle to half-measures, illogicalities, and artificial compromises.

The newly arrived Russian officials were sent out over the country during summer 1864 and were assailed by thousands of petitions complaining of the landlord's wrongdoings and clearly overstepping the new law in their demands. In every private estate, a liquidation table was now to be drawn which was destined to have a double effect. It was to be the legal means of the landlords' indemnification, and it was to fix the limits of property assigned to each peasant, together with charges and privileges. In national estates, where no indemnification was anticipated, liquidation tables were replaced by so-called donation tables. The drawing, verifying, and ratifying of these documents proved an arduous task. The most complex problem was to determine which lands would pass over to the peasants and which were to be left to the landlord. We have seen above how difficult it was to distinguish in practice between a small-holder obligated to farm work (who ought now to become a full owner) and a farmhand endowed with a patch of land (who was to be excluded from *uwłaszczenie*). The Organizing Committee accordingly drew up the following rule: Persons lodged in buildings belonging to the estate would be considered farmhands, and those living in the villages peasants. This was leaving individual fate to pure accident. Numerous were the estates which did not invest in lodgings for their manpower, and so their farmhands, who lodged in the villages, suddenly became eligible for ownership. The opposite also happened: If a small-holder unwittingly moved into a house considered to belong to the estate, he abruptly lost not only his lodging but his holding as well. Numerous other problems developed, concerning nonpeasant holdings owned by burghers, German and Jewish colonists, the petty *szlachta* (*zaścianki*), and miners in the national estates; and the major question of the servitudes. All these matters were gradually settled by the Organizing Committee, most often in a casuistic way. Generally speaking, the peasants received better treatment on private than on national estates, where the government was at once party and judge. The Polish aristocrats had more acquaintances in official circles and knew how to defend their interests, and so the peasants were treated better on the middle and smaller estates than in the latifundia. Individual decisions often depended upon the deportment of a given village (or a given landlord) during the insurrection. In the economically more advanced northwestern provinces, the capitalist changes which began before 1846 were now considered established, whereas in the east much land which had been taken from the peasants after 1846 now reverted to them and they were consequently better endowed. It can also be assumed that the more ruthless a landlord had been in dealing with his peasants in the past, the better treatment he received at the time of *uwłaszczenie*. The mild and humane squires, particularly those who had treated the peasants well out of patriotic motives, were now doubly penalized, because the peasants could legally claim more land from them and because the Russian authorities carried out the reform in a spirit hostile to them, since they were considered political suspects. Numerous were the squires of middle-sized estates who were ruined, first by the insurrection and the following reprisals and then by the reform, and were obliged to sell their estates.

Evaluation of the czarist reform in Russia and Poland is an arduous task, because the reform did not follow a uniform course. Here, the average data are particularly misleading. For Russian scholars, the immeasurable quantity of official sources presented the crucial problem. The number of village charts alone (each pertaining to one estate, i.e., several villages) exceeds fifty thousand, not including the Lithuanian and Ukrainian provinces. Some monographical work was done, concerning single counties (*uiezdy*) or guberniyas, but Professor Zaïontchkovsky undertook a general approach. He took as his starting point Lenin's classification dividing European Russia into three regions and six subregions. He selected twenty counties in twelve guberniyas as specimens of the subregions and studied with utmost care all the charts of the territory they included, which amounted to 9 percent of all Russia. There were in total about four thousand charts. His analysis descended from the estate to the village and, still lower, to the level of the individual holding. In this way he was able to correlate the several sets of data and discover dissimilar treatment of various peasant groups. On the basis of this microanalysis a synthesis was then elaborated which showed the main characteristics of the reform in each of the country's regions and subregions.

This method of research is impossible where Congress Poland is concerned. The liquidation and donation tables—the equivalents of the Russian *hramoty*—were destroyed during the last war, with only accidental lots remaining here and there. Files of the central Russian authorities are also nonexistent or inaccessible. What has remained are the records of some of the local authorities on the guberniya and county levels and the archives of some of the latifundia. One Polish historian, K. Groniowski, chose as the objects of analysis two guberniyas out of ten, one economically advanced and one backward. He studied an immense amount of evidence concerning single decisions and attitudes of officials on different levels; he classified this material according to topic and then constructed a complex but believable picture of the Russian agrarian policy in theory and in practice.

The accomplishments of the reform of 1864 in Congress Poland may seem impressive, when viewed from official records. In 1809 the peasants probably held (in what was to become Congress Kingdom) about 10.7 million *morgi*. For 1819 the analogous figure is only 7.8; for 1859, only 6.8. In the late sixties, that is, after the reform, it seems to rise again to 8.3 million. This represents an increase of 22 percent; the corresponding figure for private estates is 32 percent. These figures, however, are entirely fictitious. On the one hand, the pre-reform assets of the peasants were calculated too low because the administration, under the influence of the landlords, did not acknowledge many categories of smallholders as possessors. On the other hand, the official reports on the reform of 1864 included in the final tabulation nonpeasant categories of population such as the burghers in the "farming boroughs." An exact reconciliation of pre-reform and post-reform figures is difficult to obtain, but various historians estimate the actual gain of the peasants as 5–8 percent despite the fact that the number of peasant holdings allegedly rose from 449,000 to 678,000. This increase is exaggerated, because the first figure was purposely lowered.

The major failure of the czarist reform concerned its treatment of the landless peasants. They had been promised land from the national domains, and the promise was not fulfilled. Some of these estates were given to the Russian entail owners as compensation for the losses suffered on account of the reform; new entails were then established to recompense fresh groups of victorious generals and deserving statesmen. With the exception of the national forests, which remained state property, there remained but few lands to distribute generously. The number of landless peasants who were granted small holdings averaging about three *morgi* (four acres) each did not exceed 140,000. Russian veterans and individuals who had served the Russians during the insurrection were favored in this distribution.

The landlords, on the other hand, received 64 million rubles indemnification, but it was paid in bonds which could only be negotiated, at first, with a loss of more than 30 percent. This indemnification also covered the monopoly of the local production and sale of liquors (*propinacja*). This monopoly passed from the landlord to the state. The government, however, did not at first take advantage of the new situation. Although the innkeeper—at that time usually a Jew, since the Jews were again permitted to run inns—paid rent to the Treasury and not to the manor, he bought his spirits from the estate distillery, which functioned as before. Only in the 1890s was the state monopoly of alcohol production introduced in Russia. After that time, private distilleries produced spirits and vodka under state control, and the state supplied the town and village retail shops with liquor.

One further remark: The land tax imposed on the peasants to cover the expense of indemnification remained in force long after all the liquidation bonds had been paid off. The sum paid by the peasants through the land tax to the end of czarist rule in 1915 amounted to 110 million rubles—almost double what had been paid to the landlords.

We have omitted till now the most important concern of the reform—the servitudes. Their role in the peasant economy and in the conflicts with the big landowners has already been stressed. The ukases of 1864 specified that all kinds of servitudes allowed by custom would remain in force temporarily; at a later time regulations would fix the means of their liquidation. This was the only possible course to be taken by the czarist regime, since the National Government had guaranteed the servitudes to the peasants. Accordingly, the local commissions, in drafting the liquidation tables, collected and recorded data on the servitudes. The task was an arduous one. The peasants advanced exaggerated claims, and, acting in accordance with those claims, they willfully felled timber in excessive amounts and even grazed their cattle on the landlord's green, before his windows. The Organizing Committee ruled on such cases in a casuistic fashion. In practice, local assessments were strongly influenced by accidental factors. Where the landowner had been a patriot, the peasants were assigned more timber; where he succeeded in bribing the authorities, the servitudes were lowered to almost nothing. The rights of each peasant were delineated in minute detail: so many one- or two-horse carts of firewood to be collected during given periods in indicated parts of the forest; so many cubic meters of timber, so many dead branches, and so many bags of pine needles for litter; so many grown or young cattle, sheep, goats, pigs, etc., to have the right to graze at a given time, in different forest preserves. Gathering of berries, mushrooms, hazelnuts, and the like was also regulated, as were fishing rights. All these meticulous assessments did not eliminate conflict, the more so, since the local decisions were openly inequitable. Thus in the national forests the servitudes were entirely suppressed and only a few peasants were indemnified in land. On private estates, 65 percent of the peasants were granted grazing servitudes, 55 percent fuel servitudes, 39 percent timber servitudes, 21.5 percent litter servitudes. There were, however, large regional and local differences in the number of peasants who were to enjoy these rights and in the magnitude of the rights themselves.

According to the original meaning of the ukase, the servitudes were to be redeemed by the landlord, and the peasant was to be indemnified in land for resigning his rights. This regulation needed implementing orders, but the authorities did not hurry. The servitudes were an antiquated custom, and their liquidation was in the interest of good forestry. On the other hand, they were still indispensable for the peasants' economy, and their compulsory abolition would provoke violent protests. The Russian government saw no reason why it should anger the peasants in order to please the Polish *szlachta*. On the contrary, a continuing servitude problem would maintain a state of friction between the two classes of Polish society, which seemed convenient for the Russian regime. In 1872 the government decided that the liquidation of servitudes would be left to private agreements, requiring only that it be ratified by competent authorities.

The bargaining procedure between the squire and the commune was thus reduced to the simple question of determining the number of *morgi* per head the peasants would accept and the manor could afford. The peasants were in no hurry; nor was the squire, except in special situations. The feud could well last over decades. Control of the recognized rights invariably led to unceasing conflict. The landlords tried to curtail the rights of the village; the peasants filed petitions, brought actions, and in some cases resorted to violence. The Russian officials formally acted as mediators, adjudicating each case in accordance with the balance of bribes but, more often than not, delaying any case which was a source of personal profit. The same police officer who only yesterday encouraged the peasants to resist the squire's encroachments would now fine them for illegal grazing or cutting of trees. It was Polish public opinion that the Russian government used this bone of contention—the servitudes—in order to maintain strife in Polish society. The strife, of course, had not originated with foreign enemies, but the Russians were not interested in containing it—they even fed the fire. The regime did not recognize that this policy would have unexpected consequences. The fight over the servitudes mobilized the peasants and strengthened their class consciousness; it was later to arouse opposition not only against the landlords but against the czarist rule as well.

From an economic point of view, the dragging on of the servitudes conflict was harmful to both sides. The unique circumstance which could force the landlord to accede to the peasants' terms was a need to sell the forest, most often to pay debts. It was necessary to abolish servitudes before the forest could be felled. Therefore, the liquidation of the servitudes by private agreement brought about, not an improvement in forestry, but rather a more rapid devastation of the forests.

14

THE CONGRESS POLAND
PEASANTRY AFTER
EMANCIPATION

The further evolution of agrarian structure in the country was now to develop according to the laws of free capitalist competition. There were, however, some limits set to this competition by the government, which was anxious to control the Polish peasants and to hold them in protective custody. Even after *uwłaszczenie* the peasants remained an estate with special obligations and privileges. A distinct bureaucratical hierarchy solely occupied with these questions was maintained: a peasant commission on the guberniya level, a peasant commissar in every county (*powiat*). The duty of these officials was to protect the peasants from being wronged. All land granted to the peasants under the 1864 reform, called "ukase land," could be inherited or purchased only by another peasant; the same was true for "servitude land," given to the peasant in exchange for servitude rights. Only land which had been purchased by the peasant in another way, for example, in connection with the partitioning of an estate, could later be disposed of without limitation. Another provision limited the peasants' right to divide their holdings among successors. The share of each successor was to be eight acres (six *morgi*) at least; otherwise the division would be invalid. Small farmers not belonging to the peasant estate, such as burghers or petty *szlachta*, were not bound by such formalities, which were difficult to enforce and control.

An immediate and unquestionable result of *uwłaszczenie* was a marked improvement in the standard of living of the peasant class. This progress in the mode of habitation, clothing, and nourishment is confirmed by much evidence, although it mostly benefited the well-to-do part of the village population. There was also a sharp rise in the population, resulting from improvement of hygienic conditions. Since few persons left the countryside, the result was a partitioning of peasant property. Some peasants who owned larger holdings were able to buy more land, but a large percentage of small-holders, and particularly those who had been remunerated after 1864, were unable to retain their property. Another unsuccessful group of farmers consisted of the owners of the smaller estates who did not know how to adapt to the new conditions. Numerous estates were sold at auction during the two decades following the insurrection. They were not parceled, but sold to other landowners. Until the late eighties there was little parceling in Congress Poland. In the twenty-five years following the reform, the amount of land in peasant hands rose by only 400,000 hectares, that is, by 8.1 percent. These figures include the increase resulting from the redemption of servitudes. In the northwestern region, big properties constituted more than half the arable land.

The 1870s witnessed a continuing rise in grain prices—a trend which did not induce the farmers to introduce more economical methods. The estates adopted crop rotation and the peasants a three-field system with no land fallow, but the evolution was slow and was to take until the end of the century. Changes were also to come in farm machinery—reaping and threshing machines would become common; seeders as well as steam engines would make their appearance. Some machines were already in use on some of the bigger peasant farms. Oxen for traction were now finally replaced by horses. Sheep breeding remained at a standstill, while cattle breeding rose. Total agricultural production rose mainly because of an increase of tilled area as the result of deforestation (rather than because of a major increase in output per acre). There was, nonetheless, a marked increase in acreage devoted to better-paying crops such as wheat, barley, and sugar beets.

The world crisis in grain prices caused by cheap American wheat now being sent to western Europe was to hit central Poland relatively late—about 1884. During the next decade, local grain prices dropped by 50–60 percent. But what is more important, Congress Poland ceased to export wheat, and a commercial tradition which had lasted more than four centuries came to an end. The growth of population together with a rise in the standard of living now absorbed domestic food production. A violent displacement of the economy occurred in the course of one generation. Instead of exporting grain to the West, the country now supplied Russia with textile goods.

The fall of grain prices could not be stopped by a protective customs barrier, as was done in Germany. Congress Poland belonged to the Russian customs system, and Russia remained an exporter of grain. The agrarian crisis was therefore quite painful for the big Polish farms. Economically weaker estates were to be partitioned, while stronger ones tried to intensify their production. Not much progress, however, was to be noticed in the agrarian economy before the 1890s.

The growth of rural population together with the absence of partitioning were two factors disadvantageous to conditions in the Polish village. Two consequences were a growth in the number of landless peasants (220,000 in 1870; 849,000 in 1891), and a growth in the number of peasant holdings (593,000 in 1870; 717,000 in 1899). The average size of a peasant holding was decreasing.

A prolonged and still-not-concluded discussion has divided the specialists in Polish agrarian history on the subject of the evolution of the Polish village after *uwłaszczenie*. The theory elaborated by Lenin seventy years ago, based chiefly on Russian statistical material, is one of division into contrasting layers (*rozwarstwienie*). On the one hand, some of the peasant farmers now endowed with property had become small capitalists; they were augmenting and improving their operations, employing and exploiting wage labor, and entering the ranks of the small bourgeoisie. On the other hand, the poorer majority of the villagers was inexorably declining toward proletarianization. This theory has also been applied to central Poland, in an effort to ascertain the relative conditions and attitudes of the well-to-do peasants (*kulaki*), the intermediate group, and the poor. At the same time, both casual observations and more careful research point to another pair of phenomena. A small-holder who had a chance to save some money working off his farm might then add to his possessions by purchase of two or three *morgi*. A larger holding would dwindle when divided among three or four children after the owner's death. According to these observations, the characteristic trend in the Polish village after the *uwłaszczenie* reform was not the polarization of layers (*rozwarstwienie*), but the middle trend, the tendency for all holdings to be a uniform or average size (*średniaczenie*).

It would not be prudent to approve one of these two theories while excluding the other. Both sides quote authentic evidence, and it may be accepted that in the post-reform period some factors favored polarization while others favored uniformity. The sensible approach is to seek the sum of these various effects, that is, the actual course of events, but the problem is not as simple as that. The advocates of the uniformization theory (*średniaczenie*) are interested only in the size of the holding, and they follow the steady fall of that index. Their adversaries in the polarization (*rozwarstwienie*) camp watch not only, or even primarily, the size, but also the general character of the peasant farms: Which were being transformed into small capitalist enterprises, and which were only retarding the inevitable proletarianization of the poor villager? They assume, with good grounds, that the economic progress of the country steadily lowered the size of a farm susceptible to becoming a capitalist enterprise. In a backward region, an owner of thirty *morgi* might live under a natural economy, but in the proximity of a large market an enterprising farmer owning only fifteen *morgi* might become a capitalist. The size index, accordingly, is not enough to give an exact image of what was going on in the countryside.

What does the size index tell us? Between 1870 and 1899, the percentage of the smallest holdings under three *morgi* (four acres) fell from 21.8 percent to 15 percent. Taking into account the rise in the number of holdings, the fall in absolute numbers was not great (about 17 percent, or one-sixth). During the same period, the percentage of middle-sized holdings rose from 40.6 percent to 44.5 percent, and of the larger ones, over fifteen *morgi*, from 37.6 percent to 40.5 percent. What can be deduced from these figures? A cautious conclusion would be that during this period of almost thirty years changes were not rapid. The number of middle-sized holdings increased, which accounts for the theory of uniformity, but the bigger holdings did not fare as badly as would appear, although not every farm in this group should be considered a capitalist enterprise. Our surprise at the decrease in relative and even in absolute number of the smallest farms, should be tempered by the fact that it was illegal to divide peasant farms into lots smaller than six *morgi*. They were so divided, of course, but the divisions were not registered, so that the index of the smaller farms for 1899 is most certainly too low.

One more circumstance must be kept in mind: Averages for the whole Congress Kingdom conceal serious regional differences. We have pointed them out in the past, and do so again. The northwest was the region of strongest capitalist evolution. The southwest was traditionally a region of small-holders. The northeast, and particularly the Suwałki guberniya, contained big peasant farms at a relatively low economic level. Finally, the southeast was the region where social evolution proceeded most slowly and where structural changes appeared at a later period.

The period following the January insurrection was one of severe political repression, of military rule, and of Russification. The Polish population was barred from any participation in official functions. Polish political activities were illegal, and even participation in social and cultural affairs was rendered difficult by the suspicious Russian administration. A rapprochement between the so-called enlightened classes and the peasants was thus rendered exceedingly difficult. Immediately after the reform, some of the wealthy and conservative landowners declared that everything was not yet lost; the *szlachta* ought to accept the new reality and take advantage of it; they ought to "enter the commune" and regain their influence over the peasants while helping them in all kinds of social activities. The program remained a dead letter, notwithstanding some interesting exceptions. The majority of the landowners remained indifferent, the majority of the peasants hostile, and the Russian bureaucracy constantly controlled and counteracted all signs of interest displayed by the landlords in behalf of the peasants. In practice, thirty years after *uwłaszczenie* estates and villages were as two separate worlds. Their people lived side by side, met on workdays in the fields, on Sundays in church, but remained entirely distinct in clothes, habits, manners, prejudices, and even when not in active conflict remained uncooperative.

Important changes occurred among the landowners. Hundreds of them were "bucked off the saddle," as the current saying ran; they were losing their estates and starting afresh in town. New elements were pouring onto the large properties (*ziemiaństwo*): rich burghers, partly of German or Jewish origin, as well as former leaseholders. A small percentage of the landowners engaged in the so-called organic work while introducing agricultural improvements, running experimental farms, publishing agricultural essays, and the like. Such activities concerned the big properties and not the peasants. The village seemed left to its own devices, under the old tutelage of the church, the new one of the Russian officials and the now more efficient exploitation of the Jewish innkeeper and usurer. (Actually, the vast majority of village Jews were craftsmen and petty traders.) Communal self-government remained a fiction—the mayor (*wójt*) was in most cases an illiterate, and the yearly assembly of the commune was limited to formalities. Administrative affairs were run by the commune secretary—a half-educated lower official appointed by the Russian county chief who made a living at the expense of the community. If one wishes a somber caricature of the state of things, one has only to read the admirable short story by Henryk Sienkiewicz, "Sketches in Carbon."

The Russian bureaucracy made an enormous blunder in dealing with the peasant question. It considered the peasants a primitive and passive force, entirely alien to Polish society and capable of assimilation. It was thought in official circles that the czar's benefaction together with class antagonism toward the *szlachta* would render possible a Russification of the rural masses and, consequently, a Russification of Poland. Thus, Russian was introduced as the official language in the commune self-government, and later also as the only language in the parish schools. Attempts were made to introduce the Russian alphabet in Polish printing. The Greek-Uniate church, a denomination prevalent in the eastern parts of the country, was suppressed and its members forcibly converted to Orthodoxy. The Roman Catholic church was also attacked, with the intention of diminishing its influence on the masses. Most of the monastic orders were suppressed, and for a time there was not a single free bishop left in Russian Poland. This policy, pursued for forty years, eventually failed; even more, it brought about opposite results.

After the insurrection, almost all the peasants remained loyal to the regime. As long as the great reform was gradually being put into effect, they knew that their lot depended on the decisions of the Russian officials. Those peasants who had fought in the national ranks had perished or had gone into exile or to Siberia. Those who managed to survive had lost face and authority in the village. Other people had taken the lead: those who had been wise enough to remain indifferent to patriotic slogans; those who were now decorated with commemorative medals "for the quelling of the Polish rebellion." And they did wear these medals with ostentation, if only to spite the squire with whom they squabbled, generally about the servitudes. But such feelings were not to endure. In the course of the next two decades the majority of the peasants were slowly to realize that the Russian regime did not support them in their main class conflicts, and that the Russification policy was detrimental to their interests. It was hard to learn to read and write in a foreign language, and the result was that the peasant children were illiterate as before. It was still harder to file a petition, to bring an action, to persuade an official, to explain one's cause in court, when one had to do with an unintelligible language. The next generation, born after the suppression of compulsory labor, already understood that in order to better its position, to acquire greater liberty and political rights, it must combat not only the Polish *szlachta*, but the czarist regime as well. For such a fight, the peasants needed allies, and they were to find them—not in the residences of the gentry, but in the towns, among the ranks of the intelligentsia.

Liberal-minded journalists and novelists in Warsaw still attached the utmost importance to the peasant problem. But while they had lost hope, since 1863, for any chance of armed insurrection, they desisted from shaping new plans for far-reaching social reform. They too were partisans of "organic work," and they hoped that the program of economy, of science and education, would in due time better the lot of the masses and would transform the ignorant peasant into an enlightened citizen. They did not perceive any means of influencing the peasants other than through traditional channels: the benevolent squire, his charitable wife, the saintly priest—and such stereotypes were not often at hand in actual life. To teach the landlords that they ought to devote themselves to the welfare of the poor; to instruct the peasants that they ought to behave and follow the example of their "elder brothers"—these methods were no longer believed effective. New ways were to be found for reaching the masses.

Early in the seventies, a student of Warsaw University, Konrad Prószynski (1851–1908), had the habit of spending his vacations, together with some friends, hiking around the country, visiting historical sites, and talking with people. He was the son of a Siberian exile, a patriot and a young man obliged to struggle through life. While observing the Polish countryside, he came to the conclusion that the main reason for the peasant's backwardness was illiteracy. There was no use explaining things to him as long as he could not read. There were almost no village schools before 1863, and the new ones were Russian; besides, it would not do to await the growth of a new educated generation. One should help the adults learn to read easily by themselves. Prószynski was a born pedagogue, and after some experiments made during his summer wanderings, he hit upon the right idea. In 1875 he published a new kind of primer, intended for self-instruction, in which he applied a new method of teaching from the start the sound of whole syllables rather than of single letters. This was the famous *Promyk Primer* (Promyk ["sunbeam"] was Prószynski's pen name), which in the years to come was to be distributed in millions of copies and to become familiar to two or three generations of the Polish people. It was to win, thirty years later, the first prize at a competition in London as the best primer in the world. Prószynski began by sending his booklet free to peasants able to read whose addresses he had collected, with the characteristic injunction, "Whenever you teach one of your fellow beings to read, you do him more good than if you present him with a heap of gold." The idea was enormously successful from the start. Orders flowed in from everywhere in the country. Scores of editions followed, gradually improved. Only later did Prószynski adapt his primer to the teaching of writing as well as reading. Still later, an edition for children was prepared. The need for other reading materials was soon felt. With the help of a group of philanthropists, Prószynski opened a publishing house which issued readers, almanacs, and instruction books. The next step was to be a peasant newspaper.

After 1848, periodic leaflets intended for the common people were published in different parts of Poland; but they were uniformly patronizing and moralistic, which did not appeal to the masses. The *Holiday Gazette* (*Gazeta Swiąteczna*) was of another kind. It spoke simply of the villagers' everyday needs and worries and gave practical advice on farming, gardening, housekeeping, and legal procedures. While edited under Russian censorship, the *Gazette* did not touch on politics or teach patriotism; nor did it encourage class struggle. But it also did not preach solidarity, or reliance on the manor or the rectory. "Whenever you need anything," Prószynski used to say, "ask the *Gazette* for advice, but then, shift as best you can, in the framework of your community." This offer was accepted. Very soon, letters to the editor began to flow in from the remotest corners of the country, and a constant dialogue was established between Promyk and his readers. Then village circles of the *Gazette*'s subscribers were formed, which kept busy with promoting fruit growing or beekeeping, fertilization or field drainage. The later peasant cooperative movement was to grow out of this local initiative. The seed planted by Promyk was to actuate the countryside to move in its own behalf. The big reform of the sixties had created the possibilities; Promyk and his friends provided the incentive and later helped the movement with good advice.

The need for such activity was further emphasized when parallel initiatives began to mushroom. Other popular weeklies were founded, and existing newspapers adapted to Promyk's pattern. Self-help organizations spread over the countryside independently of his *Gazette*. Some of Promyk's early followers later took a different course—more patriotic, or more radical, or both. Prószynski was not happy about these developments. He was a conservative and did not understand the need for a political populist movement. But the populist leaders of the next generation, even when attacking Prószynski's *Gazette* for its old-fashioned apolitical style, could not help admitting that they were his spiritual children and successors.

During the two decades which followed the disaster of 1863–64, there were no possibilities for raising the Polish question in international forums. And since the *uwłaszczenie* reform, the old formula of giving land to the peasant in order to win him over to the national cause was dead. It was necessary to try a new step in order to attract the peasants; this one could no longer fit into the pattern of a capitalist society.

In 1882, for the first time, a Socialist party was founded in Poland, under the name "Proletariat." It was of course clandestine and revolutionary. It enlisted workmen and young intellectuals, but it also made an attempt to meet the needs of the peasants. One of the party's proclamations was directed "to those working on the land"; it declared that the victory of socialism would give to the poor the land of the big landowners. It did not say who was to get that land nor under what conditions, and it is doubtful if this proclamation gained wide circulation. The Warsaw Proletariat was in contact with the Russian "*Narodnaia Vola.*" There were, however, no similarities in ideology or tactics between early Polish Socialists and the Russian *narodniks*. Among the Polish emigrants in western Europe, after 1864, *narodnik* views were held by the extreme left wing, but they were not accepted in the country. The *narodniks* expected a peasant rebellion and directed their propaganda towards the people—as is known, with little success. As a result of a far less advantageous reform, the economic situation of the Russian peasant was worse than that of the Polish. The Polish peasant was not yet to be moved by political appeals. And the economic situation was not yet advanced to a stage propitious for a program of land reform, that is, the liquidation of the big estates.

15

PRUSSIAN POLAND BEFORE WORLD WAR I

The Progress of Farming

Agrarian development in the three parts of politically divided
Poland differed more and more with the passage of time. This
was also true of all aspects of economic development. The growth
of big industry, modern communications systems, and state pro-
tectionism enhanced the trend toward economic unification of
each of the Polish provinces with Russia, Prussia, or Austria, respectively. This trend toward unification was particularly strong
in respect to agriculture, since it was powerfully influenced by
the agrarian reform, both its formal content and the means by
which it was put into effect. How differently this reform was enforced in Poznania, Galicia, and Congress Poland was discussed
earlier.

The Poznanian reform was the earliest, the most gradual, and
the least revolutionary in comparison with the latter two. It
favored the big landowners more than the peasants and, among
the latter, the well-to-do element more than the poorer. The net

result was the economic dominance of big estates and big peasant farms—the two kinds of economic units most capable of further economic progress. In Poznania and Pomerania the big property owners retained 50–60 percent of the arable land, on the whole the most fertile and productive areas. They also surpassed the peasants in agricultural technology and in investments in machinery and, consequently, in the rentability of their property. Between 1850 and 1880, it was common in most of the Prussian provinces for big landowners to purchase patches of peasant land from small farmers who were in debt or were compelled to divide a heritage. The state's policy also favored the big producer, since the Junkers still formed the core of the ruling class. During the 1880s, when agriculture in Europe was suddenly imperiled by American competition, Bismarck introduced a protectionist customs barrier, and the prices of grain in Berlin dropped no more than 15 percent throughout the next decade. This drop was easily overcome by the big property owners, who managed both to increase production and to switch to more rentable profitable crops, such as sugar beet.

A steady increase of investments in the Poznanian and Pomeranian estates can be observed beginning with the eighties. Not only was the processing of grain and milk now mechanized; the tilling was now done by steam ploughs. Mineral fertilizers were introduced, and state legislation promoted integration and amelioration proceedings which involved larger numbers of farms. The results of such policies were to become visible later, around 1900. As to the peasant farms, they were also beginning to participate in this evolution. Especially on the fertile soils of the Vistula Delta, Cuiavia, and the Oder Valley, the well-to-do peasant (called *gbur* in Pomerania, *gospodarz* in Poznania) was farming better and profiting more. With a farm of fifty acres or more, he could afford modern tools and machinery; he could change to rotation husbandry, adopting clover and beet culture, or specialize in cattle breeding. The result was that the big peasant farmer was buying land from the poorer one; the phenomenon of polarization (*rozwarstwienie*) was evident and undeniable in these regions. It was less advanced, however, on poorer or mountainous soils.

The boom of farming had its counterpart in the steady growth of a rural proletariat. Mechanization in agriculture had only reached its first stage, and while much less labor was now employed in threshing or harvesting, large numbers of farmhands were still needed, especially in beet fields, for weeding and digging. Around 1880, four-fifths of the population living from agriculture in Poznania and Pomerania were wage earners. This rural proletariat was differentiated. There were the farmhands steadily employed on a *folwark* or a big peasant farm; there were the small-holders (*komornicy*)—remnants of a former epoch—who were given a patch of land in return for a specified number of paid days of labor during the busy season. There were also the owners of minuscule holdings, who earned most of their livelihoods on bigger farms; and there were, finally, foreign seasonal workmen, who will be mentioned below. Until emigration gathered momentum, beginning in the 1880s, there was a surplus of labor in the countryside, and consequently a severe exploitation of farm workers. The Prussian Journeymen Regulation (*Gesinde-Ordnung*) of 1854 imposed strict discipline on the farmhands. They were not permitted to leave before the termination of their yearly contracts; their claims for compensation were rendered almost impossible to satisfy; unions and strikes were forbidden, and then use of physical punishment by the overseer was explicitly permitted by law. This last provision was canceled only in 1900. Housing conditions were poor and wages inadequate.

This situation was to change as a result of emigration, first to the United States and after 1890 mainly to western Germany. In the eastern provinces of Prussia the emigration achieved major proportions in the 1870s. Germans and Jews were the first to emigrate, followed by the Poles. The rural proletariat furnished most of the contingent. They lived under such debased conditions that they had nothing to lose by embarking on an uncertain future. Four and a half million persons left the Prussian provinces east of the Oder-Neisse line before 1914, among them about 3.3 million Germans and 1.2 million Poles from Poznania and Pomerania. Upper Silesia was not touched by emigration, because local industry absorbed all surplus labor.

The decrease in rural manpower due to emigration was compensated for by a steadily growing importation of workmen from the East, mainly from Congress Poland and Galicia. In 1885, for political reasons, Bismarck ordered the eviction from Prussia of all foreign wage earners; 26,000 persons, mostly Poles, were obliged to leave Germany over a period of a few months. This measure appeared contrary to the interests of German agriculture, and the Junkers brought pressure to bear in order to obtain cheaper manpower from abroad. A compromise ensued in 1890. Landowners in Germany were permitted to employ Russian or Austrian wage earners (in practice, Poles from the Congress Kingdom and Galicia), but they had to be single and could be brought in for a season only. This season was set at first at six or seven months, to be prolonged later to ten or eleven months a year, so that the "seasonal" workmen departed for their mother countries before Christmas and were back to work in February. This foreign manpower was to be housed separately so as to remain isolated from the local population (the reason was the fear of a strengthening of the Polish element in Germany). The isolation, of course, made the exploitation of the immigrants easier. The Central Farmhands Board was established in 1905 as the sole agent for the delivery of foreign manpower. This board employed clandestine agitators in Congress Poland and Galicia who lured thousands of young proletarians of both sexes to Germany with promises of good earnings. At the frontier railway station, middlemen awaited, with contracts, whole groups of farmhands to be employed on one estate. As a rule, the crowd was twice as large as the number of people needed, and the middlemen could select the best people and lower the wages. The contracts drafted in German gave rise to unending misuses; in practice, the seasonal workman was helpless against his employer. Notwithstanding, the flow of willing candidates steadily grew, because of the still poorer living conditions in Russian and Austrian Poland. Before 1914, the number of seasonal farmhands employed in German agriculture reached 500,000; four-fifths of the number came from Congress Poland and the rest from Galicia. Only about 200,000 people were employed in the Polish provinces of Prussia; the majority were sent farther west, toward Brandenburg and Saxony. In this way, the Junkers were assured of cheap manpower, while the Polish proletarian from central and southern Poland could earn more by going to Saxony (*na Saksy*) than by staying at home. Thanks to his lower standard of living and enormous efforts, he was able even to save part of his wages.

German agriculture progressed markedly around the turn of the century, and the Polish provinces of Prussia kept pace with the others. Poznania at that time was often called Germany's granary. Thanks to an increase in domestic demand under a protectionist customs barrier, grain prices increased by 25 percent between 1900 and 1913. Prices of land rose still more swiftly, as a result of Polish-German competition, which will be explained later. The landowners, particularly the larger ones, grew richer each year, and they used growing credit balances for farm improvements and other investments. In respect to the use of fertilizers, Poznania was more advanced than most of the Prussian provinces. The upper levels of peasantry were also becoming more progressive, and there was growing specialization on the middle and smaller farms in vegetables, fruit, hops, poultry, etc. As to the amount of crops per acre, Poznania and Pomerania now equaled the western German standards. (The figures will be quoted later when we compare the level of agriculture in all three parts of Poland.)

These circumstances seemingly favored the stabilization of the rural structure. Notwithstanding, the assets of the big properties began to diminish, for reasons to be explained later, although on a smaller scale than elsewhere. In Poznania, estates larger than 100 hectares (240 acres) owned 55 percent of the arable land in 1882; twenty-five years later the figure was only 46 percent, and 30 percent in some regions. The latifundia fared better than the middle-sized estates, and the government extended its protection to the German aristocracy, allowing them to establish new entails, that is, indivisible and inalienable complexes of estates.

The polarization of the peasant society was clearly visible. The bigger peasant farms were growing, because they were buying land from the estates, and the number of dwarf holdings was increasing, because many proletarians invested their small savings in land. In the six regencies of Prussia inhabited by Poles there were 312,000 "dwarf" farms, 92,000 small farms, 133,000 middle-sized farms, and 38,000 big peasant farms (over fifty acres) in 1907. This last group of big farms held 40 percent of all peasant land in Poznania, 50 percent in western Prussia, and 60 percent in eastern Prussia. Only in Upper Silesia were the big peasant farms less developed; in this region there were numerous dwarf holdings owned by mine and factory workers. In the regency of Opole, such dwarf holdings occupied 12 percent of all peasant land (compared with 5–6 percent in the other provinces).

After the end of the nineteenth century, the rural population in Prussian Poland decreased not only in percentage but also in absolute figures. This was the reason why manpower had to be imported in the form of seasonal workers.

The Struggle for Land with Germanism

'The boom in agriculture, the progress of education, and the de-
'velopment of a prosperous peasantry contributed to the develop-
:ment of political activity among an important fraction of the
:Polish rural population under the Prussian rule. The course of
:this activity was to be determined by the policy of the Prussian
'(after 1871, the German) government. It was an anti-Polish
:policy, dedicated to total Germanization of the country. This
:policy was pursued under Bismarck after the unification of Ger-
:many. German was declared the only language admissible for
'official intercourse, and Polish was almost eliminated from the
:schools. Under such conditions the Polish peasantry, especially
:its upper and well-to-do groups, was ready to collaborate with
:the "enlightened" classes—the landowners, the bourgeoisie, and
:the clergy—for the defense of the Polish cause.

The first manifestation of such collaboration was the Polish
:League, which was founded in the revolutionary year 1848 by a
:group of liberal-minded landowners. This league organized a
:number of village circles composed of groups of peasants under
:the leadership of the parson. The number of peasants who enlisted
'can be estimated at about twenty thousand—mostly in Poznania,
:but also in western Prussia. A circle would assemble each Sunday
:after church, and a small contribution would be collected, gazettes
:read aloud, and political events commented upon. This kind of
:activity subsided after the revolution's downfall, when the Polish
:League was dissolved by the authorities. Nevertheless, small
:groups of peasant activists persisted in many regions; they were
:the most useful during election times.

The peasantry was to develop a more independent attitude
later, in connection with their immediate material interests. Beginning with the 1850s, the Polish landlords in Poznania and
Pomerania began to organize regional agricultural societies whose
purpose was to advance agricultural technology. These societies
combined in 1861 into the Central Economic Society, which was
interested not only in discussing professional matters but also in
defending the interests of the big properties. The members of the
societies were generally owners of the larger estates, and peasant
farmers, even though invited to join, did not find in these bodies
much concern for their problems.

In 1862, a year of growing liberalism in Prussia, the first agricultural society composed of Polish peasants was founded in the village of Piaseczno in the province of western Prussia. The founder was Walenty Stefański (1813–77), a former radical leader of the forties who was now retired from politics but still nursed ideas about promoting democracy through legal organizations with mainly economic aims. The peasant activists of Piaseczno soon founded, in the neighboring borough of Gniew, a loan society, a savings bank, an agricultural school, and a society of peasant housewives, and they advertised their activity in a local newspaper. Similar associations, called *agronomic circles (kółka rolnicze)*, began to multiply, and in 1866 the movement spread to Poznania. The propertied classes were wise enough not to oppose the idea; on the contrary, they offered the peasants their help and were thus able to control and influence them. Numerous circles were organized by or headed by priests, stewards of bigger estates, or even landlords. In 1873, the Central Economic Society proposed that the mission of organizing the circles be undertaken by Maximilian Jackowski. He was then over fifty years old, a landowner of average fortune and somewhat of a self-made man. Leaving to his son the administration of his private affairs, he dedicated himself entirely to social activities. A convention of delegates of the peasant circles accepted him as their "patron"; reelected every three years, Jackowski held this honorary position until his death in 1905. His main tasks consisted in riding about the country founding new circles and in controlling their activities. Each circle was an independent unit, but it was affiliated with the "Patronage" in Poznan, which supplied it with all kinds of professional literature concerning not only agronomy but also broader economic and legal problems important to the peasantry. Each circle held a monthly session, and once a year delegates from all the circles assembled in Poznan for what was called the *Peasant Sejm* by the Polish press. The circles organized agronomic competitions, experimented with modern tools, new kinds of crops, and fertilizers, and in general worked to bring about economic advances on the peasant farms. Not everywhere were they successful—many circles were lethargic; many went out of existence—but their number grew. There were more than 200 circles in Poznania alone around 1900; and 360, with 17,000 members, in 1910. They probably included most of the well-to-do peasants in Poznania and Pomerania, and many in Upper Silesia and

Mazuria. By statute, their activity was limited to economics, and so they abstained from electoral campaigning and antigovernmental agitation. On the other hand, the circles created an atmosphere of civic pride which certainly inspired the peasantry's stubborn opposition to Germanism. The peasants felt challenged to disprove the alleged superiority of the German oppressors by demonstrating that they were as good or better farmers and could hold their own in economic competition. An attitude such as this also fostered collaboration with the big Polish landowners, who were facing analogous problems.

The Poznanian press often extolled this immense achievement —a peasant organization inspired with patriotic feelings and working hand in hand with the big property owners in defense of the national cause. It was indeed remarkable, but there was a flaw: The agronomic circles united only the upper strata of the peasantry. Most of the poorer farmers remained outside their scope, and as to the rural proletariat, the circles were not interested in its problems. They seemed not even to know of its existence (although, of course, the well-to-do peasantry exploited hired labor on no less a scale than the big landowners). Until 1918, the rural proletariat in Poznania was a passive and unorganized element. Resolute, active individuals in the milieu fled their misery and oppression as a rule; they emigrated, but those who remained were helpless in the face of the growing army of underpaid, imported seasonal manpower.

In addition to the agronomic circles, the well-to-do peasants formed other organizations, such as savings-and-loan cooperatives, self-education groups, lending libraries, and amateur theaters. But these activities had their main influence in the towns, and the peasantry played only an accessory role. Small groups of peasant farmers participated in farmers' cooperatives (*rolniki*), which were organized by the big landowners for the purpose of selling their produce more profitably. The *rolniki* also furnished their members, on a clearing basis, with seeds, fodder, fertilizers, machinery, etc. There were about sixty Polish cooperatives of this kind, with 10,000 members, before World War I.

The growing prosperity and activity of the Polish peasantry proved to be a factor of tremendous importance when the Prussian rulers began to engage in anti-Polish activity of an economic nature. Beginning with the 1870s, the German nationalist press

unceasingly argued that administrative and educational measures were not sufficient for the strengthening of the eastern borders; that an economic policy was necessary, in order to cause the
Poles to retreat from their positions; and that not only the *szlachta*
and the clergy were to be considered disloyal toward the state
but the popular masses as well. Bismarck yielded to arguments
of this kind with reluctance. He was a conservative on this point
and chose to believe that the peasants were a servant race which
could have no voice in national affairs. In 1886 (the year after
the famous eviction of foreign manpower) Bismarck's government
established the Colonization Commission and provided it with
100 million marks in state funds. The commission's purpose was
to purchase land from the Poles and to parcel it among German
peasants. In a well-advertised speech Bismarck assured the *Landtag* in Berlin that he did not wish to antagonize the Polish peasants, who were loyal subjects of the monarchy; he wanted only
to reform the incorrigible Polish *szlachta*—but they would not be
wronged. They would get an equitable price for their estates, and
they could take this money, if they wished, to the roulette in
Monte Carlo!

This contemptuous invective was received as a moral slap by
all Polish society, not only by the gentry. Self-defense would have
to be organized, if the Poles in Poznania were not to be reduced
to a helpless proletariat. Even the propertied classes realized that
it would do no good to take up Bismarck's challenge with merely
a defense of the gentry's estates. They would have to form a
Polish parceling policy to counteract that of the government.
The first Polish initiative came in 1888 with the establishment
of the Land Bank (*Bank Ziemski*), which was financed by contributions flowing in from Congress Poland, Galicia, and elsewhere. This new bank's purpose was to help the encumbered
Polish estates by means of partial parceling among the Polish
peasants, so that the indebted landowners would not be obliged
to sell to the Colonization Commission. This scheme, however,
proved insufficient, and the Land Bank's activity was limited.

It was soon perceived that the only efficient method would be
the parceling of entire estates, including, if possible, German-
owned ones if they ever came on the market. There were many
Polish peasants with savings who were ready to enlarge their
holdings. In 1894, the Farm Parceling Company was founded,

transformed three years later into the Parceling Bank under the leadership of Ignace Sikorski. The bank mainly practiced neighborhood parceling; it sold small lots of a couple of acres to local small-holders who were ready to pay a good price to raise their status. Such parceling was easy, because it did not require investments in buildings. The Colonization Commission, on the other hand, organized large independent farms; they were sold to German colonists on long-term credit, with the provision that the credit would be revoked should the purchaser behave in a manner incompatible with the interests of Germanism. In this way, the new settlers were to remain dependent on the commission. The new German farms were economically more sound, but they were more expensive, and the long-term credit scheme immobilized the state funds involved. Competition soon evolved between the Colonization Commission and the infinitely more modest Polish parceling agencies. Before World War I, there were already twenty-four Polish parceling agencies, with 15 million marks in deposits. Some of these companies paid dividends of up to 25 percent and even attracted German speculators.

The tremendous demand for land on the part of the peasantry, together with the rapid expansion of agriculture, made parceling an excellent business. The German-Polish competition, however, was artificially raising prices. In 1887, the Colonization Commission paid on the average 568 marks for one *hectare* of estate land. In 1900 the analogous figure was 809 marks and in 1910, 1,600 marks. Such prices induced many landowners to sell—not only Poles, but Germans as well—so that they could invest in other enterprises. A singular practice evolved: The German landowner intending to sell his estate threatened the Colonization Commission by saying that he would go to the Poles if he did not get a good price; and conversely, the Polish landowner threatened the Polish Parceling Bank with bargaining with the Colonization Commission. On both sides, the press and public opinion branded as traitors to the national (respectively, German or Polish) cause those who sold land to the enemy. Nevertheless, this practice was not infrequent on both sides. With passionate interest, everyone followed the annual reports of the German and Polish parceling agencies. At first the Colonization Commission was victorious, but on the whole it was buying much more land from Germans than from Poles. In the nineties the balance turned for the Polish side; it appeared that more German land passed every year into Polish hands than the reverse. Since partition times, the Germans had steadily bought land from the Poznanian *szlachta*, but now the tide seemed to be turning, thanks to the hard labor, the thrift, and the sacrifices of the Polish peasants. This trend was indeed astounding, considering the financial and political ascendancy of the German side.

Over a period of twenty-eight years, the Colonization Commission bought 1.13 million acres in Poznania and western Prussia, but only 28 percent of this area was purchased from the Poles. On this land, 22,000 German peasant families were settled by the commission, but only one-half of them were new immigrants from the West. In the same period (1885–1913), the Polish assets in land were augmented by 250,000 acres in Poznania and western Prussia. In some of the neighboring regions of Pomerania and Silesia, the Polish peasants also scored advances. Such Polish successes, however spectacular, were illusory and frail. Even though the amount of land in Polish hands ceased to diminish or began to augment in Poznania, the fact remained that the Colonization Commission was settling more and more German peasants on formerly Polish soil, and this was more momentous than the earlier settlements of German Junkers. The Colonization Commission now planned its activity more ingeniously. New German settlements were to be concentrated in vital and, so to speak, "strategic" areas. Towns which had until now remained predominantly Polish were to be surrounded by a large belt of German villages, because it was known that in an era of rapid urbanization the rural neighborhood influenced the composition of the town population. New German areas were planned in the form of wedges in order to isolate or disrupt predominantly Polish territories.

Another and still more grim perspective lay in the changing character of the struggle. All the outbidding by German and Polish realtors seems strange to our twentieth-century minds. The omnipotent German Reich was leaving the fate of its eastern borders to the free interplay of economic forces. Such leniency was possible in the liberal atmosphere of a long-forgotten age, but only for so long as such liberalism did not endanger the basic aims of the state's policy. The twentieth century inaugurated in

Germany a new epoch of exceptional measures directed against the Poles as such.

Even then, before 1914, it was deemed unthinkable to declare openly that the Polish subjects of the Reich were to be deprived of property rights to which the Germans were entitled. Nevertheless, a law was passed by the Prussian *Landtag* in 1904 which in effect declared that the government's permission would henceforth be necessary in order to set up a new farm (in practice, to erect new farm buildings) and that the government was entitled to refuse such permission if the new farms were considered opposed to the aims of the Colonization Commission. The provision covered not only Poznania but all the eastern provinces of Prussia, east of today's Oder-Neisse line. The obvious aim of the law was to make impossible Polish parceling, since a Pole could now be forbidden to build a home on his newly purchased lot.

The new law was soon tested in a case which made it world-famous. A Polish peasant named Michel Drzymała (1857–1937) had just bought some land in the village of Podgradowice, Poznania, and was refused by police the right to erect a house. He accordingly installed on the lot an unused circus car and moved into it; it was not a house, since it had wheels. The story was well advertised in the Polish and European press as an example of German intolerance; postcards showing the image of Drzymała's car were sold, and a new and comfortable caravan was purchased by subscription and offered the national hero. The Prussian authorities were slow to deal with the case; they eventually resorted to police action and ordered Drzymała to remove the car because of security reasons. The stubborn Pole burrowed a pit in the soil and showed his new and miserable habitation to reporters. In 1910, after six years of lawsuits and harassing by police, Drzymała was eventually forced to sell his lot. The Prussian state carried its point, and Polish parceling was to be seriously handicapped in the years to come. On the other hand, Drzymała's car was to remain a vivid symbol of Prussian injustice in the eyes of the Polish nation.

In 1908, another law empowered the Colonization Commission to forcefully purchase Polish estates if not enough Polish land were willingly offered for sale. This new project produced a panic among Polish landowners, and it was deemed outrageous even by Prussian conservatives, who considered it a dangerous encroachment on private property. The law was voted in spite of much resistance, but the government did not immediately apply it on a large scale, in the hope that the menace of expropriation would induce the Poles to sell of their own free will rather than await coercion. Not until 1912 were four Polish estates comprising an area of 4,000 acres compulsorily expropriated. The year after, the Colonization Fund, which had been augmented three or four times since 1886, was fixed at 955 million marks, with an additional 100 million explicitly destined to foster German colonization in adjacent regions of eastern Prussia, western Pomerania, and Lower Silesia, where Polish expansion was considered dangerous. Finally, in 1914 a law was proposed by the government which would prohibit any kind of Polish parceling, even on a neighborhood buying-in basis. The outbreak of World War I prevented this last provision from being voted.

Compared with the later, more efficient methods of Nazi extermination, the Kaiser Wilhelm era and the system of forcing the Poles to sell their land may seem mild. It was not considered so at the time. The first exceptional laws applied to Poles in Prussia, beginning with 1904, were proof that the Prussian state could no longer count on the free interplay of economic forces to Germanize the eastern provinces. The Polish masses resisted the economic pressure and even scored advantages in the competition. This was the reason why political power had to be applied to support the Colonization Commission despite its billion-mark endowment. This pressure would probably have proved efficient; happily for the Poles, 1914 brought the outbreak of war, and 1918 the collapse of the Hohenzollern monarchy. Fifty years of national persecution by Bismarck and his successors did not succeed in uprooting the Polish peasantry from their lands. On the contrary, this persecution contributed, together with other factors, to a strengthening of that class and of its national consciousness.

16

GALICIA BEFORE WORLD WAR I

Pauperization of the Countryside

In the middle of the nineteenth century Galicia was the most ne-
glected of the Polish provinces, from the economic point of view.
Among other things, the agrarian structure evolved in an undesirable direction, as a result of the emancipation reform of 1848.
This reform had been radical in its assumptions and distorted in
its later fulfillment. Nearly every peasant became the full owner
of a patch of land, but he was burdened by indemnification payments and deprived of forest servitudes. Emancipated in theory,
the village remained economically dependent on the manor. And
since the estate owner could still force the peasants to work for
him (true, no longer for nothing, but for extremely low wages),
he was not obliged (as was the Poznanian landowner) to enhance
their working conditions.

During the first forty years after emancipation, to about 1890,
the peasant-owned tilled area in Galicia rose by 750,000 acres, that

is, by less than 7 percent. This increase was due to amelioration of some of the barren lands, to the regulation of servitudes, and, on a smaller scale, to parceling. The trouble was that the number of holdings increased much faster than the quantity of land. In contrast with the Russian system, which imposed state tutelage over the peasantry, the Galician peasant was admitted to the free realty market; that is, he was left to his own devices. He could buy or sell, mortgage or subdivide his holding as he wanted. The first result was a regularizing of the clandestine family divisions of holdings which had taken place before 1848; and during the decade following emancipation the number of holdings augmented by one-third. It almost doubled by 1900. How large a percentage of this increase was actually due to new divisions is difficult to ascertain. Statistics tell us that in 1859 two-thirds of the peasant holdings in Galicia had less than ten *morgi* (fourteen acres), and one-fourth of the peasants had even less than two *morgi* (two and one-half acres). This was only the beginning of an unhappy trend. Around 1900 four-fifths of the peasants found themselves beneath the ten-*morgi* line, although it is true that the percentage of dwarf holdings had diminished a little. The distinctive plague of Galician agriculture was the "chessboard" (*szachownica*)—the checker division of holdings. As a result of repeated family divisions, dowry acquisition, sales, and purchases, each peasant's land was scattered all over the village field—in lots so small that, as the saying ran, when a dog lay on a peasant's ground the dog's tail would protrude on the neighbor's holding. As early as 1859, there were 15 million separately registered lots in Galicia. This meant, on the average, twenty lots for each peasant, and the figure doubled in the next generation. Sensible farming was out of the question under such conditions. Let us add that the peasant was overburdened with taxes—a result of the unfavorable political situation—and denied credit facilities. As likely as not, he fell a prey to usury. From 1875 to 1884, 23,649 peasant holdings were forcibly sold at auction, often because of debts of less than twenty guldens (the equivalent of ten bushels of wheat).

This situation forced the Galician small-holder to seek additional income on the neighboring estate. And he undertook such a job on particularly disadvantageous terms, on the *odrobek* basis; that is, he borrowed money (or seed grain, or simply food) in the spring and worked it off at harvest time, at the lowest possible rate of pay. In 1874, a conservative magazine in Krakow published a curious correspondence from eastern Galicia. It told of another practice of the Polish landlords: distributing among the villagers small sums of money called *portions,* on *odrobek* terms. Each portion was to represent the value of one day of work per week—not the capital value, but the interest of the debt. Whoever accepted the portion was to work one day per week on the estate so long as he did not pay the portion back in cash, which he was not often able to do. Particularly interesting is the fact that when this practice of blatant usury (50–100 percent, according to various estimates) was denounced in the conservative press the landlords from the eastern borders protested vehemently that no such thing existed. Let us concede that these were exceptional cases; what is important is the atmosphere, the balance of forces which rendered such exceptions probable and possible.

The pauperized and overburdened villagers were incapable of technological progress. But on the large estates the situation was little better. There were forty-five latifundia in Galicia, numbering more than 15,000 acres each. Their owners, mostly Polish aristocrats, leased most of their estates, and such domains were rather poorly farmed. On middle-sized estates, if they were situated on fertile soil, some improvements were attempted, such as crop rotation, crop diversification, and tool modernization. But until the end of the century such progress was insignificant, even by standards in central Poland.

In 1861, Galicia, together with other Austrian provinces, was granted autonomy, and the Land *Sejm* (*Sejm Krajowy*) was convened in Lvov. It was elected on the basis of a curial system which allotted the seats not in proportion to the number of voters but to the importance of vested interests. The peasants in Galicia were allotted 74 seats out of 150, and it was a higher percentage than anywhere else in the Hapsburg monarchy. After 1846 the Galician peasant was presumed to be a loyal subject of the emperor, which is why the peasant curia was given almost half the seats. Remember, however, that the peasantry represented 80 percent of the population. Not all the peasants, by the way, were allowed to vote; only two-thirds of the male, adult taxpayers, ranged according to the amount of their taxes. Therefore, all landless peasants and the poorest third of the landowners were to be disfranchised. Further, the ballot in the peasant curia was to be two-grade and open, a provision which paved the way to electoral misuses. Nowhere was it stated that only peasants could be elected from the peasant curia, and so it was possible for the peasants to be persuaded to elect a landowner as their representative.

During the first session of the *Sejm*, in April 1861, about forty peasant deputies, half of them Poles, half Ukrainians, faced a majority of "enlightened" Polish patriots—noblemen, clergymen, burghers, and intelligentsia. This was the first public encounter of the adversaries of 1846. Count Adam Potocki, one of the wealthiest Polish aristocrats, rose to propose the motion, "The Polish *szlachta*, to prove its benevolence toward the peasants, solemnly renounces any claims to compulsory labor," which, as we know, had been suppressed by Governor Stadion thirteen years before. This declaration, unanimously approved, was meant to dispel suspicions that the Polish *szlachta* would put to profit the newly granted autonomy in order to reestablish compulsory labor.

Compulsory labor, however, had long since ceased to be an important issue in rural conflicts. The Ukrainian deputies answered Potocki's motion with the ominous cry, "Woods and pastures!" (*"Lisy i pasowyska!"*). The main problem in the peasants' eyes now was the servitudes, which had been denied to most villages in the preceding decade. And since on the servitude problem the landlords were not inclined to yield, the class conflict remained unsettled. As a consequence, the peasant deputies were to side with the Austrian government against autonomy and against Polish national aspirations. The "national" majority replied by evicting from the *Sejm*—because of alleged electoral irregularities—some of the most radical peasant speakers. Five years later, in 1866, the Polish nobility succeeded in coming to terms with Emperor Francis Joseph. The Poles renounced their daydreams of independence, which had lost all reality after 1863; they also pledged themselves to support the dynasty against German liberalism and Czech separatism. In exchange, the provincial administration passed into Polish hands, that is, into the hands of the big landowners.

The consequences of this change of regime were soon to be felt. Administrative pressure combined with the economic ascendancy of the manors was to influence the elections. In 1870, the number of peasant deputies in the *Sejm* sharply decreased. In 1877 no peasant was elected to the *Sejm*, and for twelve years, until 1889, the largest class of the nation was not represented in Parliament by persons of its own milieu. The big-propertied classes could organize the new autonomous province as they wished. The first provision voted in 1866 exempted the manor area (*obszar dworski*) from the commune. The commune was to consist exclusively of peasants; it was to be a small and poor autonomous unit, left under the control of the county chief (*starosta*) and of the County Council (*Rada Powiatowa*)—both subservient to the new establishment. But on his manor area, comprising the estate, the farmhand lodgings, etc., the landowner remained supreme master. The next step was the taxing policy—the manor areas were taxed much more mildly than the communes. Other legislation followed: the Road Maintenance Act, which shifted the burden of highway building to the communes; the Popular Schools Act, which exempted the manors from participating in the costs of village education, with the result that the village schools remained poorly equipped and unable to cope with the illiteracy problem; the Game Law, which compelled the commune to lease the hunting rights on village grounds to the local squire.

The most characteristic feature of the big landowners' regime in Galicia was the *propinacja*. This feudal monopoly in producing and selling alcohol was suppressed in Prussia in the 1840s and in Russia in 1864. It existed still in Galicia, although public opinion was critical of the ruling class for drawing a good part of its income from fostering drunkenness in the countryside. In 1874, accordingly, the *Sejm* passed a law which stipulated that the *propinacja* must be sold by the landowners to the Land (Province) of Galicia. There was one drawback to this decision: The province had no money with which to make the contract, and no credit, either. It was settled, therefore, that the *propinacja* owners would be paid with their own *propinacja* incomes, on an amortization basis. This was equivalent to saying that the existing system would last unchanged for the next forty years; only then would the *propinacja* be declared "amortized" and suppressed. At present the only limitation of the old monopoly was that a landowner could not run more than one inn per village. Some years later, in 1889, credit prospects appeared brighter, and so this inequitable

207

procedure could now be stopped. The *Propinacja* Fund was established, the landowners were paid a lump sum in bonds, and the liquor monopoly passed into the hands of the province. Again an obstacle: The *Sejm* stipulated that for a period of twenty-one years the landlord would have exclusive rights to lease local village inns from the state. And thus the manor inns remained in the villages, although the landlord had been indemnified by the taxpayers; the only difference was that he was now paying a moderate rent to the provincial treasury. In 1910, at last, this privilege expired, and after that, the administration sold the innkeeping concessions. The village inn was a good source of income, and so these concessions were distributed among faithful members of the government party. Innkeeping was no longer a feudal privilege, but the instrument of low-level patronage.

The peasantry in Galicia felt exploited and pauperized, communal self-government was ineffective, the peasants were not represented in the *Sejm*, and the bureaucracy was now partial to the gentry. With all this, the myth of the good emperor was bound to vanish. The time was now ripe for a new development, an independent and radical populist movement. This was possible under a constitutional government like Austria's, but its progress was slow, because the level of education in the countryside was rising very slowly.

The first populist leader in Galicia was a Roman Catholic priest of gentry provenience, Father Stanisław Stojałowski (1845–1911), an eccentric and ambitious social leader, a brilliant orator, and an able organizer. In 1875 he began to publish a popular weekly, with the aim of interesting the peasants in public life. The weekly bore the old motto, "The Polish people with the Polish *szlachta*," and it followed the conservative-clerical line. Stojałowski organized peasant pilgrimages to Rome and Jerusalem as well as patriotic peasant demonstrations in the bigger towns. Evidently influenced by the Poznanian example, he began to organize agronomic circles and autodidactic groups. The Galician conservatives proved less tolerant than those in Poznania; even these mild forms of peasant activity seemed to them a nuisance. The agronomic circles were taken away from Stojałowski (1882) and subordinated to the landowners' control; peasant meetings were harassed by police, and Stojałowski's paper was confiscated;

Stojałowski was deprived of his rectorship by the archbishop, and a slander campaign was launched against him in the press. Thus Stojałowski was forced into opposition, and soon he began to indulge in more and more violent anti-*szlachta* tirades. He was an effective demagogue and soon gained immense popularity. By 1887 he was already organizing peasant election committees under the slogan "Vote for peasants only!" He was arrested and released more than once; eventually he sought shelter in Hungary, but his disciples campaigned for him. Then came the climax: A papal bull of excommunication was suspended over Stojałowski, at the instance of the government in Vienna. The rebel priest allied himself with the socialists and won five seats for his party in the 1895 election. This was his supreme effort. One year later he made peace with the government and led his small group of deputies into the ranks of the majority—in exchange for the cancellation of the excommunication bull. His political role was now finished. A more radical Populist wing had emerged on Stojałowski's left; his influence was dwindling, although he remained extremely popular in some regions of Galicia until his death in 1911.

Stojałowski was a picturesque figure, and his role in the political awakening of the peasantry cannot be denied. But an authentic populist movement was to originate in Galicia on another basis. In 1886 a monthly journal was founded in Lvov under the name *The Social Review (Przegląd Społeczny)*. Its founder, Bolesław Wysłouch (1847–1937), a former insurgent of 1863 and a Siberian exile, was an old-style democrat who was influenced by *narodnik* ideas. He tried to revive the concept of the Great Emigration—that the Polish cause, to survive, must become the cause of the popular masses. He therefore advocated real, not merely theoretical, equality of rights for the peasants: general and proportional suffrage and participation in government liquidation of feudal relics in politics and economics. He treated the peasantry as a unit, however, without perceiving its growing differentiation. His monthly had no influence at all with the governing classes. Wysłouch became instead the patron of a growing group of peasant-born intelligentsia who were now entering the Lvov University. He inspired them to devote their energy to the service of the peasant class. This intelligentsia would, in turn, help to build a new populist movement, which would arise this time from among the peasants themselves. This was to happen only in the last decade of the nineteenth century.

Emigration and Parceling

The village in Galicia was beginning at last to emerge from secular stagnation late in the nineteenth century. Agricultural development was still feeble, and limited to middle-sized estates in the western and central parts of the province. Machines came into use on the estates only after the big strikes in about 1900, when wages of farmhands began to rise; but as late as 1910 there were only 8,000 threshing machines in Galicia, and only 1,000 of them were steam-driven. As to the peasants, the single new development in their economy was pig breeding. The number of pigs rose from 734,000 in 1890 to 1,836,000 in 1913. The sale of a porker brought important additional income for every peasant family, and the breeding's extension was only limited by lack of fodder. Galicia's population was growing, and the standard of living was rising, and so, because of its underdeveloped agriculture, it was already beginning to import small quantities of grain.

There were, however, other indices of progress, even in the countryside. First, some changes in education. The new regime in Galicia did not at first attach much importance to the lower schools, and after twenty years of autonomy two-thirds of the inhabitants were still illiterate. Improvement was visible, beginning in the nineties, and the number of rural schools almost doubled in the following twenty years. They were mostly poorly organized one-class schools, but they paved the way for self-education. There were only 55 peasants' sons in the Krakow University in 1870, and 234 in 1900.

The other factor was the emigration. The first "emigration fever" began in 1895 and was directed toward Brazil. Later, emigration to the United States became more important, although Ukrainians from eastern Galicia preferred Canada for the most part. To 1914, about one million people had left Galicia; two-thirds of the number were Poles, and they were almost exclusively peasants. The American emigration and, together with it, the seasonal farmhand migrations (*na Saksy*) reduced in some measure the overcrowding of the countryside, stimulated wage and price increases, and supplied the Galician village with a constant influx of money earned abroad and sent home by the emigrants. The yearly income from this source in Galicia was evaluated at about $52 million before 1914.

The result was a growing demand for land, and such a rise in land values that many big landowners became interested in parceling. Between 1889 and 1902 there were 237,000 acres parceled in Galicia, but in the next ten years the number increased to 607,000. It was certainly a slower movement than that in Poznania or in the Congress Kingdom, and it did not touch equally all sorts of big property. Many smaller estates disappeared altogether; the middle-sized more often sold only some part of their land; the latifundia, on the other hand, held remarkably well and even enlarged their possessions. In some regions of western Galicia the estate lands dwindled to less than one-fourth of the total tilled area.

Neighborhood parceling was the prevailing form in the province of Galicia. Whereas in Prussian Poland the process resulted from sharp German-Polish competition, and in Congress Poland, as we shall see, it was sponsored by the state, in Galicia it remained in the domain of private speculation. That excellent business attracted a swarm of speculators. The middleman bought the estate land, paying cash, and sold it back in lots to neighboring villagers on short-term installments. The Galician small-holder was ready to pay any price to get more land, and he knew that the parceling of a local estate was an event which could occur only once. The middleman always hastened a sale by threatening to bring in colonists from a neighboring county if he did not sell his lots quickly enough. The business, accordingly, was a brisk one, and in two to three years the speculator had his money back with a profit of 25–50 percent. The government was slow to interfere in these proceedings, which were ruinous for the peasants. The conservative ruling class had its own views on the problem. It advocated a partial parceling of the more indebted estates, in order to preserve them from total ruin, and the formation of large, independent peasant farms. In 1906 the *Sejm* passed a law concerning large leased farms which would grant the owners credit on exceptionally easy terms if they would pledge themselves not to divide their property. The trouble was that the state did not provide the funds required to change the country's agrarian structure.

Another new feature in the Galician countryside was the cooperative movement. It began as a corollary of the agronomical circles initiated by Father Stojałowski which had been taken over by the big landowners and left for a time in marasmus. The circles developed after 1900, and were linked with the Populist movement. There were 898 circles with 41,000 members in 1901; 1,862 circles with 85,000 members in 1913. Like the Poznanian circles, the Galician ones were advisory bodies for agricultural technology and sponsored cultural activity in the village. They undertook, besides, some trade activity, organizing the wholesale selling of the members' crops as well as the purchase of agricultural tools. Village stores were opened, sometimes on a cooperative basis, more often leased to retailers. Dairy cooperatives were also inaugurated. The main goal was to liberate the village from the monopoly of the Jewish innkeeper, who was retailer and usurer in one person. After 1910 most of the inns passed from Jewish hands to a new village bourgeoisie now in full growth—a small bourgeoisie connected with the Populist movement, not less greedy than the Jews, and prone to anti-Semitism.

According to 1902 statistics only one Galician peasant out of 20 could rank as independent, and one out of 100 as a rich man. In many counties the number of small and dwarf holdings surpassed 90 percent. There was, however, no sharp division between these various groups of small-holders. When he came of age, the son of a villager received from his parents two to three acres of land, and his wife's dowry was another acre or two. By means of hard labor, thrift, and outside work he managed to purchase more land, and then he inherited still more after the death of his parents and in-laws. His holding attained the maximum size when he was nearing fifty. Now his children were growing up and he felt obliged to "write off" some acres for them before he died. He began his career as a small-holder; he was a middle-sized owner for a short time; he died as a small-holder. And most probably he would leave each of his children a little less land than he had inherited himself. The average size of the holding lessened with each generation. It has also been statistically observed that the well-to-do peasant had more children than the small-holder, probably because he could more easily bring them up; consequently, the bigger holding was, as a rule, divided among more successors than the smaller one—one more factor working toward the standardization of the size of the holdings.

This explains why the tendency toward polarization (*rozwarst-wienie*) was much less visible in Galicia than elsewhere. Well-to-do peasants were less numerous here. They existed, however, on a relative scale. In every village, a small group was to be found which used some of its earnings to buy or lease additional land. It was probably composed of the better, more enterprising farmers. Jan Słomka, a village mayor whose memoirs have been translated into English, is a good example. These peasants probably worked together; they were certainly in control of the commune, the agricultural circle, the cooperative, and they knew how to use their ascendancy to their own advantage. A common source of inequity was the division of communal pastures, which was carried out in such a manner that the wealthier peasants acquired most of the land. It should also be noted that the wealthier peasant was more likely to be able to send his son to high school and later to the theological seminary or the university. Most of the leaders of the Populist party stemmed from this thin upper layer of Galician peasantry, and this accounts for the relatively moderate character of the movement.

The other dividing line, that between the peasants owning land and the landless peasants, was also more blurred in Galicia than elsewhere. There were 3.7 million persons actively engaged in agriculture in Galicia in 1902, about a million "owners" of relatively small holdings, 2 million "helping family members," and perhaps 700,000 landless peasants. The estates, as a matter of fact, employed a relatively small number of steady wage earners. Most of the work on a big estate was done by the poor smallholders from the neighborhood. This system was much more convenient for the big landowner, who thus paid wages only when he needed laborers; and he was sure to have a supply of unemployed hands in the half-starving village. Each summer the poor mountainous regions along the Carpathian Range sent groups of excellent mowers (*bandosy*) who were hired for harvest time on many estates of the Galician plains and even in Congress Poland. The wages of the farmhand and of the occasional journeyman were lamentable. In winter, the daily wage of a male worker on an estate was half a crown—the equivalent of four pounds of rye flour and four pounds of potatoes. As for the harvest, remuneration in kind was common; for example, the mower might receive as payment every eleventh or twelfth sheaf. This pay was to rise after the big strikes of 1902–3. But even in later years, until 1918, the rural proletarian did not enjoy any form of social security. He was also subject to the famous "home discipline"—that is, to the surveyor's stick.

Table 2 shows the differences in the agrarian structures of some of the Polish provinces, at the beginning of the twentieth century. It is obvious that the two numerically most important groups in Congress Poland were those composed of peasants with middle-sized holdings. In Poznania we observe two relatively large groups,

TABLE 2

PERCENTAGE OF THE TOTAL NUMBER OF PEASANT HOLDINGS IN GROUPS

Province	Year	Less than 5 Acres	5–12.5 Acres	12.5–50 Acres	More than 50 Acres
Congress Poland......	1905	25	40	33	2
Poznania.............	1907	67	9	19	5
Galicia.............	1902	44	37	18	1

the smaller holders and the well-to-do peasants. This is the phenomenon called *polarization*. Finally, in Galicia the two smallest groups added together represent 81 percent of the holdings, a circumstance which ought to be labeled *pauperization*.

The Populist Movement

The Galician countryside, though pauperized, was nevertheless to undertake a fight against the established regime of conservative landowners which was backed by the Vienna government and by the higher clergy. Whereas the poorer peasants sought refuge from their misery in emigration, the upper strata of the peasantry attempted to better their position by political means. To campaign for elections, to enforce a reform of voting regulations, to gain influence over the government—these were to be the steps to success. Before the 1889 elections, Wysłouch began to publish a popular weekly, *The People's Friend* (*Przyjaciel Ludu*), under the slogan "Peasants! Vote for your own people!" Analogous agitation was fostered by Ukrainian radicals in the eastern part of the country. The election proved a very limited success, since only three Polish peasants entered the *Sejm*, but this was nevertheless

214

significant, after twelve years of peasant nonrepresentation. Among these first peasant deputies were two Potoczek brothers, serious, well-to-do *gospodarze* who strongly accentuated their conservatism and Catholicism. They were later to join Father Stojałowski.

In 1894, an exposition was organized in Lvov to commemorate the achievements of the autonomous Polish administration. To mark the centenary of Kościuszko's insurrection, a panoramic picture was set up on the exhibition grounds which represented the battle of Racławice and the famous attack of peasant scythemen on the Russian guns. Numerous peasant excursion groups were shown this historic scene of peasant patriotism. On 25 August 1894, a big peasant meeting was held in Lvov which rallied 3,000 persons. There were two speakers: Jakub Bojko (1857–1944)—a well-to-do peasant from the neighborhood of Krakow, an autodidact, and a generally respected Populist writer; and Jan Stapiński (1867–1946)—a peasant's son, a journalist of lively temperament, and a pupil of Wysłouch. Unanimously, the meeting voted a resolution demanding a general and direct electoral franchise. This was the starting point of the Populist party (after 1903, the Polish Populist party—PSL).

The first program of the party was moderate enough; besides its chief postulate, an electoral reform, it insisted on the enforcement of existing civil rights laws and on a more just distribution of common charges. No concern was exhibited for the rural proletariat and no word was said about compulsory parceling of estate lands. Nevertheless, the rise of a political peasant organization whose purpose was to render the peasants independent of the *szlachta*'s tutelage was by itself an offense to the ruling classes. A clever pamphlet by Bojko entitled "The Two Souls" carried the following argumentation: "Each man has a free soul given by the Almighty, a soul which makes him the equal of other men. But the Galician peasant has still another soul lingering on—the soul of the former serf, obliged to compulsory labor. For fifty years he has been emancipated, but the soul of the *pańszcznyziak* is still there, and it obliges the peasant to bow to the earth with his hat before the squire, the rector, the official, and even the policeman. Let us break with such subservience; you should no longer be taught by persons of a 'superior' class how to behave, what to believe, and how to vote." Bojko's pamphlet was much read at the time and had many later editions. The 1895 elections brought an increase of Populist votes, and this time nine peasants entered the *Sejm*.

The political activity in the countryside was soon to lead to conflicts between the villages and the manors. Strikes of farm-hands began in western Galicia in 1898; they burst out, on an infinitely larger scale, east of Lvov in 1902. More than twenty counties were affected. The Ukrainian small-holders collectively refused to work on the estates, demanding better terms (the eighth sheaf instead of the twelfth) and more decent treatment. Other claims were raised, such as the reestablishment of forest servitudes and the right to purchase or lease a patch of estate soil. Violent incidents often occurred when the squire attempted to bring in strikebreakers or called the gendarmerie. Instances of vengeful devastation of estate sowings occurred here and there. Two facts are worth noting: Even the well-to-do peasants backed the strikers, and the Polish peasants followed the movement notwithstanding its obvious anti-Polish character. The Populists in the West sympathized with the Ukrainian peasants but did not encourage their own countrymen to follow suit. The agrarian strikes were renewed on a smaller scale in 1903 but were mostly suppressed by the authorities. A second, more powerful and violent, outburst occurred in 1906, in conjunction with the revolutionary events in Russia and Congress Poland. This time thirty-five counties were involved, and the strikes spread from the East to the mixed Polish-Ukrainian area west of Lvov. In most of the cases the squires were forced to make some concessions on the workmen's pay.

The PSL was relatively less interested in farm workers' problems than the Ukrainian radicals. This led the Polish Socialist party (PPS) to extend its agitation to the countryside. The environs of Krakow were particularly pauperized, and numerous peasant families became acquainted with factory life. To them the Socialist platform seemed more radical and therefore more appealing than the Populist one. Beginning with the late nineties, a growing number of Socialist votes were cast in the countryside in some of the western counties. The PPS, however, never managed to elaborate a consistent agrarian program of its own and so remained an outsider in the peasantry's political life.

The first ten years of the PSL's activity were a spectacular success in nearly every village. Populist cells were organized, a party newspaper was distributed, numerous meetings were attended, and a phalanx of local activists of peasant stock came into being. The party leader, Stapiński, developed as an immensely popular orator, appealing to the common people with tough and often vulgar arguments, heaping abuse on the *szlachta*, although managing to remain within the law. The party's platform was bound to become more radical; in 1903 a new point was included into the program—a demand for official help for gradual parceling of estate lands. The parceling, it was stressed, was to be voluntary and the land paid for. Nevertheless, a new big program was launched to the effect that sooner or later the estates must be subdivided, and all the land must be distributed to the peasants. This was the program of agrarian reform (*reforma rolna*), the goal of all Populist activity for the next forty years.

The Conservative party was shaken with indignation, and Stapiński was branded a bloodthirsty revolutionary. The clergy unleashed violent attacks against the Populists, and one circular of Bishop Leon Wałęga in Tarnow expressly ordered denial of absolution for any subscriber to the Populist press. This attitude was the more revealing since the Galician clergy, Bishop Wałęga included, was composed mostly of peasants' sons. The outcry proved ineffective; it neither hampered the Populist drive nor undermined the Catholic feeling of the Polish peasantry; it only impaired the authority of the village priest.

The agitation was brought to a climax in the years 1905–6, when under the influence of the Russian revolution all leftist forces in Austria united in a fight for a general franchise. A law was voted, and in 1907 the first general elections to the Vienna Parliament were held in Galicia (the curial system regarding *Sejm* elections remained in force). The Conservatives suffered a crushing defeat; seventeen Polish and twenty-seven Ukrainian Populists entered the Parliament.

Superficial observers envisaged a violent social upheaval and a frontal attack by the Populist party on the big estates of the gentry. Some of Stapiński's speeches were recalled; how, for example, he once predicted, in hot-headed rapture, that the village streets would soon be paved with gentlemen's skulls instead of cobblestones. And the peasant masses, even if not so bloodthirsty, really expected the big changes which had been promised them

217

as the result of an electoral victory. Nothing of the kind happened. The Populists were still far from control; the Conservatives, weakened in Parliament, remained entrenched in the *Sejm* and the administration. The Populist leaders, including Stapiński, did not dream of a revolution. On the contrary, they thought of a compromise with those in power, a compromise more easy to achieve now that they had shown their force. The time had come, according to Stapiński, when Parliament votes could be traded for tangible advantages for the party and the party's leaders. This attitude denoted a turn to the right—a phenomenon not uncommon among popular parties when they cease to be minorities. The turn reflected the concrete interests of the upper layer of well-to-do peasants who aspired to agrarian reform, but by orderly and peaceful means. They wanted to buy the gentry's land legally; if the estates were to be parceled by force, in a revolutionary way, the land would go "to the beggars," that is, to the landless peasants or to the small-holders.

It turned out that the Conservative party was prepared to meet Stapiński halfway. The ruling class in Galicia had split over issues of international policy. The National Democrats were challenging the Conservatives—and the Populists, when sensible, could be useful allies. A secret understanding between the former adversaries was reached just before the *Sejm* elections (1908). The administration gave its support to the Populists. Stapiński, in turn, joined the Polish Club with his followers and helped the Conservatives oust the Nationalist chairman. Having now become a component of the majority, the Populists obtained the government's support for two of their institutions, the Parceling Bank and one of their insurance companies. The party's evolution was to gain it unexpected adherents. Numerous bourgeois democrats, even some among the gentry, now accepted the poet Stanisław Wyspiański's aphorism: "The peasant's a power, and that will do!" A typical democrat's view was, "The masses have become mature, at last; let us help them, so that they may assume responsibility for the nation's fate." Beginning politicians expected a rapid career in the ranks of the Populists, who lacked experts for all the posts now offered to them. Two young aristocrats, Mikołaj Rey and Zygmunt Lasocki, joined the Populist party, as did the well-known painter Włodzimierz Tetmajer; the organizer of cooperatives Franciszek Stefczyk; the drainage and irrigation engineer Andrzej Kędzior; and Władysław Długosz, a rather dubious oil speculator who contributed a large sum to the party's fund and became a minister with the title "Excellence." Such developments could endanger the future of the Populist movement. A peasant activist, suddenly transplanted to a seat in the parliament in Vienna, was subject to many temptations for self-aggrandizement. Not all the new followers of the movement from among the intelligentsia were equally reliable, and it seemed as if the alliance with the ruling class would not benefit the peasantry as a whole. Among the rank and file of the party, opposition arose against subservience to the *szlachta*. Stapiński, who was endowed with remarkable political flair, sensed the latent danger and was preparing a new, sensational about-face, when he was suddenly assailed by some of his partisans.

The nationalist-clerical opposition, in fighting the governing bloc of Conservatives and Populists, used such slogans as "purity of political action" and "defense against radicalism." They were right, in a sense; there was a streak of demagogy and some corruption among the Populist leaders. Whereas the Conservative party cynically played up the peasant movement, against its interests, the Nationalists tried to split the Populist party by joining the moderate wing against the radicals. In their eyes Stapiński seemed dangerous as a potential radical; and he was vulnerable, because of his negotiations with the people in power. Unexpectedly, in 1913, the national press published evidence to the effect that Stapiński had accepted government funds for his party. A violent campaign was unleashed against this "corrupt monster," this "renegade" of the Populist cause. The right wing of the PSL proposed an investigation, and Stapiński found himself in a minority among his own circle. He seceded with only five deputies, although characteristically, the rank and file of the party backed him after all. The average peasant did not consider improper financial transactions by his leaders major sins. Stapiński remained a popular leader, more trusted than Count Lasocki or His Excellency Długosz. Notwithstanding, a schism ensued. Stapiński chose for his party the appellation "PSL-Left." The right wing adopted the name "PSL-Piast," recalling the legendary peasant who had founded the Polish dynasty 1,100 years before. Its leadership was assumed by Wincenty Witos (1874–1945), a well-to-do farmer from western Galicia, a shrewd politician, a peasant through and through, but a moderate peasant. He was afterward to become prime minister of liberated Poland; but even as prime minister, and even when receiving royalty, he never put on a necktie, and he remained faithful to his peasant origin. He was careful to be seen ploughing, whenever he went from Warsaw to his native village.

Less than a year separated the split in the Populist party and the outbreak of war. It is difficult to guess how the struggle between the two wings would have developed, had the war not interfered. The question of the ethics of Stapiński's behavior may seem trivial, but the problem was serious indeed. The split of the Populist movement into two wings, one moderate and ready to cooperate with the bourgeoisie, the other radical and siding with the Socialists, reappeared after 1918 in liberated Poland, and remained an almost constant feature of the interwar period. This schism reflected the growing differentiation of the peasant masses; the difficulty of an understanding between a growing peasant bourgeoisie and the more numerous peasant masses menaced with total proletarianization.

17

CONGRESS POLAND BEFORE
WORLD WAR I

Economic Progress and Parceling

We must now resume our analysis of the agrarian problems in central, or Congress, Poland, interrupted before the turn of the century. From the national point of view, this part of Poland was the most important, and a survey of its situation by 1914, following the survey of Poznanian and Galician problems, will provide us with a chance for comparison and for synthesis.

The economic crisis of the 1880s was over in the Congress Kingdom by 1893; after that, farming was again a paying enterprise, especially when run on progressive lines. The years 1905–7 were turbulent and revolutionary, but the rural economy was not weakened. The following years, until 1914, brought excellent conditions for every producer, and price rises in all commodities. The two decades before World War I witnessed a marked advance of agriculture. There was, first, an increase in the tilled area, partly due to a decrease of barren and fallow lands but mainly due to deforestation (1,750,000 acres of forests, one-fourth of the total tree cover, disappeared between 1864 and 1914). Second, harvest yields rose by 30–50 percent between 1890 and 1913, thanks to more appropriate tools and better tilling. Significantly, this progress extended now not only to the larger estates but in some measure to the peasants as well. The average gross income of a landowner was estimated in 1911 at $50 per acre, and his net income at $19; for a peasant farmer, $36 gross and $12 net income. Drainage and fertilization were in use only on the bigger estates, and even there on a relatively small scale.

The advances in agriculture in Congress Poland were considerable, but Prussian Poland, meanwhile, left the two other Polish provinces far behind. The average yield of rye rose in Poznania, between 1890 and 1913, from 6.3 to 17.4 bushels per acre. The yield of wheat rose in the same period from 9.5 to 21.2, and of potatoes from 61.5 to 168.2. In 1890, the starting point, Congress Poland and Galicia were only slightly inferior to Prussian Poland. In 1913, however, the average yield of rye was 10 in Congress Poland and 11 in Galicia; of wheat, 11.7 in Congress Poland and 11 in Galicia; of potatoes, 82 in Congress Poland and 113 in Galicia. Comparing the yield of all crops per head of farming population, Poznania remained easily in first place, with 72.8 bushels, Congress Poland came second with 26.9, and Galicia last with 18.9. Galicia's unfavorable position was due, of course, to overpopulation in the countryside, and Congress Poland lagged behind in the sphere of breeding. Its sheep flocks, numerous and renowned at one time, had all but vanished, its cattle breeding was expanding slowly, and the disorders of 1905–7 caused a diminution in the number of pigs. In 1910, there were 613 pigs per 1,000 inhabitants in Poznania, 229 in Galicia, and only 51 in Congress Poland.

The balance of trade in agricultural and livestock production in Congress Poland before 1914 was disadvantageous, with a yearly deficit of $17.6 million. This deficit was covered by a big surplus of exported industrial goods. Galicia at that time showed a small surplus of $9.1 million in her balance of trade in agricultural products. (She had, however, a big deficit as an importer of manufactured goods.) And finally, Prussian Poland (Poznania, western Prussia, and Upper Silesia) had a comfortable $122.5 million surplus in agricultural and livestock production, together with a still higher surplus in the industrial trade balance.

The two features already observed in the Poznanian and Galician countrysides, namely, emigration and parceling, are in evidence in Congress Poland as well.

As to emigration, the first "Brazilian fever" broke out in 1890, when the government of Brazil offered free passage and a promise of land to immigrants, and propagated the news with the help of recruiting agents. In the course of two years, in spite of official prohibition and of eloquent warnings in editorials and sermons, 63,000 landless and small-holder peasants left for Brazil, only to meet there different, but not less harsh, conditions of existence. The emigration to the United States also began in the 1890s; it was more successful and grew steadily until 1914, when it reached a peak figure of 90,000. It was mostly, but not exclusively, a peasant emigration; some workmen went overseas as well, as did a number of Jewish craftsmen and proletarians. It is also worth noting that Russian Poland presented a second area for emigration in the East. Not only people sentenced for crimes or political offences were sent to Siberia; numerous were those who searched for new opportunities in this immense territory, in farming, in railway building, in trade, or mining. There were about 600,000 Poles living in central Russia and Siberia before 1914; but peasants most probably represented only a small percentage of this figure. On the whole, the emigration from Congress Poland is estimated at about 1.3 million people. One of its results, as in Galicia and Poznania, was an influx of emigrant earnings, coming in large measure from seasonal emigrants—an additional factor encouraging parceling.

In 1890 the big landowners of Congress Poland still held 47 percent of the tilled area. In 1910 this figure dwindled to 38 percent. The difference, nearly 2.5 million acres, passed into the hands of small farmers—mostly peasants, but also farming burghers and poor gentry from the petty *szlachta*. Thus Congress Poland outdistanced both Poznania and Galicia in the amount and rate of parceling. In a peasant's view, purchase of land was the only conceivable way to invest his savings. Middle-sized and smaller estates were broken up more often than the larger ones, and those on poor soil disappeared sooner than those in the fertile districts. Many landowners were happy to sell some of their land, thus raising capital to be invested in improvements on the remaining part, with a substantial increase in net income. The demand for land also led to an increase in prices, which more than doubled between 1890 and 1910.

Whereas parceling was subject to wild German-Polish competition in Prussian Poland, and whereas it remained in the domain of private speculators in Galicia, in Russian Poland it was sponsored by the state in a sensible way. The state-owned Peasant Bank, wisely considered a safety valve against the threat of agrarian revolution, extended its activity to Congress Poland in the later eighties. It pursued a nationalist policy only on the eastern border (Chełm region and Podlasie), inhabited partially by Ukrainians and Byelorussians, who were considered Russians from the official point of view. In these counties (*powiaty*), about ten in number, the bank sold land only to individuals of the Orthodox faith. Everywhere else, it followed an impartial and sensible policy, permitting the purchasers to pay 70–80 percent of the price over a period of many years on easy terms. From 1895, the bank began to purchase whole estates in order to sell them to "peasant societies," the members of which, while farming separately, were collectively responsible for the payment of the installments. Only peasants, at first, could profit by these arrangements; later burghers and petty gentry were also admitted to the societies. After 1905, the society scheme was abandoned, and the bank reverted to individual parceling. In some cases it granted up to 100 percent of the purchase price. Before 1914 the Peasant Bank established 26,000 new farms on 667,000 acres, which accounts for about two-thirds of the total amount of parceled land. The "Bank" farms, on the whole, were large and economically independent. At times, specialists have debated which groups of the peasantry profited most by the policy. The majority of the purchasers come under the designation of *landless peasants* in the statistics. This is, however, only an illusion; a rural proletarian had hardly the means to invest in a farm, even on advantageous terms such as those offered by the bank. These allegedly landless purchasers were mostly sons of well-to-do peasants, endowed with capital in the course of family partitions.

The liquidation of the servitudes advanced more slowly in the last prewar years, because the peasants opposed the measure more resolutely, while making greater demands. The approval of at least two-thirds of the commune was necessary in order to reach an agreement. In 1912, 2,700 estates were still burdened with different servitudes, on behalf of 102,000 peasant farms.

There were about one million peasant farms in Congress Poland by 1914. As to their distribution by size, we present figures for 1904. There were at that time 19.2 percent dwarf holdings, 53.7 percent small ones (4.2–16.8 acres), 15.9 percent middle-sized (16.8–28 acres) and 11.2 percent large peasant farms. The typical farm was one of five to seven acres. The bigger farms, although not too numerous, were growing steadily, and constituted 37 percent of peasant land. Some of them were transformed into small estates, specializing (as in the neighborhood of Warsaw) in dairy farming and the culture of vegetables. A rural bourgeoisie was taking shape in this part of Poland as well.

At the other extreme, the landless population was growing rapidly. Varying estimates speak of a rural proletariat of 1.2 million by 1900, and of a total population of two million ten years later. The large majority was now regularly employed by the landowners or by the wealthier peasants. It was a singular variety of proletariat, earning its living under half-feudal, half-capitalist conditions. The farmhand (*parobek*) received not more than 10 percent of his wages in cash. The rest consisted of clothing (boots, sheepskins), lodging and board, if he was single, or the so-called *ordynaria*, if he was married. The *ordynaria* consisted of a specified quantity of grain, flour, grits, or cabbage—plus a patch of land for potatoes and the right to graze a cow on the squire's pasture. In exchange for the *ordynaria*, the farmhand, his wife, and one son called *posyłka* ("errand boy") were obliged to work. If he did not have a son of suitable age, he was obliged to hire help. Other groups of the rural proletariat (*komornicy, wyrobnicy*, etc.) worked under still less advantageous terms. All year round, work on the estate began before sunrise and ended after sunset. Some polemists argued that under the *ordynaria* system a farm laborer got only half the protein and one-eighth of the fat necessary for subsistence. The rural proletariat was the only segment of the population in Congress Poland that did not improve its standard of living in the entire course of the nineteenth century.

Until 1905, however, the landless peasants were a passive element. Class struggle in the countryside was led by the middle peasantry against the big landowners. The object of the struggle was more than ever control of the forests. Progressive deforestation became a problem in a country with a thin network of railways and highways. The owner of the last forest in a neighborhood, most often a latifundist, became a monopolist who could charge as high prices as he wished for fuel and timber. The peasants reacted in their own way to this injustice. In the state forests alone, 30,000 cases of illegal felling of trees were detected every year. It was a common event in the 1890s for hordes of peasants to invade the forest in order to prevent the felling of trees, which meant a catastrophe for the village. Pitched battles ensued, with Russian cossacks summoned to help the Polish landowners. Arson on estate buildings became sufficiently prevalent to force some of the insurance companies to withdraw from business in the countryside. It is significant that more and more peasant demonstrations were accompanied by nationalist slogans; that shouts of "Poland has not perished yet" were often heard in the crowd.

The Revolution of 1905–1907

It was mentioned earlier that the Russian schools and the Russian political system were the two major grievances of the peasantry. The masses responded to the challenge of Russification by organizing clandestine teaching in Polish with the help of activists from the ranks of the Warsaw intelligentsia. Their activities were to expand in the nineties to include politics as well as education. From 1886 to 1894, a weekly called the *Voice* (*Głos*) was published in Warsaw by a group of intelligentsia with Socialist or *narodnik*-like sympathies. The *Voice* became the cradle of Populism in Congress Poland, as had Wysłouch's *Social Review* in Galicia. Poland's future, said the editors, lay in her peasantry, not in the propertied classes; and the peasants should organize cooperatives and buy out the estates, now owned by egoists and sybarites. The group was far from being revolutionary; on the contrary, it was to become the nucleus of the Polish nationalism which evolved in the following decade. The National League, a secret organization founded in 1893 whose purpose was to assume a leadership role in the three provinces of Poland, attached much importance to propagandizing in the countryside. This was an easy thing in Prussian Poland, where the German danger had strengthened the leadership of the propertied classes. And in Congress Poland, where anti-Russian feeling ran high in the countryside but where a legal Populist movement was impossible under czarist rule and Socialist propaganda ignored the peasant farmers and their problems, the National League penetrated with much success. But in Galicia, on the other hand, all attempts to subordinate the Populist movement to the leadership of the National League miscarried because of the too-violent antagonism between peasantry and *szlachta*.

In 1899 the Society for National Education (TON) was organized, a clandestine body subordinated to the National League. The TON took over and significantly enlarged the network of underground teaching in the countryside of Congress Poland. The local intelligentsia in the smaller boroughs—teachers, doctors, priests, etc.—offered their help. There were soon more than two hundred TON "cells" with 6,000 members, mostly well-to-do peasants. The cells distributed the *Polak*, a clandestine gazette printed in Krakow and widely circulated. The *Polak* awakened the national consciousness of the peasants and taught them how to legally oppose the abuses of the foreign oppressor, how to fight for Polish self-government and Polish schools. There were neither radical accents nor insurrectionary slogans in this gazette, but it most certainly played a role in mobilizing the peasants for political activity. Inside this movement, usually on its fringes, more-radical social workers, such as the schoolteacher Maximilian Malinowski (1860–1948), were attempting to disengage the barely beginning Populist movement from bourgeois and Nationalist patronage.

The big event which stepped up the activity of the peasantry in Congress Poland, in the fields of both class struggle and politics, was the revolution of 1905. The class antagonisms running deep in Russia burst forth as a result of the regime's defeat in the War with Japan. Revolution in Congress Poland was a part of the Russian movement not only because this province belonged to Russia but because it played an outstanding role in the movement. Nevertheless, the Polish events had their own peculiarities and their own aims; the peasant movement in particular differed in many respects from the Russian one.

The War with Japan, begun early in 1904, awakened the hopes of all the political groups in Poland and increased their activity.

The National League's hope was that the Russian shortcomings in the Far East would force the czarist government to make concessions to Polish society. Accordingly, the TON cells were instructed to organize petitions for an enlargement of communal self-government. Meanwhile, numerous communes, particularly in the Warsaw and Płock guberniyas, put forward stronger demands, among them the introduction of the Polish language into their office work. The *Polak* joined the activity and began to advise the communes to formally vote appropriate resolutions. The Nationalist party had reason to fear a social upheaval; its leaders hoped that national slogans would divert the peasants from violent conflict with the big landowners.

On 22 January 1905, a massacre of demonstrating workmen in St. Petersburg unleashed a wave of strikes all over the country. Workers in factories, mines, railways, post offices, etc., also went on strike in Congress Poland. For the most part, the strikes were politically motivated, although economic issues were also raised. However, the subsequent unrest of the landless peasants was exclusively social in character. The villagers were well aware of the wave of strikes in the factories. Numerous workers, because of the strikes, returned to their native villages where they carried on their revolutionary propaganda. Sugar factories, scattered all over the country, were active centers of agitation. Then, spontaneously, the rural proletariat went on strike for better conditions. This occurred at the time of spring planting and affected about seven hundred estates, mostly in the Lublin and Siedlce guberniyas. Farmhands, having interrupted their work, would go to the neighboring estate and call its workers to follow their example. The strikers' demands were uniform: higher pay, a shorter working day, better lodgings, better treatment, and abolition of the much-hated *posyłka* arrangement. Some strikers demanded that the landowners be deprived of their land. Some of the owners entered into negotiations with the strikers; others called for help, but the Russian army was usually occupied elsewhere.

The peasant owners reacted much less to calls for class warfare than did those in Russia proper. Progressive parceling took the edge off class antagonisms, particularly among the well-to-do farmers. Illegal cutting of trees increased in 1905 as a result of general anarchy, but open peasant demonstrations were directed toward nationalistic, not social or economic, goals. More than two-thirds of the communes, mainly in the northern guberniyas, voted the introduction of the Polish language on the communal level, in offices, in courts, and in the village schools. The chiefs of the communes discarded their distinctive badges which were inscribed in Russian. The czar's portraits were removed from offices, and schoolchildren joyfully burned Russian textbooks. Retreating before the assault of the revolutionary forces, the government made two important concessions to the peasants: (1) Permission was granted for the use of Polish as well as Russian in the commune offices. (2) Abandonment of the official Orthodox confession was authorized. The Uniate peasants of the eastern borders who had for thirty years resisted a creed imposed by force could now publicly embrace Catholicism.

The spontaneous peasant unrest was bound to draw the attention of all political parties to agrarian problems. The Nationalist group, representing the propertied classes, fought the strikers energetically and publicly defended the landowners. At the same time it supported the goal of a Polish commune, contending that linguistic reform would settle all the grievances of the countryside. The followers of this viewpoint among the landowners, the clergy, and the well-to-do peasants tried to influence the communal debates, advocating adherence to the law and national concord. In a year of awakened revolutionary passions such proposals were not always enough. The year 1905 was also to see the beginning of an independent Populist movement in Russian Poland.

The initiative came from the "progressive democrats," a group of liberal-minded bourgeois, steering midway between Nationalism and Socialism. Toward the end of 1904, a group of Warsaw social activists, headed by Stefan Brzezinski (b. 1879), founded the Polish Populist Union (PZL) and launched a campaign of propaganda in the countryside. A clandestine weekly, the *Communal Voice* (*Głos Gromadzki*) was published. The agitators were mostly village schoolteachers and cooperative officials. Much more clearly than the Nationalists, members of the PZL spoke of an independent Poland as the goal of the revolution. They went beyond the demands of the peasantry, calling for civil rights, a democratic franchise, freedom of speech and association. They stressed the interests of the peasants as opposed to those of the landlords, although they did not advocate an agrarian revolution, but only an independent peasant organization. The PZL developed contacts in the immediate neighborhood of Warsaw. In June 1906, a convention of peasant delegates was held in Warsaw, and a resolution was voted to the effect that all nonpeasant land be expropriated with indemnification. It was not specified whether the land should be given to individual peasants or to collective groups.

The Socialists in Russian Poland were divided at that time into two opposing camps. The Polish Socialist Party (PPS) combined Socialist aims with a tendency toward national insurrection, and it favored taking advantage of the agrarian unrest in order to fight czarism. A leaflet of the PPS, printed in 180,000 copies, instructed the farmhands in organizing and carrying on strikes; it also called for a boycott of taxes and the draft. Disorderly forest incursions and willful occupation of other people's land were condemned. In principle, the PPS contemplated the nationalization of the estates, which would be leased in equal lots to small-holders and landless peasants. Such views seemed utopian at the time and were not listened to in the countryside. Nevertheless, the PPS really helped the agrarian strikers.

The other extreme leftist Socialist group, called SDKPIL (Social Democracy of the Kingdom of Poland and Lithuania), carried the struggle against czarism hand in hand with the Russian left wing. The SDKPIL also issued leaflets urging the peasants to a common fight against autocracy, but it did not have much to offer them. Most of the workmen's parties before Lenin were little concerned with the peasant question and did not perceive the need for an alliance with the peasantry. They were attracted by the rural proletariat, but this proletariat dreamed only of acquiring land, whereas, for economic reasons, the SDKPIL opposed parceling and advocated transforming the estates into cooperatives of farmhands—a prospect which did not seem sufficiently attractive.

Revolutionary tension reached a climax toward the end of 1905, when a new wave of strikes forced the government to proclaim a constitution. The regular administration seemed to dissolve in the general chaos, and this accounts for the bold attitude of some of the peasants. Some of the communes voted openly not to recognize superior authority. Whole counties had ceased to pay taxes. Armed bands of workmen—a typical feature of 1905—appeared in the countryside, particularly in the Radom and Kielce guberniyas. They wrecked Russian offices, railway stations, and liquor stores (operated by the state monopoly), removed Russian emblems and inscriptions, robbed official cash boxes, and threw bombs at police. Some peasants joined this movement. The Nationalist party tried to counteract this sabotage with patriotic demonstrations. The peasants were told that since the czar had granted a constitution, all wrongs would be righted and Polish rule introduced. A convention of 1,500 peasant activists was held in Warsaw in December. They were carefully selected from among the moderate groups of well-to-do peasants. Resolutions in favor of an autonomous Poland and against strikes or any other forms of anarchy were voted. In March 1906, the first elections were held to the Russian Parliament (*Duma*). The Polish left-wing parties boycotted the elections as totally undemocratic, and the Nationalists appeared as the only contenders. The Nationalists were shrewd enough to include on the ballot a group of peasants who appeared in the *Duma* in traditional attire and voted with the Right. They were, of course, figureheads and not actual representatives of the peasantry.

The year 1906 was a period of crisis; the government and the wealthy bourgeoisie were beginning to counterattack the revolutionary movement. Legal order was restored in the countryside and the rebellious communes brought to order. A considerable part of the peasantry, now satisfied with the enforced concessions, returned to lawful behavior. Other groups, matured by experience, now joined the ranks of the leftist parties, PZL or PPS. Agrarian strikes flared up again in 1906, 300 during the spring planting, 400 at harvest time. Sixty counties out of eighty-five were affected by these strikes. It is characteristic that successive waves of strikes involved new localities where the farmhands had not as yet attained their goals. The 1906 strikes were better organized, their demands were greater, and their course more violent than those of the year before. In cases in which the landlord refused to negotiate, a "black strike" was proclaimed; that is, the estate's livestock was not fed or attended. Some owners resorted to lockouts or to hired security guards, but most of them capitulated, agreeing to the strikers' demands. On the whole, thanks to the revolution, the farmhands of Congress Poland were able to secure an average raise in pay and *ordynaria* of about 30 percent, as well as a shorter work day.

Both Socialist parties, PPS and SDKPIL, were active in these strikes, and one of the SDKPIL leaflets even announced that all the estate lands would pass into the hands of the small-holders. This was, however, an action at the local level, unapproved by the leadership. None of the Socialist parties recognized the opportunity for proclaiming sweeping agrarian reform.

In 1907 reaction triumphed in Russia and in Russian Poland. The revolutionary parties were forced underground again. The Populist Union (PZL) was dissolved, its press closed, its leaders arrested. The National Democratic party (ND) remained alone in the field. It had changed markedly during the revolutionary years and was an open defender of the established social order. During the first parliamentary session in 1906, the ND still flirted with the idea of agrarian reform. One of its leaders, the distinguished economist Władysław Grabski (1873–1938), worked out a detailed plan for gradual purchase of most of the big properties by the state, in order to organize large, independent peasant farms. Grabski's idea was to forge a barrier of antirevolutionary forces in the countryside. But after the collapse of the revolution, Grabski's plan was discarded from the party's official program.

The ND remained active in the countryside, returning to the old "organic" program. From 1905, a somewhat greater margin of social activity was allowed. The Central Agronomic Society was founded in 1907, associating thirty local societies with 4,000 members, mostly landowners. A network of agricultural syndicates was organized on the Poznanian model in order to help big landowners and wealthy peasant farmers with the sale of their products and to supply them with various commodities. The agronomic societies in turn organized agronomic circles among the peasants, also in imitation of the Poznanian model. More than one thousand such circles existed in 1913, with 35,000 members, mostly well-to-do farmers. These circles, usually supervised by the local parson, also functioned as cells of the ND party. The same organization also tried to dominate the cooperative movement, initiated before 1900 by eminent Socialist thinkers, which had become a powerful, independent movement. In numerous villages, consumer cooperatives were founded and ran their own stores. Energetic and devoted social workers, able to gain the confidence of both the peasants and the landowners, did a lot of good in some cases. The "model" village of Lisków in the Kalisz guberniya was an outstanding example, with stores and handicrafts run on cooperative lines, with a model school, dispensary, meeting hall, amateur theater, all run by the indefatigable and widely known Father Wacław Bliziński.

The Nationalist movement had undoubted merits, inasmuch as it served to awaken the peasants from their passivity; to organize them as well as to arouse their patriotic feelings. But a state of affairs in which the awakened peasants would tamely remain under the influence of a party which did not represent their interests could not last forever. The trend to independence, clearly perceptible in 1905, later waned, but then revived as a protest against the more and more conservative tactics of the ND party. As early as 1906, a group of social workers from Radzymin County broke with the ND and founded its own weekly, named *Siewba* (an archaic word for *sowing*). The editor's office was in Tłuszcz, a village in the neighborhood of Warsaw. The editor was Jan Kielak (1877–1917), a self-taught peasant. The makeup of the paper was in pure modern style. The ideas were predominantly utopian and nebulous, concerning the peculiar mission of the peasantry, its spiritual regeneration, the transfer of all land into peasant hands, the maintenance of fraternal cooperation between the peasants and the gentry, etc. This idealistic enterprise was necessarily short-lived, but it sowed some seeds. It was the *Siewba*'s idea to organize separate peasant circles, independent of any form of influence by the clergy or the gentry. These were called *Staszic circles*, named after the famous pioneer of the Enlightenment, a friend and benefactor of the peasants. There were only 100 Staszic circles in 1914, a tiny minority when compared with those controlled by the Agronomic Society, but they were to become a kind of nursery for a generation of future Populist leaders.

In 1908 another and more important event occurred. Alexander Zawadzki (1859–1926), a popular journalist well known for years among the peasants under the pen name Father Procope, broke with the ND, partly for ideological, partly for personal reasons. His chief complaint was that the ND had betrayed the ideal of Poland's independence while pursuing a policy of compromise with czarist Russia. In 1912 Zawadzki founded the National

233

Peasant Union (NZCH) and detached from the ND a large fraction of its peasant followers. The split was a significant one, because the NZCH was eventually to merge with the Piłsudski camp.

Zawadzki's followers did not represent the extreme left wing of the peasant movement. In 1908 Maximilian Malinowski, one of the first followers of Prószynski ("the sunbeam"), began to publish a new weekly, the *Dawn* (*Zaranie*). Malinowski had been a radical since 1905; an adversary of the propertied classes without being a Socialist. *Zaranie*'s slogan was *"sami sobie"*: "Ourselves for ourselves." Malinowski advocated that the peasants go their own way, and not follow directives from the manor and the rectory. Through education, better agricultural techniques, cooperative movements, etc., the peasantry was bound to develop its own intelligentsia, a new brand of leaders who should one day become leaders of the nation. *Zaranie* counted about five thousand subscribers and four hundred local correspondents. It never instigated a mass movement, but Malinowski's followers constituted a cadre of devoted activists. One of the innovations of the group was the founding of cheap high schools for peasants' sons—boarding schools situated in the countryside, rearing places for peasant activists, radiating, in their turn, throughout the neighborhood. As had occurred in Galicia, the *Zaranie* movement was violently attacked by the clergy, and its subscribers were often eliminated from the parish community as atheists and champions of social upheaval. Another charge against them was that they enjoyed the protection of the Russian police—and it was true that the government tolerated *Zaranie* as a counterpoise to the more powerful ND party. *Zaranie* could not be legalized as a political party, nor could it advocate an ideology of independence, because it was an open movement and not a conspiracy, like NZCH. During its short career, *Zaranie* was able to train a relatively large group of civic leaders who were soon to play an important role in liberated Poland.

The parallel story of the Populist movement in the three most important provinces of partitioned Poland is singularly instructive. The rise and the success of the movement gave evidence of a significant change in the conditions and the attitudes of the peasants, over those before emancipation. In its turn, the Populist movement influenced and hastened this evolution. Its greatest successes lay, in Prussian Poland, in a visible improvement in the peasant's welfare; in Congress Poland, in an awakening of nationalist feelings; in Galicia, in the creation of a powerful political party. But even in Galicia, this party was a relatively recent one, and its leaders were poorly educated and had no political traditions. In Russian Poland, attempts to create such a party were frustrated by the czarist regime, and in Poznania by the threat from Germany, which compelled the peasants to accept the bourgeois leadership. The maturing of the peasant movement was still far from completion by 1914. Moreover, the movement was limited to a relatively small fraction of well-to-do peasants; the poorer and landless masses remained outside its scope. They were capable of striking, and even successfully, but they had neither leadership nor organization. Such was the state of things when in 1918 the Polish state "erupted" (as the people said at the time). The introduction of a general franchise in a predominantly agricultural country suddenly elevated the peasants for a short time to the rank of almost a ruling class—to their own surprise and that of the nation.

18

WORLD WAR I AND THE
PROBLEM OF POLAND'S
INDEPENDENCE

World War I broke out in 1914 as the result of numerous and various antagonisms which had run deep in Europe for decades. It will be enough to recall the conflicting Balkan aspirations of Russia and Austro-Hungary; the Anglo-German naval armament race; the French revanchist feelings over Alsace-Lorraine; and the Jugoslav Irredenta, which armed the assassin of Archduke Franz Ferdinand. If there was a major European problem which did *not* influence the outbreak of August 1914, it was the Polish one. None of the European powers was interested in Poland in 1914. And yet, while the war aims of some of the participants were frustrated bitterly, while the Western victory was achieved at who knows what price, Poland emerged in the aftermath of the cataclysm as an independent state and one of the few winners. The international situation, which had disadvantaged Poland in 1795 and 1863, and was to disadvantage her still more in 1939, this time, in 1918, was unexpectedly favorable. Of course, even the best circumstances do not automatically determine a nation's fate; there must still be the nation's will to fight, and at least a modicum of sensible policy. The fall of czarist Russia and the coalition's victory over Germany made the resurrection of Poland a possibility; and the Polish nation was able to take advantage of that unique chance.

The victory of the Polish cause was, however, a costly one, not so much in human lives (especially compared with the hecatomb of World War II), but particularly so from the economic point of view. Since we are dealing here with agrarian problems, let us but briefly mention the fact that the industry of Congress Poland was in large measure simply annihilated by Russian evacuation and German systematic dismantling. But the rural population certainly suffered no less.

Let us recall the course of military events on Polish soil in the years 1914–15. The war began with two divergent and equally abortive offensives. The Russians attacked eastern Prussia, advancing in two columns, from the east and the south; they were knocked out by Hindenburg. The Austrians advanced northward along the right bank of the Vistula and were taken in the rear and routed by General Russki. The next stage, in early fall 1914, consisted of two new offensives which passed each other. The Germans entered Congress Poland from the west and almost reached Warsaw; the Russians entered Galicia from the east and almost reached Krakow. Then came (in late fall) the famous Russian "steamroller" offensive from Warsaw toward Silesia, a movement which was blocked by an audacious German side attack on the line Toruń-Lodz. Afterward the fronts were stabilized for the winter, but in May 1915 the Russian front was broken near Gorlice, just north of the Carpathian Range, and a sweeping German offensive drove the Russians from ethnic Poland in the course of the next few months. This simple tally of events constitutes evidence that the whole of Russian Poland and almost the whole of Galicia were the theater of hostilities, and that extensive regions changed hands more than once. As for the Prussian provinces, only a few districts of Mazuria for a short period experienced enemy invasion. The worst destruction, however, was not caused by bombing, artillery fire, or trench warfare, as on the Western front.

The number of Poles mobilized from 1914 to 1918 by the three partitioning powers probably surpassed two million. The largest contingent was furnished by Austrian Galicia; the smallest by Congress Poland, where mobilization could not be fully carried through because of the rapid move of the fronts. A very rough estimate of human war losses from 1914 to 1918, on the territory of postwar Poland, is about four hundred thousand—again with the highest figure for the Austrian army and the lowest for the Russian. But the most damaging blow experienced by the Polish countryside was due to Russian evacuation in the summer of 1915. The retreating Russian armies applied the scorched-earth policy in Congress Poland. Villages were systematically burned, crops destroyed, livestock requisitioned, and the whole rural population was ordered to move eastward with the Russians. The operation had no military justification, and it was executed ruthlessly, particularly with regard to those who were not at all interested in a Russian victory. About seven hundred thousand persons were evacuated to central Russia, and those villagers who managed to hide and remain often saw their houses destroyed and their farms ruined. There were 1.9 million buildings destroyed during the war on Polish soil. The great majority were village buildings which were deliberately burned during the evacuation. Galicia suffered less of such havoc; but after the return of the Austrian military the gendarmerie began to investigate all cases of collaboration with the Russians, and thousands of persons, mostly peasants, were court-martialled and hanged on the slightest suspicion —often with no ground at all.

As to Congress Poland, it found itself by 1915 under the military occupation of the Central Powers. Two general *gouvernements* were established: a German one in Warsaw and an Austro-Hungarian in Lublin. Both administrations were set on exploiting the country to the utmost in order to help their own war economies. This policy mainly affected the town population. Factories were dismantled, raw materials requisitioned, and towns purposely put on a starvation diet so that the subsequently impoverished population should be obliged to apply for work in Germany. The policy of the German occupation government toward the rural population had a different purpose. Farming was to continue as intensively as possible in order to provide Germany with food. Landowners, especially those who were efficient farmers, and the wealthier peasants were accordingly bolstered, and their manpower, on the whole, was spared. Some kinds of activities were particularly encouraged, for example, pig breeding, which had been feebly developed. All farmers, big and small, were heavily burdened with delivery quotas for the needs of the occupying power; the landowners and the villagers alike were able, however, to retain, legally or not, a sizable surplus which enabled them to subsist and, besides, to make profits on the black market. As in all war periods, the countryside fared much better than the towns. This does not mean that agriculture flourished under the abnormal conditions. Mobilization, requisitions of cattle and horses, and shortages of machinery and fertilizers were to cause

TABLE 3

LIVESTOCK IN 1918 COMPARED WITH LIVESTOCK IN 1914
(In Percentage)

Province	Horses	Cattle	Pigs
Congress Poland (German occupation)......	78.8	80.9	165.6
Congress Poland (Austrian occupation).....	64.2	76.8	51.5
Galicia...................	71.8	81.6	29.8
Poznania................	100.7	69.4	47.8

a reduction of the tilled area and a fall of the yield per acre. On the territories which were to compose postwar Poland, the output of wheat was only 35 percent of the figure for 1913; of rye, 60 percent; of potatoes, 67 percent. Changes in the number of farm animal heads varied in the different provinces (see table 3). A particularly striking example was that of pig breeding, which was encouraged by the Germans but brought to ruin under Austrian rule.

One branch of the economy mercilessly exploited by both the occupying powers was the Polish forests. In three years, 1,500,000 acres were felled in Congress Poland with no thought of reforestation. In the heart of the famous Bialowieża forest, a powerful chemical plant was set up which was to distill from timber a wide range of militarily important substitutes. Bialowieża was an imperial game preserve, and the only abode of the European Bison. During the war this herd was almost entirely exterminated by the surrounding population—and only with utmost effort was this uncommon species saved from final extinction.

Let us now examine the attitude of the Polish peasantry under war conditions. Open class conflicts quieted down because of martial law, and the wage earner was now better paid, and especially better fed, in the countryside than in the towns. As to political activity, it varied in the different provinces. Let us briefly recall that Polish public opinion was divided into three so-called orientations. One camp sided with czarist Russia, one with the Central Powers, especially Austria-Hungary; the third, composed of the extreme left wing, rejected collaboration with any of the fighting coalitions, while laying its hopes on the expected world revolution. Division lines between the orientations ran across class and ideological connections; big landowners, bourgeoisie, and intelligentsia were to be found among Russian as well as Austrian partisans, although their attitudes underwent changes as time passed. The same can be said of attitudes within the Populist movement.

There is less to be said about Prussian Poland, because this province remained politically passive almost until the end of the war. Although the authorities in Berlin somewhat relaxed their anti-Polish measures after the outbreak of the war, the long-standing national conflict excluded a pro-German orientation. But since the Russian armies proved inferior in battle and the entente was far from being victorious, Poznanian Poles (with the exception of ultraconservative loyalists) avoided political commitments. As to the peasantry, it had long since become accustomed to following its leaders from the ranks of the gentry, the bourgeoisie, and the clergy and did not show particular initiative.

Galicia, on the other hand, was profoundly divided. The Austrian government could count, in this province, on the west-Galician Conservatives, the liberals, the Socialists, the Jews, and most of the Ukrainians. On the other hand, the east-Galician Conservatives, the clericals, and the Nationalists—for reasons not relevant to this discussion—were inclined toward Russian orientation. As to the Populists, they had just split the year before, as was mentioned earlier, over an "ethics and morals" issue. Now, Stapiński, the leader of the PSL Left, having come closer to the Socialists, declared his backing of the Supreme National Committee (NKN) formed in Krakow on 16 August 1914. The NKN emphasized the hope that the Polish cause should be linked with that of Austria-

Hungary; it also extended its patronage to the armed Polish legions which had just entered Congress Poland under the command of Joseph Piłsudski (1867–1935). The NKN was originally supposed to be a coalition of all the Galician parties. but the partisans of the so-called Russian orientation soon repudiated the use of the legions and withdrew from the NKN. The point which interests us now is the attitude of the PSL Piast and of its leader, Witos. Witos had joined the NKN but had never participated in its activity. This ambiguous course signified that the right wing of the Populist movement, while not wanting to break openly with Austria, was gravitating toward the Nationalists and, together with them, toward Russian orientation. For the time being, this condemned the Piast party to a kind of passivity.

The situation of Congress Poland as it passed under German and Austrian occupation was more complicated. When Piłsudski's legionnaires crossed the Russian border on 6 August 1914, they expected an outburst of national feeling and an insurrection against the Russians. Nothing of the kind happened. The propertied classes in Russian Poland sided with the ND party, that is, with Russia. And the peasant masses remained passive, if not hostile; they did not want to commit themselves and get into trouble with the Russians. Piłsudski's relatively feeble detachments did not impress them; nor were they attracted by radical slogans.

Under Russian rule there had been no Populist party, but the new regime created the possibility of founding one. The Germans wanted, not to inhibit the development of the conquered territories, but to promote it for their own exploitation; therefore, to gain the good will of the population, they tended to show a semblance of benevolence toward the Poles. In 1916, they embarked upon the course of building a puppet Polish state under an Austro-German protectorate. The Poles in Congress Poland were accordingly allowed a measure of political freedom unthinkable under czarist rule; they could, among other things, found new political parties, and so, late in 1915, a conference met in Warsaw which represented three distinct peasant organizations. One was the *Zaranie* group, headed by Thomas Nocznicki (1862–1944), which had been till now an ideological, rather than a political, movement. The second group was the NZCH (National Peasant Union), a splinter of the National League. The third bore the name

Peasant Union and was a relatively unimportant adjunct of the PPS, or Polish Socialist party. These three organizations of different provenience decided to unite into one Polish Populist party (PSL), thus adopting the Galician terminology. They also began to publish a weekly, the *Liberation (Wyzwolenie)*. It soon appeared that the Galician and the Congress wings of the PSL differed widely in programs and tactics, and their common name led to confusion. The Populists from Congress Poland were therefore called PSL-*Wyzwolenie*, and in 1918 they officially adopted the name *Wyzwolenie*, or Liberation, party.

Their program was a curious blend of intelligentsia radicalism and anti-clericalism which adopted the patriotic slogans of Piłsudski. Not until subsequent elections was a group of authentic peasant politicians brought to the front. Originally, the Liberation group was not an independent movement, but a dependency of Piłsudski's camp intended to act upon the peasants. Together with all of Piłsudski's followers, the Liberation belonged to the broader "activist" camp, an appellation covering the groups ready to collaborate with the occupying powers. The opposite group, faithful to the Russian orientation and led at that time by the ND party, was called "passivists." In the beginning, the passivists stood rather on the right of the political gamut, and the activists on the left (the extreme Left, the future Communists, opposed both orientations). This configuration underwent a sudden change in 1917, after the fall of czarism. The conservative landowners and the wealthy bourgeois were now ready for a rapprochement with Germany, the only power they considered able to protect them from the now-dangerous Eastern influences; they also expected to be offered the key positions in the new Polish state organized by the Germans. Meanwhile Piłsudski progressed step by step from collaboration with to opposition to the occupiers. He had counted on the creation of a Polish army, with himself in command, but he suddenly realized that the masses were ignoring him and that they did not want to fight under the German flag. He boldly grasped at the only measure which would permit him to save face and, at the same time, regain popularity: he put conditions to the Germans which would necessarily be rejected; he then ordered his followers to resign from the legions; and he let himself be arrested and deported to Magdeburg in July 1917. His party now descended again to the underground—a situation best suited to its relatively small following.

Piłsudski's about-face had a significant influence on the future career of his peasant party. Had the peasants been ordered to campaign for volunteer enlistment into the Polish armed forces (*Polnische Wehrmacht*), the party would not have found much support in the countryside. It became popular while passing over to the opposition. The peasants fared not too ill under the occupation, but they were unhappy nonetheless. The main cause of discontent was the steadily rising quota deliveries in grain, potatoes, and meat which the Germans extorted from them and which could have been switched to the black market with much more profit. The villagers, therefore, generally sabotaged the deliveries; here and there, instances of open resistance occurred. The German military's retaliatory punitive expeditions were met with fighting, and casualties resulted for both sides.

Against this background, the POW became popular with the peasants. POW—the Polish Military Organization—was the underground activist group of Piłsudski's camp, the cadre of the future Polish army. The Liberation agents now organized POW cells in the countryside, forming secret armed units, and announced for the near future a fight with the Germans for a democratic Poland. They found ready support, and while strengthening the forces of Piłsudski's camp they also fostered the interests of their own party.

The October revolution of 1917 brought new changes in the political situation in Poland. Russia had stepped out of the war, and all those opposed to the Germans, especially the ND party, now turned their hopes toward the Western coalition. On the other hand, the Socialist revolution which had triumphed in the near neighborhood radicalized the Polish masses as well. Many leftist leaders in Poland were convinced that the Russian example would help them to enforce their own program of social reform. Many moderate leftists were persuaded that the only way of preserving their ascendancy over the masses, and their independence from Russia, was to imitate the bolsheviks. Jędrzej Moraczewski (1870–1944), a right-wing Socialist and a trusted Piłsudski man, confided to his collaborators in 1918, "I am resolved upon some demagogy; we must adopt the bolshevik program."

Both tendencies—the Western orientation and the radical mim-

243

icry—influenced the Populist movement. As early as 28 May 1917, a semiofficial panel of Galician *Sejm* deputies assembled in Krakow and voted a resolution to the effect that Poland's three partitioned provinces must be united and independent and have free access to the sea. The mover of the resolution was Witos, leader of the Populist party. It was symbolic that this declaration of independence was proposed by a Polish peasant, while the old *szlachta*, represented by the Conservative party, followed, although reluctantly because of their connections with the court of Vienna.

The Populists' left wing, the Liberation party, took a momentous step: It introduced an agrarian reform into its platform which proposed that all the big estates be given into peasant hands. It is worthwhile to state here that the problem of agrarian reform did not, in twentieth-century Poland, play the overwhelmingly important role it still plays today in many countries of Asia and Latin America. The once monopolistic position of the feudal gentry had been seriously impaired since the previous century, first as a result of enfranchisement (*uwłaszczenie*) and then of parceling. There still existed vast private latifundia; most of the forests belonged to the big properties; and in some regions, such as Poznania and Byelorussia, much more arable land belonged to the estates than to the village people. But in Congress Poland and western Galicia this percentage had already fallen under fifty and in some counties even under twenty-five. The remaining big properties still exploited the rural proletariat and the village small-holders. It was, however, rather improbable that the total parceling of the estates should, alone, effect an economic panacea. There was not enough estate land in Poland to give a sufficient holding to everybody, in an overpopulated countryside; and other measures—industrialization and urbanization—would have been indispensable.

But if it was naïve to suppose that the agrarian reform would automatically cure all the miseries of the Polish peasantry, it would certainly have been a serious political blunder to oppose the idea of such an undertaking. Soviet Russia had given land to the peasantry; the Polish peasants desperately needed more land; if it was denied them, they would lay their hopes on the bolshevik experiment. This problem was well understood, not only by the Polish non-Communist Left but also by some of the bourgeois political groups—although, for understandable reasons, the conservatives fought bitterly against it. The agrarian reform was adopted in principle, in the first years of liberated Poland (1919–20). It was, however, curtailed and vitiated in the execution. The persistence of the big landowner class—even a feeble and dwindling one—was a steady source of political (not necessarily economic) weakness in Poland between the two wars.

The history of liberated Poland begins in November 1918. The Hapsburg monarchy was torn asunder, and defeated Germany petitioned the entente for an armistice. In western Galicia and Congress Poland, the POW organized the disarming of the occupying forces, which showed no resistance. Lublin was liberated some days earlier than Warsaw, and it was here, on 7 November, that the Provisional Populist Government of the Polish Republic was installed. It was a thoroughly leftist government, headed by the Socialist leader Ignacy Daszyński (1866–1936). Its manifesto proclaimed, among other things, fully democratic voting regulations, an eight-hour workday, extensive social security rules— and, moreover, the agrarian reform and the nationalization of the forests.

The Liberation party entered the Daszyński government and gave it full support. Witos was also invited and even came to Lublin, but, on second thought, he declined the offer and unobtrusively left the town. This was another significant symptom. On the eve of a new chapter of Poland's history the peasantry was far from united. There were regions where the peasants tried to establish the agrarian reform themselves by attempting to drive all landowners away. Everywhere unions of farm wage earners were organized which engaged in violent strike warfare against the landlords, for a better standard of living. At the same time, moderate Populist politicians offered their cooperation to the bourgeois parties, in exchange for a moderate agrarian reform. As a result of the first elections—entirely free and democratic elections, although boycotted by the extreme Left—about one hundred and twenty peasants entered the *Sejm* (which counted less than four hundred members). No parliamentary government was possible without Populist support; but since the Populists were divided into a right center, which sided with the nationalist bourgeoisie, and a left center, which was nearer to Socialism but influenced by Piłsudski's men, the actual force of the Populists in the *Sejm* was negligible.

The political split of Populism—a result, among other things, of personal rivalries and provincial differences—was conditioned in a deeper sense by the differentiation of the Polish peasantry itself: one group, well-to-do and more or less satisfied with the existing social order and trying to preserve it; the other, less privileged and more revolutionary. Only later, when Piłsudski's authoritarian regime denied the masses participation in power, and when the Great Depression immersed in bitter misery the whole of the countryside, did a unique Populist party emerge as an important partner in the fight for democracy.

During the first years of independent Poland swarms of peasant activists arrived in Warsaw straight from their villages to function as deputies, high officials, and ministers. Witticisms multiplied at their expense; they were accused of churlishness, of abusiveness, of putting their own interests (their party's or their class's) over the nation's welfare. Some of these accusations might have been true; certainly they are understandable. But on the whole one must say that the immense majority of the Polish peasantry and its political representatives clung unwaveringly to the platform of a Polish national state—even when reborn Poland appeared less favorable to the popular masses than it had seemed to promise. In the first crucial years of 1918–20, and still more during the next and more terrible ordeal of World War II, the Polish peasantry felt and acted as patriots. We can consider this attitude the result of a long and complicated process which transformed the serf obliged to compulsory labor into an independent farmer and a citizen conscious of his responsibilities. Many factors—economic, social, educational, and political—played a part in this process, as did the Polish revolutionaries and democratic activists. The chief merit, however, ought to be attributed to the peasants themselves. With great laboriousness and tenacity they fought for the ownership of their land and defended it against all adversaries at home and abroad.

APPENDIX
Legislative Documents

A. Constitution of 3 May 1791, Article 4

The farming population, from which flow the most abundant riches of the country and which constitutes the most numerous part of the nation and consequently its most vital force, is now, for the sake of justice, humanity, and Christian duty as well as our own obvious interest, brought under the protection of law and of the national government. We establish that henceforth all freedoms, conferments, or agreements authentically concerted by the landlords with the peasants of their domains, whether such freedoms, conferments, or agreements be concluded with whole communes or separately with each villager, will constitute their common and mutual obligation, belonging under the protection of the national government, in accordance with the essential conditions and contents of these conferments and agreements. Such agreements and resulting obligations, if accepted freely by a landlord, will also bind his descendants and the rights of new purchasers, who may not change them arbitrarily. In like manner, the peasants in any domain may not repudiate voluntary agreements, and the privileges and obligations connected therewith, otherwise than in such a way and under such conditions as were settled in the said agreements, which will bind them strictly, forever or for a specified time. Having thus guaranteed the landlords all the profits due them from the peasants, and wishing to efficiently promote the welfare of the whole population, we proclaim full freedom for all immigrants and for all those who, having left the country, now desire to come back. Any person newly arriving, or one returning, to the republic, as soon as he puts his foot on Polish soil will be free to practice his industry how and where he will, to contract agreements concerning settling, labor, or rent; and until he makes such agreements he will be free to settle in town or in village, to dwell in Poland or go to any country he wishes to, after having fulfilled the obligations he has voluntarily contracted.

B. Decree of Frederick Augustus, King of Saxony, Duke of Warsaw, 21 December 1807

Article 1. Every farmer, peasant, or journeyman who has not already been granted the right of property is free to move from his residence and go to live in the area of the Duchy of Warsaw, where he will choose by free will.

Article 2. He must, however, first give an account to the landlord, who has no right to restrain him, and to the authorities of the county, who must report to the government every person leaving or arriving in their district.

Article 3. Every farmer, peasant, or journeyman who wishes to remain in his present residence is assured freedom to dwell there for one year, provided he performs the same duties to which he has been liable till now. The landlord, during that time, has no right to force them to leave or to impose any more duties than those in effect till now.

Article 4. On every judicial summons, the authorities empowered to it will register voluntary agreements of perpetual sale or temporary lease, under conditions negotiated by common consent between farmers and landlords, whether in the same villages where they have dwelt till now, or in different villages with other landlords. A court official must function as a public witness, with the responsibility of seeing that the parties negotiate a free agreement. Is there indeed a voluntary contract, or is there fear, constraint, or deceit? Every detail of the proceedings must be included in the records.

Article 5. When leaving the village in which he has dwelt till now, the farmer must relinquish the landlord's property—livestock, tools, and seeds. He can be freed from that duty only by proving that he lost this property after 1 October 1806, by plague or other calamity. All other claims of the landlord denied by the farmer must be taken to court. Since he has the right to sue for his property, in no case may the landlord take it from the farmer against his will.

C. *Edict of Frederick William III, King of Prussia,* *14 September 1811* *(Excerpts)*

Part 1, concerning not owned but hereditary peasant holdings:

§3. Among these holdings are numbered all lands which were passed by inheritance to their holders' descendants or collaterals, as well as those on which, when vacant, the landlord was legally bound to place one of the successors of the previous holder. Estates given in usufruct without such a pledge, for an indeterminate period or for a definite number of years or for life, do not belong to this category but must be considered temporary leases.

§4. All possessors of hereditary peasant holdings and possessions, whether they are called full- or half-peasants, single-holders or cottagers, or any other common local name, and whether they belong to ecclesiastical, governmental, or private estates, are granted the title to their holdings, subject to the obligation to compensate the landlords according to the regulations given below.

Labor duties are also abrogated, subject to compensation, with the exception of some types of duties indicated in paragraph 16.

In exchange, all claims of the peasants against the landlords concerning the maintenance of buildings, the lending of livestock, all kinds of grants-in-aid, and locum-tenens in taxpaying will also cease. The peasants will be compensated for such rights according to their value.

§5. We desire that the separation of the landlords from their subjects take place by mutual agreement, and we allow them two years, starting from this date, to accomplish it. If such an agreement does not materialize, the following regulations will be applied—on the motion of one of the parties or of the state.

§6. The matters commonly concerned in such an agreement and therefore liable to compensation are as follows:

    a. The rights of the landlord:
      1. The right of property
      2. The right to labor duties
      3. Tributes in cash and kind
      4. The livestock lent to the holder
      5. The servitudes of the landlord on peasant grounds
    b. The rights of the peasants:
      1. The right to be helped in misfortune
      2. The right to collect brustwood and branches; other rights to the woods
      3. The duty of the landlords to construct and repair buildings
      4. The duty of the landlords, in cases of poverty, to acquit the peasants from the obligation to pay taxes and other public charges
      5. Grazing and wood servitudes

§7. Only a few of these matters, such as tributes in cash or kind, livestock, and servitudes, can be evaluated more or less exactly. The following can be appraised only approximately:

    a. The right of property, which may have a large or small value according to circumstances
    b. Labor, which, however definite, does not have a uniform utility because of the means of its performance
    c. Most of the landlord's charges, which are sometimes numerous and at other times few in number, so that past experience does not supply a comparative scale because of the lack of continuity in needs and benefits
    d. Acquitted taxes, since acquittal occurs erratically

In order to arrive at an assured base for compensation, and not to frustrate our beneficial goal by insuperable difficulties, we consider it necessary to set forth the following regulations, which are based on generally accepted principles.

§8. We prescribe—

  a. that in hereditary holdings the tributes and charges of the peasants are not to be raised;
  b. that, on the contrary, they are to be diminished if the holder is unable to sustain himself;
  c. that the holdings must be maintained in such a manner that they are capable of bearing the state charges.

Thus, according to general principles of state economy and state law, the state has a superior right to ordinary and extraordinary taxes and contributions, whereas the tributes due the landlords are limited in that the subjects must be left the means for subsistence and for discharging their duties toward the state.

§9. We complement herewith the problems of subsistence and taxpaying, by stating that both must be assured when the tributes and charges toward the manor do not exceed one-third of the total profits from a hereditary holding.

§10. With the exception of cases quoted below, it will be the rule that, concerning hereditary holdings, the landlords will be compensated for their titles of property, labor duties, and other charges when their subjects have ceded them one-third of all their grounds and renounced all extraordinary grants in livestock, repairs, and locum tenens in taxpaying.

§11. While freeing the landlords from the above duties and obliging them to accept the stipulated compensation, we also order their present subjects to relinquish their claims, and we set forth the following regulations:

§12. It will be the general rule that compensation must be given in the form of one-third of all the grounds: fields, gardens, grazing lands, and woods. The parties are free, however, to settle on compensation in capital or rent in kind or cash.

If such a settlement does not occur, the landlord may agree

251

to compensation in rent. But if he claims land as compensation, and the peasants refuse, the General Commission will determine if land must be given.

D. Enactment of Viceroy Joseph Zajączek, 30 May 1818 (Excerpts)

Article 1. Each village consisting of at least ten dwellings may have its own mayor.

Article 2. Part of a village belonging to one landlord may be committed to the administration of another, if it consists of at least ten dwellings.

Article 4. Several villages belonging to one landlord may form one commune, administered by a single mayor.

Article 7. The villages administered by one mayor will form one rural commune.

Article 8. The owners of the villages are mayors by law. They can discharge their duties themselves or through mayors or their deputies proposed or appointed by them. The Governmental Commission for Internal Affairs and Police, however, can, on sufficiently important grounds, refuse to confirm the proposed mayor.

Article 15. The mayor keeps all official files in order, supervises the collection of taxes, decides the equitable distribution of public charges and duties, sees to tidiness and order in the commune. He also guarantees the security of persons and property; obviates all damages brought on the whole commune or on single persons by malice or license; maintains the ways, bridges, and crossings; seizes tramps, vagabonds, and runaways and remands them to the commissary-delegate; administers conscription for the army, keeps the Communal Book and communal statistics. He is careful not to admit into the commune anybody without proper attestation and sends unauthorized persons back to their rightful places; he complies in general with all the requirements of the Governmental Commissions and reports to the commissary delegates on all the above subjects at times prescribed by the commissions.

Article 16. The mayor of each village may appoint as an assistant a head of the village (*sołtys*), who will remain under his authority.

E. Manifesto of the National Government of the
Republic of Poland, Krakow,
22 February 1846

Poles! The hour of insurrection has struck. Poland, torn to pieces, rises and unites. Our brethren in Poznania, Congress Poland, Lithuania, and Ruthenia have already risen and are fighting the enemy. They fight for their most sacred rights, which were wrenched from them by guile and force.

You know what has happened and still happens: the choice of our youth rotting in prisons, outrages perpetrated on the old men who supported us with advice, priests deprived of authority; in short, everybody who fought, in deed or thought, for Poland, has either had his livelihood destroyed or rots in prison. The moans of millions of flogged, imprisoned, deported, and tortured brothers have caused our hearts to bleed. The invaders have wrenched our glory from us; they have denied us our language and the right to confess the creed of our fathers. They obstruct every means of bettering our social structure, arm brethren against brethren, and calumniate the most deserving sons of the country. Brethren! Only one more pace and there will be no Poland and no Poles. Our grandsons will curse our memory, crying that we have left them only rubble and desert out of what was once the most beautiful land on earth; that we have let our poor people be put in chains, confess a foreign faith, speak a foreign language, and be the slaves of those who have robbed them of their rights. Our fathers' and our martyrs' dusts are calling us from the tomb, invoking vengeance; our infants are imploring us to preserve their mother country; all the free nations of the world are calling on us not to let fall the sacrosanct cause of nationality. God himself calls us and will one day claim an accounting from us.

We are twenty million; let us insurge in a body so that no force will overpower us! Ours will be a kind of liberty which has never before existed on earth. By fighting we shall secure a social system in which everybody will enjoy the goods of the earth according to his merits and capabilities and in which privileges will no longer be permitted. Every Pole will find a safeguard for himself, his wife, and his children; all persons handicapped in body or mind will find, without humiliation, unfailing help from society; the land, now possessed by the peasants only under certain conditions, will become their unconditional property; rent, compulsory labor, and all similar charges will cease, without remuneration to the landlords; and the national servicemen will be rewarded with homesteads in the national estates.

Poles! From now on we do not acknowledge differences among us. We are now brothers, sons of one mother country and of one father, the heavenly God! Let us invoke his help, and he will bless our arms and grant us victory. But so that He will hear our prayers let us not pollute ourselves by drunkenness or plundering; let us not stain our sacred weapons by license or by murder of unarmed dissenters or foreigners. We do not lead a fight against nations, but against our oppressors.

And now, as a sign of unity, let us put on the national cockade and take this oath: "I swear to serve Poland, my country, in counsel, word, and deed! I swear to sacrifice all my personal views, my fortune, and my life for her! I swear unconditional allegiance to the national government formed in Krzysztofory House, Krakow, on 22 February at 8 P.M., and to all the authorities ordained by them, so God help me!"

The present manifesto should be published in the *Official Journal* and in circulars distributed throughout Poland. It should immediately be proclaimed from the pulpit in all the churches, and posted in public places in all communes.

F. Imperial Patent of Ferdinand I, 17 April 1848
(Excerpts)

1. All compulsory labor and other duties evolving from the serfdom of the propertied peasants, as well as of the cottagers and small-holders, should cease on 15 May 1848.

2. The existing servitudes remain intact, although the serfs are obliged, if they wish to enjoy these rights on the landlords' soil, to pay a suitable charge. Its original determination is made by voluntary agreement between the serfs and their lords.

3. If, as a consequence of the partition of an estate, the serfs enjoy the right of servitudes evolving from serfdom on territories belonging not to their own but to another master, these servi-

tudes remain in force; the serfs, however, are to reimburse the
state treasury, which has acquitted them from their charges.

4. In exchange, the landlords are freed, beginning with 15 May
1848—

    a. from paying the urbarial tax;
    b. from the duty of granting aid to their serfs in need;
    c. from the duty of establishing and keeping the land books;
    d. from the duty of pleading in contentions involving their
        serfs;
    e. from contributing to the cost of maintaining village police;
    f. from paying the costs of bringing conscripts to their place
        of induction and of feeding them (such costs will be assumed
        by the communes in the future);
    g. from contributing to the costs of treatment in cases of epi-
        demic disease, venereal disease, and cattle plague.

5. In consequence of the expected arrangement of first-instance
authorities, the landlords will also be freed as soon as possible
from the burden of levying taxes and from the costs and responsibilities connected with the exercise of civil justice and political
administration.

7. All these alleviations will constitute for the landlords partial
reimbursement for the loss of their serfs' labor and other duties.
In evaluating the landlords' indemnity, the treasury will calculate such alleviations as one-third the value of the former duties.
A further restitution will consist in the value of the servitudes
if they cease by mutual agreement; or, if they remain in force, in
the payment by the serfs for the use of such rights. For the rest
of the legally due urbarial and dominial charges the landlords
will be indemnified by the province according to the assessment
figured in the Land Tax Books, with a deduction of 5 percent for
collection costs.

8. The ways and means of covering the future indemnity to be
paid the landlords by the treasury will be more precisely determined by legislation.

9. Before the final assessment of the said indemnity, advances
will be paid the landlords and other persons entitled to urbarial
duties, these advances to be deducted from future remuneration.

10. Regulations concerning the evaluation of the advances and the means and terms of payment will shortly be set forth in a separate circular.

13. Parties who feel wronged in the final assessment of the indemnity are entitled to file complaints to the Civil Court, according to regulations to be issued at a convenient time.

We trust that landlords and serfs will acknowledge these dispositions, which we have enacted after carefully analyzing the public's needs and urging circumstances for mutual profit, as new proof of our unceasing solicitude for their welfare. Propertied peasants, cottagers and small-holders, whose duties we abrogate— even with sacrifices by the public treasury—are particularly expected to become worthy of the attention bestowed upon them: by their obedience to law; their calm and orderly demeanor; their avoidance of all attempts against persons and property; their unshakable fidelity and benevolence toward us and our government; as well as their sincere collaboration with the landlords, including tilling their land for moderate daily pay.

G. *Ukase of Emperor Nicolaus I, 7 June 1846*

Considering—

1. that the peasants in our kingdom of Poland, after having been granted personal liberty, have since 1831 experienced important alleviations of their duties in the state domains;

2. that their existence becomes more and more settled, thanks to measures gradually undertaken;

3. that, on the contrary, the peasants living on private estates, depend solely upon the discretion of the landlords because of the lack of constant legal rules;

4. that the landlords arbitrarily evict the peasants or impair their ownership of old holdings, whence comes the increase in the number of landless peasants and their frequent migrations, which are detrimental to the welfare and morality of that useful class;

5. that peasants in private estates, who are fearful of losing their ancient holdings, are often compelled to accept harsh

conditions and bear onerous duties which are either arbitrarily pressed upon them by the landlords or are based on custom alone;

we therefore recognize it as indispensable—before publishing general rules concerning the peasant arrangement—to settle the elementary principles, which are as follows:

Article 1. The farmers dwelling in private towns and villages and tilling for themselves at least three *morgi* of soil will, as long as they correctly perform the duties attached to their holdings, use the holdings and other conveniences; and the landlords cannot arbitrarily evict them, impair their holdings, or raise their duties. On the other hand, the farmers are free to leave one estate for another, provided they carry out the existing police regulations and give an account to the landlord three months in advance of each new economic year.

Article 2. Holdings vacated by peasants must be filled by the landlord, within two years at most, with other peasants; the holdings may not be incorporated into the manorial demesne.

Article 3. All gratuitous extra labor days and compulsory-hire days levied on private estates (under various names) without legal authorization will be abrogated by the Administrative Council—on private estates run by the owners themselves, beginning 1 January 1847; on estates which were rented out before 1 January 1846 by legal contracts, beginning with the expiration of the contracts.

Article 4. In order to settle all contests between landlords and peasants as conveniently and quickly as possible, the Administrative Council will enact, in place of the present, admittedly onerous procedure, appropriate regulations delineating precise jurisdictional procedures for handling these affairs. Meanwhile the same council will recommend that the executive authorities take the utmost care to see that the duties and charges owed the landlords by the peasants do not surpass those based on the legal title—after the abrogation of extra labor and compulsory-hire days—which existed on 1 January 1846; and that in contests of landlords versus peasants strict justice is dispensed and protection granted, according to law, to whom it is due.

Article 5. Executive authorities will extend the necessary help and protection to landlords who intend to conclude rent agreements with the peasants. Such agreements, however, together with detailed conclusions, should be forwarded by the Guberniya Authority for ratification by a higher authority which will be appointed by the Administrative Council.

Article 6. Perpetual usufructuaries of land belonging to the state, the educational, and other public funds, and to the communes are legally bound to leave the burghers and peasants dwelling thereon, with their present holdings, and they may not charge them with new duties exceeding those covered by inventories or other titles. Future contests will be settled by competent administrative authorities.

Article 7. The fulfillment of this, our will, and its gradual development are committed to the care of our viceroy (*namiestnik*) and to the Administrative Council of the Kingdom of Poland.

H. Decrees of 22 January 1863

The Central National Committee in its capacity as National Provisional Government—taking into consideration the fact that making the peasants freeholders has long been delayed, notwithstanding the general wish of the country, by the usurping government; and, further, taking into consideration the fact that granting full title to the peasants of land they formerly possessed by paying or performing compulsory labor or other duties impairs the property of the present owners—issues the following decrees:

Article 1. Every kind of land property possessed by any husbandman to the present time—whether by labor services, rents, or other title—together with the messuage which belongs to it, dwellings and farm buildings, as well as the rights and privileges attached to it, becomes from the day of this decree the exclusive and hereditary property of its present possessor, without any form of obligation whatsoever, whether gifts in kind, labor services, or rent, upon the sole condition that he pay the taxes levied upon it and render the required services to the country.

Article 2. The former proprietors of the holdings granted to the husbandmen will receive suitable indemnities in the form of government stock.

Article 3. The principles of evaluation of the indemnity and the nature of the stock will be settled by separate decrees.

Article 4. All ukases, laws, etc., published by the usurping government on the subject of the so-called peasant problem are declared null and void.

Article 5. The present decree applies not only to private estates but also to national estates, lands bestowed by the crown, church property, etc.

Article 6. The carrying out of these decrees is confided by the Central National Committee, in its capacity as National Provisional Government, to the military and Palatinate chiefs.

The Central National Committee in its capacity as National Provisional Government—taking into consideration the fact that throwing off the foreign yoke demands a large armed force and that no one can be excused from military service; and, further, taking into consideration the fact that every citizen subsisting from the work of his hands must, when away at war, have his livelihood as well as that of his family secured—issues the following decrees:

Article 1. Cottagers, small-holders, journeymen, and all citizens subsisting only from their wages will, after fighting for their country in the ranks of the national army, receive with full title at the end of the war holdings of at least three *morgi* from the national estates. The wives and children of soldiers killed during the war will also receive holdings.

Article 2. The carrying out of Article 1 is confided by the Central National Committee, in its capacity as National Provisional Government, to the military and Palatinate chiefs.

I. Ukase of Emperor Alexander II, 2 March 1864
(Excerpts)

Article 1. The grounds in peasant possession, that is, the peasant holdings in private and entail estates and in public and government estates, are now to pass with full property title to their peasant holders.

Article 2. Beginning 15 April 1864, the peasants are freed forever and without exception from all charges levied by the landlords, such as labor duty, ransom in cash, tributes in kind, rent, etc. All claims of arrears and deficits of these charges are to come to an end, and they may not be reinstated in the future. The peasants will be bound, instead, to pay to the treasury the land tax established by this ukase.

Article 3. The landlords of private, entail, and public estates will receive from the government compensation for the abrogated peasant duties. Apart from this, the landlords of estates in which the peasants have been granted the ownership of their holdings by this ukase are freed from the duties of helping the peasants in the event of calamity and of lending them livestock, tools, and sowing grain.

Article 5. On private and public estates, all peasants will become owners of their holdings, whether the holdings fall under the Imperial Ukase of 7 June 1846 or not. That is, all holdings—even those smaller than three *morgi*—are included. Exceptions to this regulation are specified in Article 10.

Communal property such as office and school buildings as well as land used in common without the landlord's participation (e.g., communal grazing land) will also become peasant property.

Article 6. In addition, the peasants are entitled to full property title to holdings falling under the ukase of 7 June 1846 which were held by them at the time of its proclamation, even if the holdings are now vacant or if, in defiance of Article 2 of the ukase, the landlords have appropriated them without giving other grounds in exchange. The peasants may apply to the local commissioners or to the Commission of the Interior, within three years from 15 April 1864, for grants of the holdings.

Article 7. The abandoned holdings mentioned in Article 6 which are not claimed by peasants within the specified period and the grounds arbitrarily taken away from the peasants after 7 June 1846 to which they have not filed claims may be incorporated into the manorial grounds.

Article 8. If after 7 June 1846 an exchange of land has taken place between peasants and landlords on an estate of any kind, without legal approval and solely according to the landlord's decision,

260

the peasants may claim possession of any grounds they held on 7 June 1846 and must abandon the manorial grounds given them in exchange.

Article 9. Together with the land acquired by each peasant, all dwellings and farm buildings situated on that land, and the livestock, tools, and sowing grain, pass into his possession.

Article 10. Excepted from the grounds acquired by the peasants in accordance with the present ukase are:

a. The inns, mills, brickyards, and forges set up by the landlords

b. The holdings of shepherds, gardeners, and other manorial servants if their dwellings are situated adjacent to the manor or the demesne and are not in the village

c. The holdings of foresters if their holdings are situated not in the village but adjacent to the manor or the demesne or are in the landlord's forest

d. Manorial lands temporarily leased to the peasants by written contract, if they have been farmed out together with manorial buildings

e. Holdings acquired by the peasants with full property title before the proclamation of this ukase

Article 11. Even after acquiring title to their holdings, the peasants retain the right to servitudes they enjoyed previously on the basis of prestation tables, contracts, oral agreements, or common use, such as the right to obtain timber and firewood; the right to gather branches, dry wood, and needles; the right to graze their stock in the landlords' forests or fields. If on 7 June 1846 the peasants were in possession of any such rights, and if they were later deprived of them illegally, these rights are to be fully restored in the form practiced before 7 June 1846.

Article 12. The rights of the peasants to the servitudes cannot be abrogated otherwise than by mutual agreement, ratified according to regulations, between the landlord and the peasants; or by the landlord's demand but under the indispensable condition of compensating the peasants. Cases in which the abrogation of servitudes can be permitted on the landlord's demand, as well as regulations concerning the method of evaluating the peasants' compensation, will be separately settled.

Article 13. In the state domains and entail estates the peasants become full owners of all their holdings together with all the servitudes now in use.

Article 14. The right of ownership of their holdings, with the exception of those specified in Article 10, is granted to all peasant landholders, whether they are colonists, full- or half-peasants, cottagers, small-holders, etc.; whether their titles of possession are determined on the basis of official tables of charges, specifications provided by the law of 1862, prestation tables, privileges, and written or oral term or termless contracts. Titles for those with no contracts, who hold their land according to custom, are determined independently of the circumstances—whether they have been obliged to pay rent, to pay ransom in cash (according to the law of 1861), to pay tribute in kind, to perform compulsory labor, or have been liable to a combination of such charges.

BIBLIOGRAPHY

Primary Sources

The pertinent sources are both extremely numerous and extremely incomplete. Two important questions have never been recorded: the material conditions of peasant life and the psychological
motivation behind peasant attitudes. Some of the most important
archival sources are outside of Poland and of difficult access: in
Lvov, for Austrian Poland (Galicia); in Moscow, for Russian
Poland. Numerous archival materials were destroyed in Warsaw
during the last war. On the other hand, a new category of material, almost inaccessible in prewar times, has now been opened to
researchers: the records of numerous private estates.

Many printed sources have long been known and exploited—
official statistics, agronomic newspapers, pamphlets concerned
with the agrarian reforms. These well-known sources are uni-
lateral, superficial, and fragmentary; statistics from the early
nineteenth century are unreliable. Private correspondence and
memoirs, have one major defect. They are mainly of nobility

263

provenance; occasionally from the middle classes. Peasant memoirs are practically nonexistent for the period before emancipation. The few extant are not typical; they tell the stories of peasants who left the village: one becomes a soldier, another a teacher, still another goes on a pilgrimage on foot to Rome and Jerusalem, etc. Only toward the end of the nineteenth century memoirs written by peasants came to light. Some of them are remarkable and interesting, but they are concerned with the later part of the period.

Archival sources are mainly of two kinds:

1. Records of domain administration. They were much better preserved on big estates—those belonging to the state and to aristocratic families—than on small estates. The big estates were seldom directly run by the owner; as a rule, they were farmed out. Consequently, there is no trace in the records of such important matters as the handling of compulsory labor, the raising of crops, the income and expenses of a single, middle-sized farm. The records of a latifundium give us summarized data about the rent paid by peasants or leaseholders, the income from innkeepers, the sale of timber, and the maintenance costs of the manor, the stable, and the gardens. We get, of course, exact data concerning estate and village grounds, the amount of compulsory labor, the rights of felling and grazing to which the peasants were entitled, the so-called regulations consisting in changing compulsory labor to rent. Only a fragment of this information concerns the middle-sized estates, which were the most common category.

2. Sources associated with agrarian reforms undertaken by the state. Immediately after the partitions, the three governments which had partitioned Poland began to record materials concerning the agrarian conditions in their new provinces. There are the questionnaires (*indaganda*) in Prussia, several cadastres put through in Austrian Galicia, the prestation tables of 1846 in central Poland, etc. The schemes of all the sources are the same: they enumerate the quantity and quality of land owned by each peasant, together with incumbent charges (labor and rent). The exactness of these data may be questionable; on the other hand, they served as norms for the future.

The emancipation reform generated another group of sources. They are especially useful because they show the assets of each peasant before and after the reform. The documents are fully preserved for the Poznan province and for Galicia. They are extremely voluminous, and therefore difficult to use. The documents for central Poland (the Congress Kingdom) are lost, for the most part. Paradoxically enough, this is the reason why research work concerning the agrarian reforms is more advanced for Russian Poland than for the two other provinces.

Polish postwar historiography has achieved a good bit of work relative to these problems, but much is still left to be done. There is a preliminary approach to the history of Polish agriculture (cultivation as well as breeding) in the precapitalist period, especially in central Poland. There are books concerning the different groups of peasants, among others, the landless peasants. Other books discuss the administration of individual estates; the different aspects of the feudal exploitation. Numerous examples of the peasant class struggle have been studied. The agrarian programs of political parties and the peasants' attitude toward national insurrections have also constituted the subject of many exhaustive studies. A very brief synthesis of the peasant's emancipation was written ten years ago by Śreniowski. Since then, more-detailed monographs, about the Prussian reform and the reform in the Congress Kingdom, have appeared; but the parallel story of the reform in Galicia has been practically untouched by modern research. More recently, younger specialists have tackled the postemancipation period, particularly in the Congress Kingdom, and there are many differences of opinion concerning vital problems. The main difficulty lies with figures—the estimation and interpretation of statistical data; we meet here far-reaching divergences, which render difficult, and even dangerous, the drawing of conclusions.

Abbreviations for Publishers in Secondary Sources

KiW   Książka i Wiedza, Warsaw
LSW   Ludowa Spółdzielnia Wydawnicza, Warsaw
MON   Wydawnictwo Ministerstwa Obrony Narodowej, Warsaw
Oss   Zakład Narodowy im. Ossolińskich, Wroclaw
PTPN Poznańskie Towarzystwo Przyjaciół Nauk, Poznan
PWN   Państwowe Wydawnictwo Naukowe, Warsaw
PWRL Państwowe Wydawnictwo Rolnicze i Leśne, Warsaw
WŁ   Wydawnictwo Łódzkie, Lodz
WP   Wiedza Powszechna, Warsaw

Secondary Sources

There are but few up-to-date books on Polish modern economic history written in a language commonly studied by Western students. Most of the works cited below are in Polish. Nineteenth-century publications have been omitted, and only the more important editions of sources are included.

A general survey of Poland's history will be found in *The Cambridge History of Poland*, vols. 1–2 (Cambridge, 1950–51), as well as in the *History of Poland*, edited by PWN (Warsaw: PWN, 1968). (The chapters covering the eighteenth–twentieth centuries are due to E. Rostworowski, S. Kieniewicz, and H. Wereszycki.) The newest Polish textbook on nineteenth-century Poland is S. Kieniewicz, *Historia Polski, 1795–1918* (Warsaw: PWN, 1968). Volume 2 of J. Rutkowski's *Historia gospodarcza Polski* (Economic History of Poland) covers the period 1795–1918 and may be useful for its statistical data. *Zarys historii gospodarstwa wiejskiego w Polsce* (An Outline of the History of Polish Agriculture), vol. 2, published under the direction of J. Leskiewicz (Warsaw: PWRL, 1965), concentrates mainly upon agronomic technology. A. Jezierski, *Handel zagraniczny Królestwa Polskiego, 1815–1914* (The Foreign Trade of the Kingdom of Poland), Warsaw University Editions (Warsaw, 1867), contains the important statistics of the Polish grain trade.

Sources for individual chapters of this volume are given below.

Chapter 1

Księgi Referendarii Koronnej (The Books of the Referendaria Court), vols. 1–2, edited by A. Keck and W. Pałucki (Warsaw: KiW, 1955–57), contains a selection of court cases concerning conflicts with peasants in the Crown estates from 1786 to 1794.

The evolution of agronomy and the rent reforms: B. Baranowski, *Gospodarstwo chłopskie i folwarczne we wschodniej Wielkopolsce w XVIII w.* (Peasant and Estate Economy in Eastern Great Poland in the Eighteenth Century) (Warsaw: PWN, 1958); C. Bobinska, *Studia z dziejów wsi małopolskiej w 2 połowie XVIII w.* (Studies on the History of the Village in Little Poland in the Second Half of the Eighteenth Century) (Warsaw: KiW, 1957); E. Rostworowski, "Reforma pawłowska P. K. Brzostowskiego, 1767–1795" (P. K. Brzostowski's Reform in Pavlov, 1767–1795), *Przegląd Historyczny* (1953).

266

The problem of the peasant's rights to the soil: K. Orzechowski, *Chłopskie posiadanie ziemi na Górnym Śląsku u schyłku epoki feudalnej* (Peasant Land Holdings in Upper Silesia during the Decline of Feudalism) (Opole, 1959). The political programs: S. Staszic, *Pisma filozoficzne i społeczne* (Philosophic and Social Writings), vols. 1–2, edited by B. Suchodolski (Warsaw: PWN, 1954); H. Kołłątaj, *Listy Anonima* (Anonymous Letters), vols. 1–2, edited by B. Leśnodorski and H. Wereszycka (Warsaw: PWN, 1954), contains the annotated texts of the leading reformers of the time. See also B. Leśnodorski, *Les jacobins polonais* (in French) (Paris, 1965); and J. Kowecki, *Uniwersał Połaniecki i sprawa jego realizacji* (Kościuszko's Manifesto of Połaniec and Its Execution) (Warsaw: PWN, 1957).

Chapter 2

The Russian provinces: L. Zytkowicz, *Rządy Repnina na Litwie, 1794–1797* (Repnin's Government in Lithuania, 1794–1797) (Wilno, 1938).

Prussian Poland: J. Wąsicki, *Ziemie polskie pod zaborem pruskim* (Polish Lands under Prussian Rule), vol. 1: Southern Prussia, 1793–1806; vol. 2: New Eastern Prussia, 1795–1806 (Wroclaw: Oss, 1957–63); D. Rzepniewska, *Gospodarstwo folwarczne na Mazowszu, 1795–1806* (The Folwark Economy in Mazovia, 1795–1806) (Warsaw: PWN, 1968).

Galicia: R. Rozdolski, *Stosunki poddańcze w dawnej Galicji* (Serfdom Relations in Former Galicia) (Warsaw: PWN, 1962). Volume 2 of this book consists of an edition of sources, mostly in German.

The political programs: C. Wycech, *Spisek Franciszka Gorzkowskiego na tle ruchów społecznych w końcu XVIII w.* (F. Gorzkowski's Conspiracy on the Background of Social Uprisings at the End of the Eighteenth Century) (Warsaw: LSW, 1960); Pawlikowski's pamphlet *Czy Polacy mogą się wybić na niepodległość?* (Can the Poles Recover Independence?) has been re-edited with a commentary, by E. Halicz (Warsaw: MON, 1967).

Chapter 3

The genesis and meaning of the December Decree, 1807, are analyzed in volume 2 of H. Grynwaser, *Pisma* (Writings) (Wroclaw: Oss, 1951). The evolution of the countryside: H. Grossman, *Struktura społeczna i gospodarcza Księstwa Warszawskiego* (The Social and Economic Structure of the Duchy of Warsaw) (Warsaw, 1925), contains valuable statistics.

Chapter 4

The essential texts (in German) are to be found in M. Kniat, *Dzieje uwłaszczenia w W. Księstwie Poznańskim* (History of the Emancipation in the Grand Duchy of Poznań), vols. 1–2 (Poznan, 1939–46). A general survey: *Dzieje wsi wielkopolskiej* (History of the Great Polish Countryside), edited by W. Rusiński (Poznan, 1959). The consequences of the Reform: S. Borowski, *Kształtowanie się rolniczego rynku pracy w okresie wielkich reform agrarnych, 1807–1860* (The Shaping of an Agrarian Labor Market in the Period of the Great Reforms, 1807–1860) (Poznan: PTPN, 1963). The attitude of the propertied classes: H. Owsińska, *Sprawa chłopska w świetle publicystyki poznańskiej, 1823–1848* (The Peasant Problem in the Poznanian Press, 1823–1848) (Warsaw: PWN, 1955).

Chapter 5 and Chapter 6

The legislative texts are in S. Kieniewicz, *Przemiany społeczne i gospodarcze w Królestwie Polskim, 1815–1830* (Social and Economic Changes in the Kingdom of Poland, 1815–1830) (Warsaw: KiW, 1951). Z. Kirkor-Kiedroniowa, *Włościanie i ich sprawa w dobie organizacyjnej i konstytucyjnej Królestwa Polskiego* (The Peasants and the Peasant Question at the Time of the Organization and under the Constitution of the Kingdom of Poland) (Krakow, 1912), is important for its analysis of the inquiry of 1813. K. Deczyński's memoirs, *Żywot chłopa polskiego na początku XIX w.* (Life of a Polish Peasant at the Beginning of the Nineteenth Century) (Warsaw, 1907), have been edited by M. Handelsman. M. Meloch, *Sprawa włościanska w powstaniu listopadowym* (The Peasant Question during the November Insurrection) (Warsaw: KiW, 1948), and R. F. Leslie, *Polish Politics and the Revolution of November 1830* (London, 1956), contain introductory surveys of the preceding period of fifteen years.

Chapter 7

The statistical material is to be found in W. Grabski, *Historia Towarzystwa Rolniczego* (History of the Agronomic Society), vol. 1 (Warsaw, 1904); I. Kostrowicka, *Produkcja roślinna w Królestwie Polskim, 1816–1864: Próba analizy ekonomicznej* (The Vegetable Production in the Kingdom of Poland, 1816–1864: A Tentative Economic Analysis) (Wroclaw: Oss, 1961); W. Pruski, *Hodowla zwierząt gospodarskich w Królestwie Polskim* (The Breeding of Domestic Animals in the Kingdom of Poland), vol. 1 (1815–80), vol. 2 (1881–98), vol. 3 (Warsaw: PWRL, 1967–68); H. Rożenowa, *Produkcja wódki i sprawa pijaństwa w Królestwie Polskim, 1815–1863* (The Production of Vodka and the Problem of Drunkenness in the Kingdom of Poland, 1815–1863 (Warsaw: PWN, 1961).

For an analysis of the discussion on the three-field system see J. Łukasiewicz, "Uwagi na temat systemów rolniczych w Królestwie Polskim w 2 połowie XIX w." (Remarks on the Agronomic Systems in the Second Half of the Nineteenth Century), *Kwartalnik Historii Kultury Materialnej* (1965).

The situation of different groups of the peasantry: F. Bortkiewicz, *Nadziały i powinności chłopów pańszczyźnianych w dobrach prywatnych Królestwa Polskiego* (Holdings and Duties of Compulsory-Labor Peasants in Private Estates of the Kingdom of Poland) (Warsaw: PWN, 1958); H. Chamerska, *O położeniu i zbiegostwie czeladzi folwarcznej w Królestwie Polskim, 1830–1864* (The Situation and the Desertions of Farmhands in the Kingdom of Poland, 1830–1864) (Warsaw: PWN, 1957); D. Rzepniewska, *Sezonowi najemnicy rolni w Królestwie Polskim w połowie XIX w.* (Seasonal Farmhands in the Kingdom of Poland in the Middle of the Nineteenth Century) (Warsaw: PWN, 1957).

Chapter 8

The most important texts of the democratic Left, with commentaries: *Towarzystwo Demokratyczne Polskie: Dokumenty i pisma* (Polish Democratic Society: Documents and Publications), edited by B. Baczko (Warsaw: KiW, 1954); *Lud Polski: Wybór dokumentów* (The Polish People: A Selection of Documents), edited by H. Temkin (Warsaw: KiW, 1957); H. Kamieński,

Wybór pism (Selection of Writings), edited by Z. Poniatowski (Warsaw: KiW, 1953); C. Wycech, *Ksiądz Piotr Sciegienny: Zarys programu społecznego i wybór pism* (Father Sciegienny: An Outline of His Program and a Selection of His Writings) (Warsaw: LSW, 1953); M. Tyrowicz, *Julian Maciej Goslar* (Warsaw: LSW, 1953).

Chapter 9

Rok 1846 w Galicji (1846 in Galicia), edited by J. Sieradzki and C. Wycech (Warsaw: PWN, 1958); S. Kieniewicz, *Ruch chłopski w Galicji w 1846 r.* (The Peasant Movement in Galicia in 1846) (Wroclaw: Oss, 1951); R. Rozdolski, "Do historii krwawego roku 1846" (Contribution to the History of the "Bloody Year"), *Kwartalnik Historyczny* (1958).

Chapter 10

S. Kieniewicz, *Społeczeństwo polskie w powstaniu poznańskim 1848 r.* (The Polish Society in the Poznanian Uprising) (Warsaw: PWN, 1960); M. Tyrowicz, *Dzieje ruchu rewolucyjnego na Sląsku, 1846–1849* (History of the Revolutionary Movement in Silesia, 1846–1849) (Katowice, 1960); S. Kieniewicz, "Sprawa włościańska w Galicji w 1848 r." (The Peasant Problem in Galicia), *Przegląd Historyczny* (1948).

Chapter 11

Materiały do dziejów uwłaszczenia w Królestwie Polskim (Materials concerning the Uwłaszczenie in the Kingdom of Poland), edited by K. and S. Sreniowski (Wroclaw: Oss, 1961).

A general survey: S. Sreniowski, *Uwłaszczenie chłopów w Polsce* (The Enfranchisement of the Polish Peasants) (Warsaw: PWN, 1956). An analysis of the government's policy: Grynwaser, *Writings,* cited under chapter 3. See also Kieniewicz, *January Insurrection,* cited under chapter 12; J. Chmura, *Problem siły roboczej w rolnictwie Królestwa Polskiego* (The Problem of Labor in Polish Agriculture) (Warsaw: PWN, 1959); Z. Stankiewicz, "Serwituty w dobrach rządowych Królestwa Polskiego" (The Servitudes in the Government Domains in the Kingdom of Poland), *Przegląd Historyczny* (1958).

Chapter 12

Chłopi i sprawa chłopska w powstaniu styczniowym (The Peasants and the Peasant Problem in the January Insurrection), edited by S. Kieniewicz and I. Miller (Wroclaw: Oss, 1962). S. Kieniewicz, *Sprawa włościańska w powstaniu styczniowym* (The Peasant Problem in the January Insurrection) (Wroclaw: Oss, 1953); R. F. Leslie, *Reform and Insurrection in Russian Poland, 1856–1865* (London: University of London, 1963). For the peasant uprising of 1861, see Grynwaser, *Writings*, vol. 3.

Chapter 13

K. Groniowski, *Realizacja reformy uwłaszczeniowej 1864* (The Introduction of the Enfranchisement Reform) (Warsaw: PWN, 1963); *Studia i materiały do dziejów Lodzi i okręgu łódzkiego: Uwłaszczenie chłopów i mieszczan-rolników* (The Enfranchisement of the Peasants and the Farming Burghers in the Lodz Area), a collection of studies under the direction of H. Brodowska (Lodz: WŁ, 1966).

Chapter 14

K. Groniowski, *Kwestia agrarna w Królestwie Polskim, 1871–1914* (The Agrarian Problem in the Kingdom of Poland, 1871–1914) (Warsaw: PWN, 1966); H. Brodowska, *Ruch chłopski po uwłaszczeniu w Królestwie Polskim, 1864–1904* (The Peasant Movement after the Enfranchisement in the Kingdom of Poland, 1864–1904) (Warsaw: PWN, 1967).

The story of Prószyński-Promyk: S. Kieniewicz, *Dramat trzeźwych entuzjastów* (The Drama of the Sober Enthusiasts) (Warsaw: WP, 1964).

Chapter 15

S. Wysłouch, *Studia nad koncentracją w rolnictwie śląskim, 1850–1914* (Studies on Concentration in the Silesian Agriculture, 1850–1914) (Wroclaw: Oss, 1956); W. Jakóbczyk, *Studia nad dziejami Wielkopolski w XIX w. Dzieje pracy organicznej* (The History of the Organic Work in Great Poland in the Nineteenth Century), vols. 1–3 (Poznan: PTPN, 1951–67); M. Pirko, *Niemiecka polityka wywłaszczeniowa na ziemiach polskich, 1907–1908* (The German Expropriation Policy in Poland, 1907–1908) (Warsaw: PWN, 1963); K. Wajda, *Wieś pomorska na przełomie XIX i XX w: Kwestia rolna na Pomorzu Gdańskim* (The Pomeranian Village at the Turn of the Century: The Agrarian Problem in Gdansk Pomerania) (Poznan, 1964); B. Drewniak, *Robotnicy sezonowi na Pomorzu Zachodnim, 1890–1918* (The Seasonal Farmhands in Western Pomerania, 1890–1918) (Poznan, 1959).

Chapter 16

The evolution of the agrarian structure: W. Styś, *Współzależność rozwoju rodziny od jej gospodarstwa* (The Correlation of the Evolution of the Peasant's Family and of His Farm) (Wroclaw: Oss, 1959).

The Populist movement: *Materiały źródłowe do historii polskiego ruchu ludowego* (Materials Concerning the History of the Polish Populist Movement), vol. 1 (1864–1918), edited by K. Dunin-Wąsowicz, S. Kowalczyk, J. Molenda, and W. Stankiewicz (Warsaw: LSW, 1966); S. Kowalczyk, J. Kowal, W. Stankiewicz, and M. Stański, *Zarys historii polskiego ruchu ludowego* (An Outline of the History of the Polish Populist Movement), vol. 1 (1864–1918) (Warsaw: LSW, 1963); A. Garlicki, *Powstanie Polskiego Stronnictwa Ludowego Piast* (The Foundation of The Polish Populist Party Piast) (Warsaw: LSW, 1966).

Chapter 17

Walki chłopów Królestwa Polskiego w rewolucji, 1905–1907 (The Struggle of the Peasants in the Kingdom of Poland during the Revolution, 1905–1907), vols. 1–3, edited by S. Kalabiński and F. Tych (Warsaw: PWN, 1958–61); Z. Kmiecik, *Ruch oświatowy na wsi. Królestwo Polskie 1905–1914* (The Educational Movement in the Countryside of the Kingdom of Poland) (Warsaw: PWN, 1962); W. Piątkowski, *Dzieje ruchu zaraniarskiego* (The History of the Zaranie Movement) (Warsaw: LSW, 1956).

Chapter 18

M. Handelsman, *La Pologne, sa vie économique et sociale pendant la Grande Guerre*, vols. 1–2 (Paris, 1932–38); J. Molenda, *PSL w Królestwie Polskim, 1915–1918* (The Polish Populist Party in the Kingdom of Poland, 1915–1918) (Warsaw: LSW, 1965).

INDEX

274

French Revolution, 2, 8, 31, 34–35, 40–42, 45, 60, 106

Frizia, 60

Galicia: under Joseph II, 35–39; after Joseph's death, 40, 101, 113; untouched by democratic propaganda, 110, 117; temperance movement in, 116; in 1846, 118–24; in 1848, 127, 133–37; after Emancipation, 203–4; autonomy of, 205–7; emigrants from, 193; before World War I, 210–20; in World War I, 237–38

Garnek estate, 149–50

Gdansk, 8–10, 58, 90, 92, 107

Gdów, battle of ,122

German colonists: in 18th century, 12; after the partitions, 34; in Congress Kingdom, 97; attitude of, in 1863, 168; acceding to ownership, 175. *See also* Colonization Commission

German conquests, in the Middle Ages, 61

Germanization policy, 131, 192, 195, 198–202

Germany: 116, 124, 192–93, 236–37; its Polish policy during World War I, 238–39, 241–42

Głowacki Bartos, 25, 162

Gniew, 196

Gogol, Nikolai, 33

Gołuchowsi, Agenor, 137

Gorlice, 237

Gortshakov, Michel, 149–50

Gorzkowski, Franciszek, 41–42

Goslar, Julian, 118–19, 123

Grabski, Władysław, 232

Gradzicki, Ksawery, 149

Grudziądz, 107

Harvest yields, 7, 93, 95, 182, 194, 222, 239

Hauke-Bosak, Józef, 169

Heltman, Wiktor, 105, 110

Hindenburg, Paul, 237

Holy Cross Mountains, 168

Hrubieszów estate, 74

Humań massacre, 19, 33, 108

Hungary, 39, 49, 209

Hunger: in Upper Silesia, 131; in Galicia, 133

Hunting rights, 159, 207

Indemnification of landlords: in Prussia, by the peasants, 66–67; denied by Democrats, 105; in Galicia, discussed in Parliament, 136; evaluation of, in Galicia, 137–38; promised by National Government, 161–62; granted in Congress Kingdom, 172, 174, 177

Inns, in villages, 92, 116, 159, 172, 177, 208

Insurrections: as a factor hastening social reforms, 5; of 1794, 15, 24-28, 31–32, 34, 215; of 1830, 77, 80–86, 102; of 1846, 119–22; of 1848, 128–30; of 1863, 162–69, 173, 184; peasant participation in, 27, 83–85, 121, 123, 130, 164–67

Intelligentsia: radicalism of, 28; bearer of democratic ideology, 109, 155; engaged in national propaganda, 186; peasant-born, 209–10

Inventories, in the western guberniyas, 141–42

Ireland, 116, 130

Italy, 42, 124–25

National consciousness of peasants: lack of, immediately after emancipation, 186, 206; growth of, in Poznania, 197; in Congress Kingdom, 226, 229; in Galicia, 208; in independent Poland, 246

National estates. *See* State-owned estates

National Government, of 1846, 119–20, 160, 253

National Government, of 1863, 162–63, 165, 172, 178, 258–59

Nationalist parties, 218–19, 228–29, 231–34, 240–41, 243. *See also* League, National

Nazimov, Rescript, 155

Negroes, American, 49

Newspapers, populist, 188, 226–27, 229, 233

Nicholaus I, Emperor of Russia, 107, 140, 256

Niemen River, 13, 32, 44

Nocznicki, Tomasz, 241

Noteć River, 12

Nowogródek County, 32

Oczynszowanie. *See* Rent reforms

Oder-Neisse line, 68, 192, 201

Oder valley, 68, 70, 191

Odessa, 33

Odrobek. *See* Loans to Peasants

Opole regency, 194

Orchowski, Alojzy, 28

Organic work, 185–86

Organizing Committee, 174–75

Orientations, political, in World War I, 240–41

Orthodox confession, 167, 186, 224, 229

Ownership of the soil, granting of: advocated by Jacobins, 28; denied to peasants, in 1807, 48; granted in Prussian state domains, 59; advocated by Czartoryski, 104; formulated in Poitiers Manifesto, 105; proposed by landowners, 115; proclaimed in Galicia, in 1848, 133, 254–56; characteristics of Galician reform, 137-39; as a procedure unknown outside Poland, 151; advocated by T. Potocki, 152–53; proposed by Agronomic Society, 156; envisaged by Central National Committee, 160–62; proclaimed by National Government, 162–63; extended to Lithuania and Ukraine, 170–71; decreed by Russian Government, in 1864, 172–73, 259–62; the decree carried through, 174-75; results of, in Congress Kingdom, 176–77; economic consequences of, in Galicia, 203. *See also* Regulation reform

Pańszczyzna. *See* Compulsory labor

Parceling: in Prussian Poland, 198–201; in Galicia, 211; in Congress Kingdom, 181, 223–24; opposed by Socialists, 230

Paris, 42, 102–3

Partitions of Poland, 8, 30, 32

Paskevich, Ivan, 96, 111, 117, 141

Patriotic Club, 84, 102

Patriotic party, 21, 22

Patriotic Society, 81

Paul I, Emperor of Russia, 32, 42

Pawlikowski, Joseph, 21, 42

Pawłów, 13-15

Petersburg, 32, 42, 172, 228

Piaseczno, 196

Piłsudski, Józef, 241–43, 246

Pistorius apparatus, 91

Płock district, 50, 55–56, 162

Pŏdgradowice, 201